THE
HARLEM
FOX

J. Raymond Jones, 1967. Courtesy of *The New York Times.*

THE
HARLEM
FOX

J. Raymond Jones and Tammany, 1920–1970

JOHN C. WALTER

State University of New York Press

SUNY Series in Afro-American Studies
John Howard and Robert C. Smith, EDITORS

Published by
State University of New York Press, Albany

Printed in the United States of America

For information, address State University of New York
Press, State University Plaza, Albany, N.Y., 12246

Library of Congress Cataloging-in-Publication Data

Walter, John C. (John Christopher), 1933–
    The Harlem Fox : J. Raymond Jones and Tammany, 1920–1970 / John C.
Walter.
        p.   cm.—(SUNY series in Afro-American studies)
    Bibliography: p.
    Includes index.
    ISBN 0–88706–756–5.   ISBN 0–88706–757–3 (pbk.)
        1.   Jones, J. Raymond (John Raymond), 1899–   .   2.   Politicians—
New York (N.Y.)—Biography.   3.   West Indian Americans—New York
(N.Y.)—Biography.   4.   Afro-Americans—New York (N.Y.)—Biography.
5.   Afro-Americans—New York (N.Y.)—Politics and government.   6.   New
York (N.Y.)—Politics and government—1898–1951.   7.   New York
(N.Y.)—Politics and government—1951–   I.   Title.   II.   Series.
F128.5.J72W35 1988
974.7'1043'0924—dc19
[B]   88–7038
                                                                                            CIP

10 9 8 7 6 5 4 3 2 1

This book is dedicated to Ruth H. Jones, my late wife, who dropped out of high school in order to earn a living but whose strong character and dedication to excellence made it necessary for her to complete her high school diploma and to achieve a Bachelor of Arts, Master of Business Administration and Ph.D. in Economics (ABD). She was my very best friend and counselor. And to my son-in-law, Dr. Ashley Brian, who taught me the importance of a scientific education for the children.

Contents

Acknowledgments

WITHOUT THE COOPERATION of the illustrious graduates of the Carver Democratic Club and members of the "Jones gang," among others, this book would not have been possible. The names are too numerous to cite here, but they know who they are, and I am grateful to them for taking the time to answer my questions. Thanks are also due to my researcher, Leisa Jenkins, for the unflagging energy and ingenuity she displayed in tracking down hard-to-find information, whether at Smith College or the New York Public Libraries.

I will always be indebted to my Smith College colleague, Professor Johnnella Butler, for editing the entire text, exclaiming over and over, "The passive voice, the passive voice . . . when will it end?" At deadlines, some rewriting escaped her scrutiny; any unnecessary use of the passive voice in this book are entirely of my own doing.

Because the completion of the book was delayed by my illness, speed was most essential once I returned to work. Mrs. Barbara Michalak was the fastest and most accurate typist I have ever encountered, and to her I offer my heartfelt thanks.

I will always be grateful to my former student, Ms. Lucette Mercer, for initiating communication between J. Raymond Jones and me. This book is the culmination of that small beginning, and I am sure she will be pleased to know that I have not forgotten her.

Finally, I am forever indebted to the late Mrs. Ruth Jones who, from the very beginning, encouraged her husband's cooperation with me, and in her usual blunt and straightforward manner, deemed my earliest draft, "promising."

To any of the others who assisted this project but I have failed to include, they may rest assured that they too have my most sincere thanks.

Preface

IN 1972, I BEGAN COLLECTING materials for a projected book on Caribbean immigrants in the United States. During this endeavour, I visited the Schomburg Collection of the New York Public Library and chanced upon a thin file on J. Raymond Jones, an immigrant from the Virgin Islands. The file consisted mostly of clippings from Black newspapers, but as I read through it, I realized that here was a man who had achieved great prominence in New York City politics, finally becoming the Chief of Tammany Hall in 1964. This was a good find, so I noted on my index card: "(1) get additional information from white newspapers, and (2) check if he's alive."

Other projects intervened after 1972, and I did not return to the immigrants until 1982 when, as a professor at Smith College, I had a student from St. Thomas, Ms. Lucette Mercer, to whom I remarked that perhaps she might have heard of this J. Raymond Jones. To my surprise, she said that she knew him quite well, that Mr. Jones' wife was her father's boss at the Bureau of Customs in St. Thomas, and that he was alive and well. After this conversation, I wrote in the Jones file, which had become a little thicker: "Interview soon." This occurred sooner than I anticipated, because a few months later, in June 1982, I received a letter from Mr. Jones himself, which read in part:

Dear Dr. Walter:

It is with great pleasure that I write you on matters concerning the writing of my biography. I am presently coordinating that project, which would result in the publication of this book. your name was brought to my attention by Lucette Mercer, who advised me of your interest in this project.

The College of the Virgin Islands has undertaken the job of facilitating the financing of the book, and I have begun to identify persons who will work on the taping of the interviews and doing research. However, I am in need of a chief investigator who will either be responsible for the principal writing of the book, or will oversee the writing by a staff. That person should have fairly intimate knowledge of New York politics since the 1920's and of United States political development since World War II. Miss Mercer has discussed with me your reputation as an historian, and to some extent, your area of expertise.

Of course, I could not resist such an invitation, because a book about the "Harlem Fox" would be an ideal precursor to a book on West Indian immigrants. Besides, I thought, here was a person who had lived a long time and had known everybody who was anybody in the West Indian community in New York City. I would be able to ask questions about people for whom I had inadequate information. I thought also that Mr. Jones would most likely add to my list of notable immigrants.

Prior to 1983, I had written a number of articles on West Indian immigrants. Jones had these writings assessed, he informed me later, so he knew who I was when he expressed confidence that we could work together. He informed me, candidly, that there had been two previous attempts at collaboration. In the first instance, the collaborator had become distracted by other concerns, and nothing came of the work. The second attempt Jones abandoned because a satisfactory tone could not be achieved.

As he talked about these false starts, I got the feeling that J. Raymond Jones felt this would be the last attempt; otherwise, he'd abandon the project altogether. I hastened, therefore, to assure him that from the little I knew of his career there would undoubtedly be an audience for the book, and that I felt we could easily work out a satisfactory tone for the manuscript. I inquired, though, why in the first place he wanted a book about his political career. He said that he thought "the times and the manners" (one of his favorite phrases) had changed many times during his career, and that the time had now come for him to say something about his life, which he thought might be of value to Black and white politicians, and especially to the younger people. Jones felt that college students did not know how politics really worked, and that as a Black man who had achieved much, perhaps these "youngsters" (as he called collegians) might realize through his experience the numerous and attractive possibilities that a life of politics afforded. He thought also that there are not enough books about successful Black people. This, he believed, was unfortunate, not only for deserving Blacks, but for students of all races who had no opportunity to read about the contributions of Black people to American society.

Since I agreed with all his reasons, we turned to how we would work together. "I will tell the story," he said, "and you can fill in the historical details." "Okay," I said, "but I will still have to check as far as possible everything you say." "Of course, of course," he said, waving the ever-present cigar he never smokes. "You are the historian. I leave those details to you. You can check whatever I say with whomever you wish. We can talk about it and come to some conclusion." On this note, we agreed to begin taping the next morning. I arrived bright and early, and the questions continued, with interruptions only for lunch and supper, into the night. This was to be the pattern every day for four and a half weeks.

After this, I returned to the mainland for a mandatory week's rest. This was in July, but Jones was anxious that I should meet some of "the gang." In early August I found myself high above New York at the Windows on the World Restaurant with more than twenty members of "the gang," Jones looking very much like a potentate in his wheelchair.

From this meeting, I got a sense of how J. Raymond Jones had worked with these men and women, including such current stars as Percy Sutton, Basil Patterson, Congressman Charles Rangel, and Manhattan Borough President David Dinkins. I spoke to every one at that meeting and verified telephone numbers and addresses for future interviews. It was an encouraging and heady affair, because all those present were enthusiastic about the project and expressed a real desire to assist. Buoyed by this experience, I returned to Northampton to schedule interviews and organize research.

Nearly two years later, in the spring of 1985, after completing the first draft, I became very ill and lay in a coma for twelve days while friends, colleagues, and physicians were unsure that I would make it. I did, but could not renew work until January 1986. I suspect Raymond Jones must have despaired during that whole depressing year; nonetheless, his first concern was always my health, and for that I was and am grateful.

In working through the first draft with Jones, I was assisted by my colleague Dr. Johnnella Butler and Mrs. Ruth Jones, Ray Jones' wife. I could not have learned everything I wanted from Ray without them. A number of times when Ray was reluctant to detail certain events, such as the attempted bribe by Kennedy forces, Mrs. Jones would give a meaningful cough and Ray would proceed. Reluctant to characterize his enemies and opponents, Jones resisted telling me why he disliked Earl Brown and Antonio Rasmus; but when Dr. Butler sweetly asked the same question, he chivalrously spelled out their "repugnant behavior." On a number of such points, he would give in to "the ladies," because he thought they had a better sense of the limits of disclosure than we men. Such are the predispositions of an essentially Edwardian gentleman.

The second draft was ready in the summer of 1986, and once again Dr. Butler and I journeyed to St. Thomas. This three-week session, though taxing, was easier than the previous one because we could clearly see the well-developed themes and the linear coherence of Jones' political life.

Jones was especially pleased with the background I provided on the Garvey movement, particularly the American perception of Garvey. I recall that he exclaimed after I had read the Garvey section to him, "You did a wonderful job on that one. That's exactly how I want it said." His pleasure derived from his belief that perhaps it would contribute to clearing up the misunderstandings about Marcus Garvey. He argues that very few people understand what the man was about, since his complex social movement is almost impossible to decipher unless one was a part of it.

By late fall 1986, the third draft was complete, and once again I journeyed to the Virgin Islands for what we called the "polishing session." Jones wanted everything to be absolutely right, and since we were not so concerned this time with facts, it was tone and temper that had become important. A word that simply would not do the job was thrown out, while an anecdote deemed unnecessary was given short shrift. Although I returned to the mainland within three weeks, this process continued until July 1987. It consisted of innumerable telephone calls from Northampton to St. Thomas, but at all times the discussion was cordial and lively. By March, we knew the book would be published, and that this endeavour, which we had begun to call an "odyssey," would soon reach a very satisfying conclusion. It was the best of times.

It should be noted that all effort to get this book published J. Raymond Jones left to me. Questions of title and authorship were not discussed, because it was understood from the beginning that I would be the author and Jones would be the title. In consequence, our work was always congenial, even though Jones had to read and approve every single word. We seldom disagreed as to context, because by the summer of 1986, the text read as if Jones and I were speaking with one voice. I knew by then how he thought, what he thought about, what he considered important. I also well understood the manner in which he wanted to tell his story, so well in fact that at times he'd lean back majestically in his chair, and with a look of satisfaction on his face, say to me, "I wish you had been around when I was in politics. We could have gone a long way." This was very gratifying to me, because I wanted to do this book very much, in the belief that in Jones' life there is enough to merit serious consideration by students and scholars as well as practicing politicians.

We early decided that, in order to create intimacy and immediacy, the work would be in the first person. Putting it in the first person would give the impression that I had merely edited Jones' narrative; however, we preferred the first person atmosphere and decided to explain the division of labor in the preface. Therefore, for the record, it is Raymond Jones who

relates his activities, while the corroboration, historical and political context, and continuity of the story has been left to me. Consequently, I
personally interviewed a large number of his colleagues, including former
Mayor Robert Wagner of New York City, Judge Herbert Evans, former
Borough President Percy Sutton, the businessman Bruce Llewellyn, current Manhattan Borough President David Dinkins, and others. Some I
contacted for a written interview. In addition, I obtained a complete file on
Jones from the *New York Times*, as well as information from the *Amsterdam
News*, the *New York Post*, *Jet*, *Newsweek*, and other periodicals. Throughout,
I consulted a large number of secondary works; the most pertinent are in
the selected Bibliography.

Only in a very few instances was Raymond Jones' memory at fault.
When he thought this might be so, he would say to me, "We have to check
this out." This meant I had to check with the appropriate participants, the
sparse documents in Jones' possession, newspaper files, and appropriate
secondary sources. These forays were time-consuming but a joy because of
the affectionate but respectful way in which Jones' former colleagues spoke
of him. Former Mayor Robert Wagner, for example, took time out from his
busy law practice to graciously answer all my questions. He thought of Ray
Jones as "a man who knew how to separate the role of political leader from
that of a statesman. Above all, he was very honest."[1] Judge James L.
Watson of the U.S. Court of International Trade impressed on me that
"the name 'The Fox' was not one which was taken lightly, because he
[Ray] was a wise, perceptive person, who tried to, and did, use every
resource at his command for the good of the community as well as the
Party."[2] Julius C. C. Edelstein, in 1984 the Senior Vice-Chancellor of the
City University of New York, wrote: "I would say that his [Jones'] major
weakness, if any, consisted of the fact that he had neither the talents nor
the vices of a demagogue."[3] These encomiums were encouraging, but
since most of Jones' official and personal papers had been lost with the
closing of the Carver Club building and during his retirement move to St.
Thomas, I wanted an unbiased review of Jones' recollections as well as any
additional pertinent information. All the people interviewed were most
helpful. At no time were there any contradictions in essential fact.

In the end, nothing of substance remained unresolved, and by the time
we were ready for the publishers, Jones and I felt that the story of his
political life had been told in such a way as to achieve the ends for which
it was intended. No corners had been cut and no embarrassing or controversial topics avoided. In sum, we have accomplished what we set out to do,
and we are satisfied with the integrity and honesty of the work. We now
leave it for the readers to judge.

Introduction

WHEN J. RAYMOND JONES arrived in New York City at the end of World War II, Mayor John F. Hylan and Irish politicians dominated the city. Very few of the Germans who had run New York City politics in the nineteenth century remained except for Robert F. Wagner, Sr., whose son became mayor in 1953. The new ethnic group making headway, the Italians, would not make their presence undeniably felt until the election of Carmine DeSapio as Chief of Tammany Hall in 1949. While the Germans had established their predominance in the eighteenth, nineteenth and early twentieth centuries because of what one might call "prior power"—that is, having been there in the first place—the Irish established themselves as a consequence of their sheer numbers, resulting from wave after wave of immigrants from the mid-nineteenth century on. The Italians, of course, benefitted later from their own similar wave. A graph would reveal a direct relation between rising numbers of immigrants from each of the various ethnic groups and their ascendance to power in the politics of New York City and New York State. In similar fashion, Jews settled in New York City in increasing numbers in the late nineteenth and early twentieth century and then achieved political prominence, as Irving Howe has documented historically in *World of Our Fathers*. Afro-Americans and West Indians moved in such increasing numbers to New York City between 1890 and World War I that by the time of the Jazz Age, Langston Hughes, the great Afro-American poet, saw Harlem as a Mecca for Blacks, especially artists.

These waves of migration and immigration greatly colored and profoundly focussed the political atmosphere. When Jones arrived, not only were increasing numbers of Blacks arriving from the South and from the Caribbean, but a subtle and little-noticed change was also taking place on the political scene. In New York and nationally the Republicans dominated Black politics until the Depression, having established the political allegiance of the Negro population due to Lincoln's legacy as the Great

1

Emancipator. By the 1920s Black politicians in New York City and the rest of the country depended upon the largesse of federal rather than local governments. As a consequence of his relationship with Black troops in the Spanish-American War, Theodore Roosevelt on becoming President in 1901 had furthered the benign paternalistic Republican attitude toward Blacks throughout the country. His chief Negro supporter, Booker T. Washington, as shown by the careful studies of August Meier in *Black Political Thought in America, 1880–1915* and Gilbert Osofsky in *Harlem: The Making of a Ghetto*, largely controlled federal patronage in New York through his lieutenant, Charles W. Anderson.

Born in Oxford, Ohio, in 1866, Anderson had migrated to New York City. By 1893 he was private secretary to the State Treasurer, later became himself Clerk of the State Treasury and then Supervisor of Accounts for the State Racing Commission. All these were state jobs, because Negroes, Republican or Democrat, had little power within Democratic-controlled New York City. During the 1904 Republican Presidential campaign, Anderson organized in New York City the Colored Republican Club, which worked for the re-election of Theodore Roosevelt as President of the United States. (James Weldon Johnson, the outstanding literary and legal personality, succeeded to the leadership of this club after Anderson's resignation.) As a result of Anderson's yeoman work for President Roosevelt, and in defiance of Southern challenges to the President's appointment of a Negro as Collector of Customs of the Port of Charleston, South Carolina, Roosevelt appointed Charles Anderson as Collector of Customs for the Second District of New York in 1905. Anderson retained this job, the highest position held by a Negro in the City of New York, for ten years, even during the first administration of Democrat Woodrow Wilson, who quickly dismantled Republican Negro patronage.

In the latter part of the nineteenth century, T. Thomas Fortune, the founder of the Afro-American League, had constantly harangued Negro New Yorkers to consider voting for the Democrats and to remove themselves from the Republican Party, which had in fact done little for them since 1876. These exhortations eventually took effect in 1898, when the efforts of a number of Negroes on behalf of the New York mayoral candidate, Robert Van Wyck, resulted in the formation of the United Colored Democracy, a permanent Negro auxiliary of Tammany Hall, established by Tammany Chief Richard Croker. That same year, Croker established an Italian auxiliary, beginning the Italian drive for power, which culminated in 1949 with Carmine DeSapio. It is an interesting commentary that Richard Croker chose Edward E. Lee as leader of the United Colored Democracy. Although he had considerable authority and power in the United Colored Democracy, Lee, the chief bellman at the Murray Hill Hotel, remained illiterate all his life.

By World War I, the United Colored Democracy had become quite powerful in New York City, its well-educated leaders drawn mostly from southern and West Indian immigrants. In 1915, the year Booker T. Washington died, Ferdinand Q. Morton assumed its leadership, and under his guidance increasing numbers of Negroes attained low-level city patronage jobs. Morton himself soon became the first Black member of the Municipal Civil Service Commission, a job he retained until 1947.

J. Raymond Jones came to New York in 1918 at a time of political and demographic flux. Blacks in all the boroughs, with the exception of Staten Island, were beginning to flex their political muscles as their population increased, more so in Brooklyn and Manhattan, but soon also in the Bronx and in Queens. The Democratic Party increased its power in state politics with the election of Alfred Smith as Governor in 1918,[1] and in 1928 Franklin D. Roosevelt, who was to become President of the United States in 1933.

Raymond Jones' first affiliation, however, was not with any political party, but rather with the Marcus Garvey movement, the Universal Negro Improvement Association. As an active member of this nationalist organization, Jones began to realize the potential not simply of the Negro vote, but of political organization, and the relationships between large-scale organizations, political power, and a clear sense of prideful identity. Jones worked with the Garvey movement on a number of business ventures that prospered moderately and from which he learned to make successful personal investments. By his middle years, he was sufficiently wealthy to be independent of patronage jobs.

With the decline of the Garvey movement, Jones cast around to find some way to gain entry into the power structure of New York City in order to "better himself" and make a contribution to the Negro cause. The Democratic mayoral primary of 1921 provided that opportunity. Seeking to garner Negro votes for Democrat John F. Hylan, Jones and his friends propagandized on behalf of candidate Hylan and preserving the five-cent subway fare. Jones did not expect any of the insignificant individual cash rewards given out after Hylan's victory, but thought that a few city jobs, the kind that white election workers routinely received, would be forthcoming. When this turned out not to be the case, he decided to "integrate" the Democratic Party in order to insure a say in its governance and disbursement of patronage.

Jones and his friends from the Five Cent Fare Club, mostly members of the Garvey organization, were mostly of Caribbean ancestry. Caribbean immigrants had formed other such Democratic Party clubs in New York

City at this time, opposing the United Colored Democracy, the organization of indigenous Afro-Americans. The formation of these new clubs unaffiliated with the U.C.D. marked a schism in Black Democratic ranks in New York City. Furthermore, the U.C.D. with its one leader, Ferdinand Q. Morton, functioned as an auxilliary, subordinate entity to Tammany Hall. The new clubs, however, did not follow one leader throughout Manhattan, and maintained at best a tenuous and edgy relationship with Tammany. Located in various Assembly Districts, these new club leaders knew each other, effected a loose cooperation, and aimed to be accepted on equal terms within the Democratic organization. From these new clubs, the effective integration of Blacks in the Democratic Party in New York City began to take place in the 1930s.

To a great extent the decision by Raymond Jones and other West Indian immigrants, as well as a number of younger indigenous Blacks, to form independent clubs, came as a consequence of their attempts to join the all-white clubs rather than the U.C.D. Darwin W. Telesford, a lawyer and immigrant from the West Indies, related his experience of going to Martin J. Healy's Democratic club of the 19th Assembly District in Harlem and being told that he should approach another club under the leadership of the U.C.D., because Negroes were not welcome in Healy's club.[2] Jones relates a similar experience at this same club, the Cayuga, in 1921.[3] Ironically, many of these racially discriminatory white clubs were located in Harlem where Negroes comprised the majority of the population.

Jones' full-fledged leadership came somewhat later than his colleagues' because he belonged to one of the few integrated clubs, John Kelly's, in the 22nd Assembly District, a bit north and outside of Harlem proper. Consequently, while clubs in parts of Harlem with a Black majority elected Black Democratic district leaders beginning with the election of Herbert L. Bruce in the 21st Assembly District in 1935, it was not until the period between 1937 and World War II that increasing numbers of Black district leaders were elected in Harlem. Jones himself did not obtain a district leadership until 1944, in an Assembly District almost equally Black and white. By then the U.C.D. and the new clubs had been absorbed into the Democratic Party—a development catalyzed by the continued migration of Blacks to New York in the interwar years, Fiorello La Guardia's long mayoral tenure, and World War II.

Jones' early apprenticeship in the Tammany organization began during one of the worst times for that institution, but one of the best for Black political advancement, the 1930s. During the preceding Jazz Age of the 1920s, Tammany had enjoyed a great deal of power and influence simply because the governor and the majors of New York City had been

Democrats. Al Smith, Governor of New York State for most of the 1920s, was generally known as a creature of Tammany, and Franklin D. Roosevelt, in his first term at least, was a product of Tammany's vote-getting power beyond New York City. But by 1930, Tammany had fallen into disrepute as a consequence of the press' exposure of its graft, fraud, and chicanery; the subsequent investigation by Judge Samuel Seabury, from 1930 to 1932, caused the resignation of Mayor Jimmy Walker in the latter year. The revelations of the Seabury Investigation turned Roosevelt entirely against the Tammany organization, and he carried the feeling of distrust with him into the presidency in 1933. He cut off federal patronage to Tammany, and instead patronized Mayor La Guardia and the American Labor Party. Roosevelt's animus and the election of reformer Herbert Lehman as Governor was not enough to end Tammany's power in New York City, however. It still had an ally in the person of Joseph V. McKee, who, as Acting Mayor for part of 1932, was such a creature of Tammany that when he was asked who would be his Police Commissioner, he replied, "I don't know. I haven't got the word yet."[4]

Apart from Roosevelt's disaffection, the Seabury Investigation, and the campaign of William Randolph Hearst to expose Tammany's corrupt behavior,[5] the election of La Guardia in 1933 dealt the most serious blow to the Tammany organization. With Tammany now out of power, the mayor managed all city patronage, and with Federal patronage now funnelled through La Guardia, Tammany Hall had to woo all those constituencies previously taken for granted. One of those constituencies, of course, was the Black population.

Despite the presence of La Guardia in office between 1933 and 1945 and Smith's disaffection with the National Democratic administration, Herbert Lehman, the Democratic Governor of New York at this time, allied himself with Alfred Smith. In fact, Lehman owed much of his popularity, as well as his election, to the efforts of Smith, a Tammany creature until his death. Therefore, Tammany held some patronage lever-age from the state from 1932 to the end of Lehman's governorship. Warren Moscow, in *The Last of the Big-Time Bosses*, notes how Lehman was elected in 1932:

Al Smith, the revered elder statesman, was fighting hard for Lehman, who had always contributed generously to Smith's campaigns. He leaned across the table and said to Curry, "If you don't go along with Lehman, I'll take the party away from you by running for mayor of New York next year."

"On what ticket?" sneered Curry.

"On a Chinese laundry ticket I could beat you and your crowd," Smith retorted.

Curry knew Smith spoke the truth, that he could never best the great former governor in a contest for the support of New York City voters. he threw in his cards, and there was no fight on the floor of the State Convention. Lehman was nominated and was supported by Tammany on election day that year and in each of the six successive occasions that he ran for Governor or U.S. Senator.[6]

In 1936 a referendum changed the governance of New York City from a Board of Aldermen to a City Council with proportional representation. This system, beginning with the election of 1937, further undermined Tammany's hold on the old Board of Aldermen, and made it even more necessary for the Democratic party to take into account the Black population. In addition, although the Seabury Investigation had ended in 1933, various crusading federal and state attorneys-general continually pressured Tammany because of its well-known involvement with members of organized crime. This involvement, begun during the Jazz Age and intensified during World War II, continued until the Kefauver hearings of the 1950s.[7] Legal attacks on this unholy alliance created severe disruptions at Tammany Hall, and increased the need for new allies. Men like Raymond Jones and much of the Negro population were ready.

In the same year that La Guardia first won the mayoralty of New York City, effectively undermining the power of Tammany, Jones found himself the protegé of John Kelley, the leader of the 22nd Assembly District (A.D.) and a power in what may be called Northern Harlem. In 1939, encouraged by Kelley and other members of the 22nd A.D., Jones made his first political foray for District Leadership in the Tammany organization in the 19th A.D. in the heart of Harlem. This move was based on demographics. Harry C. Perry, current leader of the 19th A.D. through the assistance of his half-brother, Tammany Chief Christy Sullivan, had been chased out of his former downtown district by thugs led by Charles "Lucky" Luciano. As Moscow tells it, this is how Perry reached Harlem:

In 1939 Christy Sullivan was leader of Tammany Hall, but without strength in his own right. He was a figurehead for the Ahearn crowd, who had succeeded the Sullivans as rulers of the East Side. But Sullivan took himself seriously and bitterly resented the decline of Irish hegemony in Tammany affairs. Asked why he had declined to seat De Sapio, Sullivan gave reporters the excuse that he had no alternative but to stick with Finn because the latter, as sheriff, controlled 150 patronage jobs.

This reasoning was thin. Finn had neither the gumption nor the know-how to use control of those jobs as a threat to Sullivan's leadership. Sullivan was really just staving off the seating of another Italian on the Tammany executive committee, which for so long had been the almost exclusive turf of the Irish.

Tammany's racism was both conscious and unconscious. By design, there were no black district leaders. Harlem had not yet overflowed its dikes and spilled out south of 116th Street or north of 145th, or even west of Amsterdam Avenue. The territory inside its existing borders had been carefully divided among four assembly districts so that no one black segment could outvote the white territory to which it had been attached. There were a few Jewish district leaders, but the flair of the Irish for politics kept Irishmen as leaders in most of the predominantly Jewish sections. The Puerto Ricans had not yet arrived in numbers substantial enough to spread out of Spanish Harlem. The sole Italian district leader had been forced in at gunpoint in 1931.

The story was never printed in the newspapers at the time, or afterward, but Prohibition-bred mobsters operating under orders from Charles ("Lucky") Luciano—the first traceable Mafia chieftain—had walked into the office of City Clerk Harry Perry in the old Tweed Court House 100 feet north of City Hall. They told Perry, Christy Sullivan's half-brother, that he was to give up his downtown district leadership. The gunmen, significantly patting their holsters, said, "Lucky says you're through."

Perry quit, telling friends that the alternative was to have his people shot down in the street. He was succeeded by Albert Marinelli, in whose behalf Lucky's gunmen had carried the message. It was the first instance of an underworld sortie against Tammany, and it was for years the only one, but the incident left Sullivan with a personal reason for his distrust of Italians in politics.[8]

Jones did not succeed in his foray against Perry, although Perry's district was predominantly Black. Perry, now realizing that he would always be in trouble in this district, soon after resigned, and a friend of Jones, Daniel L. Burrows, succeeded to the leadership. Back in the 22nd A.D., realizing the changing population distribution there (by World War II, almost one-third Irish, one-third Italian, and one-third Black and Puerto Rican), Jones decided in 1941 to support two other members of Kelley's club, Congressman Joseph Gavagan and Assemblyman Daniel Flynn, in order to oust Kelley because of what Jones perceived to be his insensitivity towards the Black population.

With Kelley gone, Jones, Gavagan and Flynn held the power in the club. But the possibilities for Jones' leadership of the 22nd A.D., given its demographic distribution, seemed dim, so in 1943 he ran against Herbert Bruce for the district leadership of the 21st Assembly District where Bruce had been District Leader since 1935. This election Jones also lost, but his willingness to oppose Bruce with the backing of the Tammany leadership gained him influence at Tammany Hall, then ruled by Clarence Neal and Bert Stand. Luck played a role here, for in 1944 Joseph Gavagan accepted a judgeship on the New York State Supreme Court and Daniel Flynn went into the Navy, leaving Jones the virtual leader of the district. However, with Blacks making up only one-third of the district's population, it was unlikely that Jones would become the permanent leader of this neighborhood.

But fortune smiled again. In 1944, two simultaneous political moves worked in Jones' favor. First of all, reapportionment of the districts reduced the number of Assembly Districts in Manhattan from 23 to 16, while rearranging and enlarging them, and dividing certain districts for leadership purposes into East and West, North and South, or subdistricts A, B, and C, as necessary. As a result, the 22nd A.D. was divided, with part of it incorporated into the new 13th Assembly District, with Jones as its de facto leader. At the same time, the incumbent Tammany Chief, Michael Kennedy, fell into disfavor with Bert Stand and Clarence Neal, kingmakers in the Tammany organization, who preferred to see Edward Loughlan as Tammany Leader. Since Jones had been friendly with Stand and Neal (they succeeded with Jones' vote to engineer Loughlan's election), they split the 13th A.D. in two, and gratefully awarded Jones the leadership of its eastern half.

The year before he assumed the leadership of the 13th Assembly District, Jones had formed his own political club, the Carver. This club was unique, not simply because it was racially integrated but, unlike the Kelly-Gavagan club, the Carver was Black-led. It therefore became *the* club in the new 13th A.D. East, which, though predominantly Black, was not overwhelmingly so.

At the end of the Second World War, white former politicians returned home in droves to parlay their war records into political capital. Among them were such later standouts as New York Senator Jacob Javits, far away in Boston the young John F. Kennedy, and in Manhattan, William O'Dwyer, former crime-busting Brooklyn District Attorney. In 1941 O'Dwyer had run against La Guardia with the endorsement of the entire New York City Democratic leadership. He did so well that, in 1945 as a Brigadier General, he was endorsed by the Democrats as their savior. But all was not well. Democrats had been out of power since 1933, twelve years, and La Guardia had made serious inroads to the Black community. The repair engineer of the machine had to be found. Although the Reverend Adam Clayton Powell, Jr., the charismatic new Congressman from Harlem, would have seemed the logical choice, it was to J. Raymond Jones, already called "The Fox," that O'Dwyer turned. O'Dwyer regarded Jones' contribution so highly that the new mayor appointed Jones his personal secretary and proclaimed him his "eyes and ears in Harlem." As such, Jones represented the new breed of Black politicians who, rather than seeking socialist or separatist nationalist alternatives for their constituents, maintained a cultural nationalist posture within the framework of integration and capitalism. As A Democrat, Jones figured significantly in the resurgence of Tammany Hall, which had been in limbo since La Guardia's election in 1933.

In 1947, Mayor O'Dwyer elevated his Harlem "eyes and ears" to Deputy Commissioner of Housing and Buildings, making Jones the highest-ranking, most highly paid Black political appointee in New York City. The press noted his appointment, discussed and wrote about it, and Congressman Powell notwithstanding, J. Raymond Jones, District Leader, 13th A.D. East, member of the New York County Democratic Executive Committee and Deputy Commissioner, became the most powerful politician in Harlem, a personage to be reckoned with throughout the entire city. Indeed, "The Fox" had arrived. But Jones' rise to eminence coincided with the balkanization of the Democratic party, which had begun in earnest with the 1933 election of Mayor La Guardia.

By 1945, Jones, at age 46, having mastered the ins and outs of New York politics, was well on his way to becoming a pivotal figure in the Democratic Party. He was already known as an expert on election law, petitions, and campaign strategies. Because of F. D. R.'s and Governor Lehman's eventual estrangement from the Party in New York City, a number of Reform groups organized during the 1940s. After the death of President Roosevelt, Lehman and Mrs. Eleanor Roosevelt provided the leadership for the Reform Democrats who, clothing themselves in the mantle of "good government," challenged the old leadership. Since Jones was now seen as part of the Tammany Regulars, the Reformers continually sniped at him, with considerable aid from the *New York Times*. Jones' career was not helped when Mayor O'Dwyer's seeming friendship with unsavory characters led to O'Dwyer's resignation in 1950. The Kefauver Investigations in the early 1950s revealed much of Tammany leadership still involved with gangsters, and Jones concluded that it was time to leave politics entirely. This he did in 1953.

On the surface, Jones' decision to leave politics might seem to be self-serving and sanctimonious; however, his life story shows him to be governed by a consistent sense of ethics. Throughout his political career, he was investigated several times on charges of bribery and fraud. While a number of people were forced to resign and even went to jail, Jones was never proven guilty of any of the charges, a fact many argued was a testimony to his high ethical standards, while others saw it as testimony to his extreme cunning. It seems more likely, on the basis of available evidence, that Jones remained an essentially ethical and straightforward person throughout his career, a formidable accomplishment given the pressures, blandishments, and general climate of the times. Of course, he was cunning too!

Between 1953 and 1958, absenting himself from New York politics, Jones held a patronage job as a judge's secretary. At odds with the Tammany leadership and with the elements of the party he considered crude and gangster-ridden, Jones left the scene to flamboyant Congressman Adam Clayton Powell. But by 1958, Powell too was exiled by Tammany for his support of President Dwight D. Eisenhower in 1956. Because the party, under the strong direction of Carmine DeSapio (whom Jones distrusted), had exiled Powell, Jones decided to assist the beleaguered Congressman. He realized that the momentous changes taking place in the social and political life of the United States and New York City had now created new political, economic, and social opportunities for Blacks too good to be missed. Aiding Congressman Powell now would provide the perfect vehicle for a political comeback. The moment could not have been more felicitous.

In Montgomery, Alabama, two years earlier, the successful bus boycott ending segregation in public transportation had had a profound effect upon the perspective of New Yorkers, especially those in Harlem. It was the time of the bus boycott in Jacksonville, Florida, and the Little Rock, Arkansas, protests to end school segregation when the National Guard was called out to protect Black people from the onslaughts of benighted white people. None of this was lost on the Black population, and assisted in creating new attitudes in New York altering the political and social relations between Blacks and whites. The Democratic Party took notice, but belatedly.

The decision to aid Congressman Powell in 1958, Jones calculated, would bring about a return to power to settle old scores and start new initiatives. Powell welcomed this aid, for he knew not only of Jones' technical skills, but also of his high standing among the voters. Jones had always been seen as a more stable, astute, dependable figure than the flamboyant and charismatic Powell. So it was no accident that the very next year, Ray Jones won the election to District Leader in Harlem and that discussions began about supporting him as a future Tammany Chief.

In the 1960 Presidential elections, Jones' power and influence was of such magnitude that Speaker of the House, Sam Rayburn, invited him to the Capitol to insure his support for Lyndon Baines Johnson's nomination for President at the Democratic Convention. At this meeting they struck a deal whereby, if Jones were to support Johnson on the first two ballots, should there be that many, the Speaker would arrange that Congressman Powell become Chairman of the House Education and Labor Committee soon after. It should be noted that the deal was not made with Adam Powell, but with Raymond Jones. This deal later caused Jones a great deal of grief from John F. Kennedy's brother, Robert, the chairman of Kennedy's Presidential campaign, and started a feud that escalated in 1964 upon Robert Kennedy's election as Senator from New York State, and only ended in 1967 when Jones resigned the leadership of Tammany Hall from ill health and Senator Kennedy's harassment.

John Kennedy's campaign regarded Jones' support as so important that a campaign representative offered him a bribe to support the candidate, a bribe which he turned down, but did not make public until the writing of this book. Although Lyndon Johnson lost the nomination, he gained the

Vice-Presidency, and through his advocacy, Jones' wife, Ruth, was appointed Collector of Customs for the U.S. Virgin Islands, a well-paid job which many Democrats coveted. Congressman Adam Clayton Powell also reaped his rewards. In January 1961, Powell was duly chosen Chairman of the Education and Labor Committee, at that time one of the most powerful committees in the House.

Jones' return to politics could not have been better timed, for 1961 was also an election year for Mayor of New York City. To Jones' good fortune, this would not be a normal election year. In fact, all five Democratic County Leaders, led by Tammany's Carmine DeSapio, had decided to dump Mayor Robert F. Wagner, Jr. The mayor was in serious trouble, fighting for his political life.

It is a very significant fact in the history of New York City politics that the mayor in these extreme circumstances turned to J. Raymond Jones to run his campaign. Wagner especially needed Jones' petition expertise, for the leaders of his own party were blocking his nomination. Of added value, however, was Jones' stature among New York's Black constituency, for he was known and respected in all five counties. Black votes were most important, and any serious defection from Wagner would seal his political doom. Jones and his cohorts would prevent that. In my interviews with former Mayor Wagner, he assured me that J. Raymond Jones played the pivotal role in that searing primary fight. When it was over, Raymond Jones emerged as one of the most powerful political figures in New York City. Yet even then, Jones was not a politician in the ordinary sense, because apart from being District Leader of the 13th A.D. East, he held no elective office and functioned strictly as an organization man.

During Mayor Wagner's last term, the schisms in the Democratic Party since the La Guardia era widened. Edward Costikyan, the Tammany Chief from 1961 to 1963, found it impossible to bring the Reformers and Regulars together, though he tried valiantly. He soon realized that his efforts were hopeless, and in 1964 he retired. The party now needed miraculous powers to prevent a Republican takeover of the city in 1965. Since the small miracle of Robert Wagner's 1961 election was most associated with Jones, the Mayor and the Regulars logically turned to him to lead the party in New York County.

Raymond Jones' election as Chief of Tammany Hall in November 1964 made him its first Black leader. Black people and progressive whites throughout the city and its environs were ecstatic amid the bitter irony that the Democratic Party was in the worst possible shape, literally bankrupt, with irreconcilable differences between the Regular and the Reform Democrats. Even worse, the Republicans, flexing their political muscles, had developed a number of attractive candidates who could at any time seriously challenge the Democrats for the mayoralty. Indeed, two years later, Republican John V. Lindsay triumphed as mayor, a triumph underwritten by Reform Democrats and disenchanted Blacks.

A study of the leadership of Tammany Hall during the tenure of J. Raymond Jones yields very important information and lessons, for the politician was concerned with revitalizing an economically moribund and faction-ridden organization. Under the most stressful conditions, Jones provided leadership and viability for the Party for longer than could have been expected. Indeed, the leadership abilities of Raymond Jones were never before tested as they were in the fight to reorganize the New York State legislature in January 1965. In that month, following a Democratic sweep of the House and Senate the previous November, the Legislature could not get itself organized because of the conflict between Reform and Regular Democratic leaders. Involved in this dispute was Mayor Robert Wagner's desire to have two of his candidates from New York City placed as Speaker of the House and Leader of the Assembly. To County Leader Jones fell the job of resolving the issue. After a bitter and debilitating campaign, Anthony Travia was elected Speaker of the House and Joseph Zaretsky, Senate Majority Leader.

Robert Kennedy's election to the U.S. Senate from New York further complicated Jones' tenure as Tammany Chief. Seen by many as a political messiah, Kennedy's charisma bedazzled large numbers of New York City Blacks, and he drew their votes away from the Regular Democrats. Kennedy had come to New York City as a Reform Democrat, tilting against "a suspicion of corruption" which he implied hung around Jones and other Regular Democrats. This allegation formed a central part of what came to be called the "Surrogate Fight of 1966," in which Kennedy and his group were deemed the winner.

Yet in this conflict, as in all the others between Senator Kennedy and the Regular Democrats during Jones' tenure as County Leader, a better and cleaner system for the nomination and appointment of judges was not the real issue. At stake was who would be the most powerful Democrat in New York State after Mayor Robert Wagner's departure. Robert Kennedy fully believed it should not be J. Raymond Jones, and the battle over the Surrogate Judgeships was in itself a surrogate fight for the control of the Democratic Party in New York City and State.

Yet despite the election of Kennedy's candidate, no new rules were adopted for the nomination and election of judges. In fact, the *New York Times* eventually admitted that Jones had, prior to the Surrogate struggle, substantially improved the system for judicial appointments and elections. Indeed, given the circumstances, it could not then be improved beyond the Jones initiative. Even Justice Arthur Klein, Kennedy's successful candidate, resigned a few years later claiming that he could not "change the system."

During his struggle with Robert Kennedy, Raymond Jones achieved a number of notable successes. In 1965, he engineered Constance Baker Motley's elevation to a Federal judgeship, the first Black woman to be so honored. This was an accomplishment of great importance within the state and an event noted throughout the country. The ability of Jones to move Mrs. Motley from State Senator, a first for a Black woman, to the Manhattan Borough Presidency, another first, to a Federal judgeship, testified to his skill to move candidates of ability through a tricky political process into very significant and important positions in city, state, and federal governments.

In 1966, when it became clear that Senator Robert Kennedy would continue relentlessly to oppose Jones' leadership, the Manhattan Borough Presidency became available. Although the law forbids City Councilmen from electing one of their own to fill that vacancy, Jones could have resigned as County Leader and City Councilman and arrange his election to three undisturbed years as Manhattan's Borough President. This he rejected, because his rule was always to assist younger, qualified, and aspiring individuals—in this case, State Assemblyman Percy Sutton. Jones' refusal of the Borough Presidency was consistent with his never seeking political office for himself throughout his career. He settled mostly for positions from which he could advance qualified Black people into pivotal positions in New York City and elsewhere.

When Republican John V. Lindsay became Mayor of New York in 1965, J. Raymond Jones already had served the city for two years and had completed a year as County Leader. Because of his immense prestige, Jones exercised great influence in the Council, and Lindsay came to depend on him. His council colleagues also deferred to his knowledge of New York City politics, and placed him in charge of a number of the most powerful committees, including the chairmanship of the important Committee on the State Legislature.

In the waning weeks of 1966, Jones, as the New York County Democratic Leader, watched in dismay as his on-and-off friend Congressman Adam Clayton Powell became encircled and entrapped by large numbers of his congressional colleagues, shouting for his ouster from the House. Adam had indeed been indiscreet and foolish on too many occasions, but the response to his transgressions went far beyond the norm. It seemed obvious that the hysterical ravings of the congressman's detractors resulted not from Powell's peccadillos, but from his longstanding opposition to racism. The scene was deeply disturbing.

Early the next year, rumor had it that former Vice-President Richard Milhouse Nixon, as a candidate for the Presidency, would pursue a "Southern Strategy." Raymond Jones knew what that meant. He had seen it before. Nixon would win. Of that he was certain. Why? The "backlash" that his good friend President Lyndon Johnson had predicted was happening. Realizing the threat, Jones surveyed his own backyard. Already, unmistakable signs of the disease were apparent in New York, and the names of "law and order" conservatives were being promoted as candidates against "liberal" Democrats. Two new developments were the last straw, for now even Regular Democrats were defecting to the "conservative" camp. In this further fractured and politically regressive atmosphere, J. Raymond Jones could not live. He resigned as Tammany Chief in March 1967, and as District Leader a few months later.

Predictably, Richard Nixon won the presidency of the United States in 1968 on a "law and order" platform, and the next year Mario Procaccino won the Democratic nomination for mayor on the same platform. To John Raymond Jones, forty years a loyal Democrat, having attained the party's highest honor in New York County, the time had come to repudiate his party's nominee for mayor and support his Republican opponent. The choice was a painful and unhappy one, but the decision was never in question; humanity must triumph over bigotry and party loyalty. Now as an unrestricted City Councilman, he announced his support for John V. Lindsay in September, and, with sadness but hope, witnessed Lindsay's victory in November. Jones had struck his last formal public blow for decency and humanity in New York City politics. He retired in December, aged 70 years.

Any aspiring Black politician would do well to study the careers of politicians such as Mayor Tom Bradley of Los Angeles, Lieutenant Governor James Wilder of Virginia, former Congresswoman Shirley Chisholm, and J. Raymond Jones. All these individuals joined their party early, advocated defensible and practicable positions, and worked hard for their adoption. They all made contributions to their party before they demanded rewards.

To join a political party and to work one's way up is not as simple as it sounds. One cannot just go down and register as a regular Democrat or Republican and expect to become immediately a part of the party's leadership. The route, even in the 1980s, is still up through the organization, unless, due to community standing, the party courts a person, as was the case with Constance Baker Motley in 1964. There simply isn't any other way! For aspiring officeholders to whatever level, the journey begins at the party's local club. The support of "family ties" in the party is necessary for political advancement. One therefore usually has to pay one's dues by working as a poll watcher, a petitions gatherer, eventually perhaps as the captain of an election district, maybe one day a district leader, and so on up the ladder. Seldom does an elected or party official gain the post without having gone through at least some of these stages within the organization. A more active incorporation of Blacks into the U.S. political parties at the lowest level and progressing through these stages is the surest way of achieving power and influencing policy. When this is done, particularly in areas where the minority population is at or approaches majority, neither party has any choice but to sponsor minorities for appointive and elective offices. The memoirs of J. Raymond Jones illustrate this truism repeatedly, not only for Jones, but for all his political colleagues.

The greater Black participation in the party and its various activities, the better the everyday political education of Black people, because increased dissemination of information to the Black community can only come about by the dispersion of Black people throughout the parties. This is a most important point because, although increasing numbers of the Black population are receiving a "higher education," these young Black people have not been taught much about the realities of the political game. All too often, for instance, college graduates are under the impression that parties exist only for providing elected officials. They either ignore or are unaware that there are thousands of jobs available that, on the face of it, are not political jobs, but indeed cannot be gotten without political connections and sponsorship. For example, appointive judgeships cannot be obtained without the sponsorship of party officials. Even at state universities, as exemplified in the 1986 confrontation between Massachusetts Governor Michael Dukakis and the committee to select the state's Chancellor of Higher Education, the appointment of the Chancellor is not simply based on academic, professional merit, but on politics. Unaware that such jobs exist as political plums, Blacks will aspire to them but fail because they have no political leverage. This was why J. Raymond Jones, before his retirement, lamented the local political clubs' decline in membership and influence.

The wide distribution of these clubs once provided a quick education to the uninitiated men and women who, aspiring to political careers, came relatively ignorant into the political arena. Malcolm Cowley in his book *Exile's Return* commenting on American education of 1916, said:

In school, unless we happened to be Southerners, we were divested of any local pride. We studied Ancient History and American History, but not, in my own case, the history of western Pennsylvania. . . . We had high school courses in Latin, German, Chemistry, good courses all of them, and a class in Civics where we learned to list the Amendments to the Constitution and name the members of the Supreme Court; *but we never learned how Presidents were really chosen or how a law was put through Congress. If one of us had later come into contact with the practical side of government—that is, if he wished to get a street paved, an assessment reduced, a friend out of trouble with the police or a relative appointed to office—well, fortunately the ward boss wouldn't take much time to set him straight.*[9] (Emphasis supplied)

Cowley's enlightening and profound observation in 1934 could not be more correct. Despite the now flourishing schools of "public policy" in the universities, it remains largely true today. Therefore, the decline of political clubs in Black and mixed communities is especially unfortunate, for they once promoted a strong sense of political community, resulting in a greater awareness of the importance of politics and of its potential for everyone. Although Shirley Chisholm in her autobiography is scathing towards the white-run political clubs she worked with and against in Brooklyn's 17th Assembly District, in explaining her seeming sudden rise to prominence in 1968, the year she entered Congress, she writes:

What they fail to realize is that in Brooklyn there have been Black people working toward political freedom for more than twenty years. They do not know the effort of groups like the Bedford-Stuyvesant Political League, the Unity Democratic Club, and others that in all the Bedford-Stuyvesants of this country have been working, organizing, collecting and fighting toward freedom from white political control of black communities.[10]

Whether it is through the traditional club structure or through some other type of organization, it is strikingly obvious that in the career of Jones, Chisholm, and all the other Black officeholders that there have to be readily identifiable organizational structures in Black communities which the community can support and from which it can expect assistance, both economic and political. In this regard, more is better. However, an opposite approach is being advocated by political wizards, and this approach the Reverend Jessie Jackson has tried and will probably try again. But how viable is it?

Edward Costikyan, the New York County Leader before J. Raymond Jones wrote in 1980:

If laboring in the political vineyards and working your way up seem like just too much work, cheer up. In the 1980s there is an easier way. Start at the top. Among those who have successfully followed this route are Senator Daniel Patrick Moynihan and former Senator James Buckley of New York, Senators John Glenn and Howard Metzenbaum of Ohio, Governor Jerry Brown and former Governor Ronald Reagan of California, Senator Charles Percy of Illinois, Senator Lloyd Bentsen of

Texas, Senator Bill Bradley of New Jersey. Among those who are waiting to follow this route are Henry Kissinger, former Treasury Secretary William Simon, former Miss America Bess Myerson, and perhaps a host of successful businessmen, college presidents, television personalities, and others who are looking for new worlds to conquer.[11]

After sketching the career of Senator Moynihan, he adds:

The Moynihan switch signifies that in the politics of the 1980s it's not necessary to have spent years climbing up the ladder. Senator Henry Jackson started as an elected County Prosecutor, was then a Congressman, and then over four terms a senator. He sits in the same body as Moynihan and Bradley, no more or less than they, but different. There is now a new and faster route to the top. It is another proof of the old non-Euclidean political proposition, which is: *Rule 9. In politics, a straight line is never the shortest distance between two points.*[12]

All this is very interesting, and perhaps the Reverend Jackson read Costikyan, but on close examination this glib prescription does not undermine what may be called the "Jones Rule:" *The Black politician is best served by choosing his party, paying his dues, and then seeking power.*

It is significant that none of the people mentioned by Costikyan is Black. Were he to have filled his book with names, very, very few would be Black, because outside the purely political arena, and in the everyday life of America, very few Blacks have been able to achieve the required prominence to come in from the top. Virtually bereft of such opportunity, the Black political aspirant is left with little real choice but to toil in the party trenches for at least a convincing period. Considering the barriers to the alternative approach, such toil is sometimes satisfactorily remunerative and the bonus is that it usually provides the Black politician with support from white constituents.

In 1984, the Reverend Jessie Jackson attempted the "over-the-top" route to the highest office in the United States. He was, predictably, unsuccessful. It appears that in 1988 he will again try the same route, but the prospects are not now any more encouraging. Nonetheless, Jackson's campaign has already yielded larger benefits. It has definitely brought significant numbers of Black "non-voters" to the ballot box. This is important, because even in the 1980s, Blacks have continued to vote in numbers far below their potential, and a significant segment is not even registered to vote. In fact, since the peak year of 1972, the rate of increase in Black elected officials has slowed significantly in the South,[13] and the editors of the 15th edition of the *National Roster of Black Elected Officials* note that in the rest of the nation there has been a similar decline.[14] In their overview they conclude:

In 1985 blacks continued to make progress in winning electoral office, but the rate of increase remained far below the double-digit rates of the early 1970s. This can perhaps be explained by the fact that the great majority of blacks who seek public office depend heavily on electoral support from other blacks to win; but there are fewer and fewer majority-black places that do not already have BEOs. Thus, increasing the number of BEOs may require not only stricter enforcement of laws protecting black voting rights but also an ability on the part of black candidates for public office to attract more votes from groups besides their own.[15]

Indeed, that is exactly what Jessie Jackson is trying to do, and he has been far more successful than former Congresswoman Shirley Chisholm, who unsuccessfully attempted to run for the presidency in 1972. But Jackson's problem is that the position he seeks was not factored into the Costikyan equation; that is, no one, Black or white, runs for the presidency of the United States without having paid party dues. Since Jackson has never been a mayor, Congressman, or even president of the local school board, he is regarded as an upstart and an usurper. As such, he will never become President, except by a miracle. Such occurrences are extremely rare these days.

More attainable in the 1980s are governorships and senatorships. Such real possibilities exist from the confluence of two new developments in American political life. First, Black leadership has now reached such a level of political maturity that no office in the land is considered beyond Black attainment. This confidence, the development of political sophistication, and the willingness to attempt participation in all areas of politics (a willingness not present before 1960) is revolutionary. Second, just as revolutionary, although seemingly less so, is the willingness of whites, even in southern states, to vote for Black candidates for high office. The case of James Wilder's election to Lieutenant Governor of Virginia in 1986 is most revealing, and while Mayor Tom Bradley lost his bid to become Governor of California in 1984, the fact remains that he was the nominee of the Democratic Party. Wilder certainly could not have been elected Lieutenant Governor on Black votes only, nor could Tom Bradley become his party's standard bearer without white votes. All this bodes well for the future of Black politicians and the Black community, but it is instructive that, in the case of Bradley and Wilder, both had been long-standing participants in party politics.

Despite these encouraging developments, there still linger serious problems in American political life, for Black political progress has been less than satisfactory even in the 1980s, and indeed the near-term outlook is certainly not as encouraging as it could be. Eddie Williams, Director of the Joint Center for Political Studies, has noted that although the number of Black elected officials in the United States rose from 6,056 to 6,424 in

1985, this calculation amounts to little more than a six percent increase.[16] These figures show that Blacks hold only approximately one and one-half percent of the elective offices in the United States, when their voting-age population is approximately twelve percent. Mr. Williams also points out that the Black rate of increase in elective officeholding in 1985 was only one-third the annual rate between 1970 and 1976. In Williams' view there is a desperate need for improvement, but this "will depend on the ability of Black candidates to appeal to non-Black electorates."[17] Here lies the rub; for this, the political life of J. Raymond Jones is instructive.

Although Jones started his political career over 60 years ago in a Harlem that is today Black, his early lessons in the techniques of racial and inter-racial politics were learned in a district that was then racially mixed. Throughout his political life he sought independence of the Black community from the domination of white racists, but at no time did Raymond Jones advocate racial politics for its own sake. As he rose in power in New York City, his dedication to integrated party politics earned him the trust of his non-racist white colleagues. This trust allowed him to promote a significant number of Black people to high positions in the Democratic Party and into prominent jobs in business and government. All these people shared his hope for an integrated future society cured of bigotry. There would then be no need for racial politics. That time has not come yet, but Jones' record shows that with a thorough understanding of our political and economic systems and of their interrelationships, and by the assiduous application of intelligence and forethought, aspiring Black leaders can lift themselves and their communities, regardless of their racial mix, to a level never before achieved. His life and those of the leaders he has tutored testify to that fact.

Chapter 1

Youth and Adolescence

I WAS ELECTED Chairman of the New York County Democratic Committee in the late fall of 1963. Though the title was fast becoming meaningless, I was now called the "Boss of Tammany Hall." What is perhaps surprising is that I never thought of myself as the boss of anything; yet I had desired the post, had thought it would be mine three years earlier when it went to my friend, Edward Costikyan, and was pleased for myself and all my supporters when I was elected. What I desired and tried to do as Tammany leader were the same things I had been trying to do nearly all my life—to involve as many people as possible in New York city and state party politics and thereby in the democratic electoral process.

Because I was a Black man, my early political base was restricted to Harlem, but I was fortunate to be involved in city, state, and national politics between 1930 and 1970, a time which saw tremendous changes in social relations in the United States. By 1963, these changes made it possible for me to be regarded not only as the "Harlem Fox" but also as Leader of Tammany.

The road to Tammany Hall, or for that matter Harlem, was not direct, for I was not born in the United States, but in Charlotte Amalie of the Danish West Indies (on the island of St. Thomas, Now part of the U.S. Virgin Islands). Once in New York, I was determined to make something of myself and my adopted community. By 1921, I knew politics would be the vehicle. The route to that realization was as circuitous as my passage to the mainland, but once I had made the decision, I pursued my goals with sober purpose, biding my time when necessary, and seizing opportunities swiftly as I recognized them. My life has been an odyssey, full of thought, action and, political strife. Yet, all in all, it has been an exalting and exhausting eighty-seven years and I am told that I have made a few lasting contributions.

At 87 years of age I look back now with a feeling of amazement and awe at the long distance I have travelled from inauspicious beginnings. I was born on November 19, 1899, in what is now Charlotte Amalie, in the Virgin Islands, the only child of Ansedella Perdereaux of St. Thomas, and Alfred Percival Jones, an immigrant from Barbados. When I was five, my father died, leaving my mother and me to face the world alone. In St. Thomas at that time, however, we were never really isolated, for our community was tightly knit and something of the extended family without the ties of blood kinship operated there. This close community caused me much distress, for I was an adventuresome fellow, and my mother's favorite maxim was, "The Bible say don't spare the rod and spoil the child." Her philosophy was all too often put into practice by this extended family; any time members of the community saw you doing anything they considered improper, it would be reported promptly to your mother. Any youngster in St. Thomas, suspecting that a report had been made at home, had better be prepared when he got there, for there was no question that Mother would be ready.

Reflecting during my adult years on my mother's willingness to so generously apply the rod, I finally realized what was at work. It was really a matter of upholding community standards. Black St. Thomas, before the coming of the Americans in 1916, was firmly middle-class in its aspirations, and since by reason of property and education my family was already in that category, any erosion of that status was viewed with horror. In those days, a sharp contrast to now, good conduct and proper manners were the hallmark of the good person, and any evidence of deviation merited prompt punishment, which many times in the heat of adult disappointment was untempered by justice.

It is impossible to be certain of what source supplies important beliefs in one's adult life, but as a youth, I knew what was fair and what wasn't, and the concern for fair and judicious treatment finally led me to an estrangement from my mother, a decision to leave St. Thomas, and the pursuit of a political career in which I believe I tried to act with fairness. Until the time came to leave St. Thomas; however, I played by the rules as best I could. I attended All Saints Anglican Church, went religiously to Sunday School classes, and zealously pursued my studies at Lincoln Junior High School, from which I graduated in 1915 as the top male student of my class. Graduation was, therefore, a mixed emotional experience. I was happy to graduate with honors, but I was bothered by the fact that there was no senior high school to attend and that indeed my prospects now looked dim.

It was the custom in those times for students graduating at the top of the junior high classes to be sponsored for a scholarship to Denmark. During my last year at Lincoln, it was widely believed that I would be recommended and accepted, but the European war abruptly eliminated that possibility. So on graduation day, after a year of happy anticipation, I realized there was no place for me to go.

During my school years, my mother had decided that I should be apprenticed to my godfather, a shoemaker. This was an unhappy development, for I had grown to know something of the world and its possibilities through the books available to me through my godmother's family, the Normans, and the public library. Though I was very young and understood things imperfectly, I considered myself something of an intellectual. After all, I had read widely in world history. I knew of the exploits of Alexander the Great, of Hannibal's extraordinary march through the Alps, and of the incredible journeys of Marco Polo. I had read with keen interest, and no less enjoyment, the Greek classics. I knew Oedipus Rex, Electra, and Medea, and I was not unacquainted with the works of William Shakespeare. For a young person schooled so heavily in history and the classics, settling down at the age of 16 years was unthinkable. As for becoming a shoemaker, sitting on a stool with an awl, sewing the tops of shoes to the sole, or repairing old broken-down shoes day after day, was out of the question. No, I was very clear on the matter; I had no intention of becoming a shoemaker.

Therefore, my shoemaking apprenticeship was brief. I was determined, nevertheless, to find some occupation that would suit my temperament, since my skills were nil. In quick succession, I was an apprentice tailor, joiner, and printer. On this last job, speed was important, and in my desire to be the fastest, one of my fingers was crushed in the job press. I immediately concluded that I would not excel in this line of work and abandoned further exploration of that trade.

When my finger healed, I decided to explore the harbor for an opportunity. Earlier, while I had been at Lincoln, I and a number of other boys would visit the docks in serious pursuit of business. Quite a number of ships from a variety of nations would visit St. Thomas during any given week, and my friends and I soon discovered that sailors would buy conch shells on which local scenes were painted and other such novelties. This was a lucrative trade for us, but it was also a very good education. One perforce picked up a bit of German and French as well as a knowledge of what goods appealed to various nationalities and what to expect for them.

In time, my activities at the harbor took on serious entrepreneurial proportions. Though any trade was ad hoc, I made a respectable sum of money—or more than most lads my age. One did not make money, however, without acquiring a quick knowledge of the rates of exchange and a feeling for overhead—a concept of which I knew nothing formally, but which I sensed. Apart from the novelties we traded, there was Bay Rum and Florida Water, and I quickly learned how many boxes of foreign cigarettes equalled a bottle of Bay Rum plus overhead. I learned, too, the concept of "how much the market would bear" in times of scarcity. This was exciting business, made even more so when I realized that I had a talent for swiftly converting Deutsche marks into French francs, and francs into dollars. To me this was exciting business, but to my mother it was dubious until she realized I was not playing and was, in fact, making money.

All this ended abruptly with the advent of the war. Few ships visited after 1914, but I had been attracted by the economic opportunities of the harbor, and it was inevitable that I would return there after I had found other occupations wanting. But the absence of ships, except the occasional warship that put in for stores and liberty, meant that I had to find a normal harbor job, for there was clearly a recession in my old "import-export business." In fact, my first job there, that of water boy, indicated a loss in stature. This occupation I viewed as temporary, however, for surely an opportunity would present itself through which I would be allowed to prove myself. In fact, it was this youthful confidence that caused my memorable encounter with the steam hammer.

I had frequently watched the operator of the steam hammer as he drove steel beams into the sea bed at the West India Dock Company where I was employed, and I knew that it was a job I could do. Intent on proving myself, I decided one day, with no trepidation, to operate this machine when it was left unattended. No one was more surprised than I when in the next instant after seizing the ropes, I found myself treading the warm waters of the Caribbean. And it was a fact that I was in warm water of more than one kind, for before I had reached terra firma, I had come to the conclusion that the waters at home would not be temperate either.

It was this concern with the climate that caused me to delay my return home until very late. This tactic was not successful, for as I approached my home it became very clear that the gate and all the doors and windows were locked. I have said before that my mother was very strict, so, though upset, I was not entirely surprised. I marshalled my courage and knocked on the window of my mother's room. No response came. After a repeat performance, I knew that I would be on my own for the night.

Since I could think of no place to go, I retreated to a set of brick stairs across from my house and there I sat to consider my fate. As the night grew darker and my brick seat harder, I decided that the time was near to leave

St. Thomas. I recalled that my grandfather, a carpenter, had left St. Thomas for Puerto Rico long ago to build homes for the U.S. army after the Spanish-American War. Not only was my grandfather there, but also two aunts. By midnight, Puerto Rico had begun to look very attractive to me.

I slept on the steps that night, an experience which by morning I had come to regard as adequate penance. My mother, however, said I had become too rebellious and that my spirit had to be broken. I was made to kneel in a gravel bed for fifteen minutes with arms frontally outstretched with a brick in each hand. This punishment I considered much too undignified, and in my humiliation all reservations about leaving St. Thomas for Puerto Rico vanished.

Resolved though I was, the actual business of departing presented a problem. Though I had a small fund hidden away, I knew that it would not be enough to pay my passage to Puerto Rico and support me for any appreciable time. For a while I was troubled by this difficulty, but I recalled that many people I had read about had travelled far as stowaways. If they could do it, so could I. After all, I viewed my situation as definitely untenable.

I also recollected that a Danish motor vessel still made regular trips between St. Croix, St. Thomas, and Puerto Rico. This ship would be my conveyance, and within a few days, I put the plan into action. Since I was something of an old hand around the harbor, I experienced no trouble in getting aboard the vessel and ensconcing myself in the anchor chain locker. Luckily I encountered no difficulty on board ship or in disembarking in Puerto Rico, and soon I arrived at my aunts', who happily took me in. I was now a man, but soon the sobering business of finding a job deflated my new-found euphoria.

I have noted before that my youthful contacts with ships and sailors, combined with my reading of great naval explorers, had fostered a romantic view of a sailor's life. To travel to exotic places, to learn all kinds of languages, to see strange animals— all these meant adventure. Then there was the business of how all this was done. I was in awe of the captains, who, I thought, were the only ones who understood the deep mysteries of guiding a ship over vast expanses of water without any landmarks. Determined to learn these mysteries, I decided to become a sailor.

I was hired on the S.S. *President*, a German ship of the Hamburg-American Line. Dreams of travel were not to be realized, however, for shortly after I hired on, the United States declared war on Germany and the ship was impounded while in San Juan harbor. But it was during the impoundment proceedings that I discovered, much to my surprise, that I was an American.

Everybody had been asleep on board that early Sunday morning when American soldiers with 45 calibre pistols in their hands woke us up and ordered us on deck. We were told that the United States had declared war on Germany and that the ship was impounded. After a lot of commotion and questioning, I realized that I was one of only two Black people on that ship;soon after the Americans had questioned me about place of birth and domicile, I was politely informed that I was now an American citizen since the United States had bought St. Thomas the year before, in 1916. The announcement created a strange feeling, since, until that morning, as odd as it may seem now, I still considered myself a Dane. Such is the metabolism of youth, however, that I did not dwell on it. American or Dane did not matter. Adventure beckoned, and that was more important.

Since I had aunts in Puerto Rico and my grandfather owned property there, I was allowed to disembark, and I journeyed back to my aunts' home in Santurce, where I received a wary welcome. I still did not intend to stay long in Puerto Rico, for I now considered myself a dashing sailor, therefore twice a week I journeyed into San Juan in search of a new berth. Within a month I was successful.

My new job was as a fireman on the S.S. *Pampa*, an Argentine Navy freighter, and I got it, not because of any experience as a fireman, but because the German personnel officer discovered that I could converse in his language, albeit in a rudimentary way. My idea of the fireman's job was strictly a landlubber's—that is, to go around putting out fires. This understanding was very rudely erased when, taken below decks, I was confronted with the boiler room. The boiler's machinery seemed monstrous. I was instructed to throw shovelsful of coal into the four fireboxes, which were simply very big steel boxes with openings for coal to be thrown in. The fireman was required to raise his shovel as high as five feet for the highest box and throw the coal back as deep as eight feet.

Of course, I had never done this, but I wanted the job, and so I picked up the shovel and tried my first throw. Needless to say, the coal went everywhere except in the firebox. It wasn't that I was weak or lacking in height, for I was at least six feet tall by then and quite strong. What I sorely lacked was technique and my failure to display it was a big embarrassment for me. My boss, a big Black Brazilian fellow, was not too concerned with my mental state, because he promptly cursed me in a very profane manner while pushing me around. This was too much. The verbal abuse I did not mind, since I felt that in a way I deserved it; but the physical shove, given my already bruised ego, was intolerable. In response, I, to use a phrase, decked him. My triumph was short-lived for, in gentlemanly fashion, I permitted him to rise, at which point he proceeded to knock me down and subdue me by *sabate*, a form of fighting I had not seen before.

Although my initial experience on the job was not encouraging, the engine room crew apparently liked my style. My fistic opponent became my friend, and the Chief Engineer, a German, took an especial interest in my welfare. By the time our ship reached Buenos Aires, I was an accomplished fireman and was paid as one. My hard work apparently impressed the Chief Engineer, who offered to help me become an Argentinian citizen and to arrange my schooling in steamship engineering.

This offer did not tempt me, however, for I had now heard so much about New York City, a place where the streets were virtually paved with gold, that nothing could prevent my going there. Since I did not sign up for continued work on the *Pampa*, I was turned over to the American Consulate, which I persuaded to send me to New York instead of Puerto Rico. In this curious way, I arrived in New York City where, dazzled by the excitement of the place, I somehow lost the desire to return to sea. In my youthful enthusiasm, I convinced myself that this was my kind of town and that I would find, in full measure, all the wondrous things I sought.

When I was in Puerto Rico, I knew a family, the Woods, who now lived quite well in Harlem. To the Woods I went, and they provided me with a room in their apartment for a modest rent. They had a boarder, Christophina Bastian, a beautiful immigrant from St. Thomas, who became my first wife.

Now that I was in New York and settled in a nice environment, two things became very urgent. One, I had to get a high school education and, two, I had to find a job. Finding a job was easy in 1917, but going to high school wasn't. In those days, fortunately, there were private high schools that held classes in the evenings. These schools were for the most part run by immigrant Jews and most of the students were Jewish. I was accepted at one located at Fifth Avenue and 114th St., where I immediately enrolled in the university preparatory courses.

At that time I had no definite plans for going to college, because I married Miss Bastian and was about to begin a family, but the desire for liberal, humane learning was still very strong in me, so I avoided vocational topics. For this attitude, I ran into trouble with my young wife. Being of a self-described "practical disposition," she protested vigorously against my seemingly foolish interest in the humanities. To her, a liberal education was for white people, since she noted, with weighty evidence that in America very few Black men went anywhere with such an education. Since I knew very little then of the great Black men and women in America who had overcome adversity and distinguished themselves, I was unable to justify my position in any pragmatic way. Nonetheless, I was convinced that there was useful knowledge to be gained and beauty to be enjoyed in my studies. It was in complete faith, therefore, that I carried on, despite interruptions, and eventually obtaining my diploma. Many years have passed since then and although circumstances beyond my control prevented me from obtaining a college degree, I have never regretted the time, effort, and money I spent on this endeavor. In fact, as the occasion permitted, I would take college courses that provided me with information for my political, business, and social life. This penchant for learning contributed to the eventual dissolution of my first marriage, but I was fortunate in my second marriage to find a person who understood my yearning for knowledge.

While I pursued an education, I worked. My first job was as an elevator operator in the Hearst Building at 2 Williams Street. Office space in this building was occupied by theatrical personalities and the staff of Hearst Publications.

Approximately one week after starting on this job, I had my first experience with what it was really like to be Black in America. While taking passengers down, I heard a woman's voice screaming, "Stop the car! You're hurting me! Call the cops!" I immediately stopped the elevator, looked around in the car, but no one seemed to be in distress. I surveyed the passengers who for the most part had straight faces; but on two faces, there were smirks. I restarted the car; two floors down, the screams were repeated, at which point an elderly gentleman in the car demanded that the sounds cease. Confused and a bit scared, I discharged my passengers and went to discuss the matter with a fellow elevator operator who found my story amusing. He told me that two of the passengers in the car were ventriloquists, able to throw their voices so it would appear that the sounds were coming from under the elevator. Many whites, he told me, believed that Blacks were innately superstitious and easily frightened, and therefore easy victims for this kind of prank. I reflected briefly on this information, and once more decided that it was time for a change of venue.

I had heard that work was plentiful on the docks, and recalling my experience in St. Thomas, I decided that the docks would be more tolerant, less mean and claustrophobic than a public elevator. In this, I was sadly mistaken. On my first try I was hired, and for a few days I thought my reasoning had been flawless. All this self-congratulation was swiftly erased on my sixth day, when I made the unforgettable acquaintance of Griffo.

Griffo was an integral part of the dock system which at that stage of my life I could not even have imagined. But he was real, and in my ignorance he caused me real trouble. In brief, Griffo, a small Black man, was the moneylender on my section of the docks. The way it worked was simple. The foremen made a point of letting any non-union worker hired know that Griffo was there to assist you financially. Anyone "in the know" would borrow money from Griffo, whether he needed it or not. On payday he repaid Griffo, but at two or three percent interest per day. Also, if Griffo cashed your check there was a small fee. On my first day at work, the foreman had carefully pointed out Griffo, but he had been a bit too delicate in the explanation of Griffo's role for such an unsophisticated newcomer as myself. As a result, I blithely ignored Mr. Griffo and within a few days I paid the penalty. I was unceremoniously fired. No expression of regret would reverse my fate. I had been uncooperative and perhaps was viewed as a potential troublemaker, and so it was farewell to the docks.

There was no question that I viewed this development with frustration, anger, and disillusionment, and for a few days I was thoroughly depressed. Fortunately, my new landlord, Mr. Hoffman, had connections with the Pullman porters, and when I told him of my problem, he quickly engineered a job for me with the troop transportation service. Initially, I welcomed this new job with delight, for although it took me away from home for days at a time, this was compensated for, in my mind anyway, by the excitement of travel. Unfortunately, the reality turned out to be quite different from the fantasy. My job as a porter was to keep the troop cars clean and, where appropriate, attend to the personal needs of the inductees. The usual run was from varying points in upstate New York through Florida and the south to San Diego, California.

The trip was uneventful until we reached Jacksonville, Florida, where I was switched to a car of southern recruits. I had the responsibility of sanitizing their car and the disinfectant was somewhat noxious. One day I made the mistake of using too strong a solution and objections were raised by the southern inductees. They began to shout insults at me such as "Boy, why did you do this?" "Boy, do that." "Nigger, do this." "Nigger, do that." All this intensified as the train traveled farther across the deep South. This was my first experience with groups of southern white Americans.

I was unaccustomed to this kind of harassment and let it be known that I resented these indignities. The southern recruits, however, interpreted my reaction as the show of an uppity Nigger who didn't know his place; when the train reached Georgia, the recruits physically attacked me, thinking, I believe, that the time had come to put me in my "place." I finally escaped to another car where I found sympathetic support from northern recruits with whom I had worked earlier in the trip. They blocked the passageway to insure my safety. I remained in this haven until the train reached Mississippi where the Pullman supervisor came aboard and listened to my complaints and those of my friends. Despite the serious nature of the matter, he decided that I should return to the same car. I did not look forward to this, and on the advice of a northern friend, I bought a revolver from one of them and hid it in my closet before returning to the southerner's car. Although I could detect animosity, nothing happened until the train reached New Orleans.

Since Louisiana at this time was the first wet state that we had reached in the South, the recruits were eager to indulge. A number of them tried to let bygones be bygones, and tried to cajole me to leave the train and purchase liquor for them, which I refused to do. They complained constantly that they had no porter, that I had deserted them. When the train arrived in New Orleans, the southerners attacked me again. Outnumbered, I was quickly knocked down, but because of my previous experience, I did not even try to get up. As I proceeded to crawl on my hands and knees toward the locker in the passageway where my "equalizer" was stashed, my tormentors vigorously applied their feet to my backside. But when I finally reached the closet, and pulled out my Saturday night special, all those great "He-men" scattered like chickens. Three shots later, I could claim unequivocal victory, though I had succeeded, luckily, in shooting only the roof of the Pullman car.

The joy of triumph was short-lived for, within seconds, I came back to earth and realized I was in serious trouble. Somewhere along the line I knew I would be arrested. My greatest desire, therefore, was to get out of the South and to Los Angeles where I thought I stood a fair chance of receiving justice. Providence was on my side, for nothing happened until we reached Yuma, Arizona, where a sheriff boarded the train, politely informed me in one breath that I had been drafted back in New York and was also now the father of a son. But there was also the business of my gunplay to resolve, and here I was thankful that the sheriff saw himself as a westerner rather than a southerner. Years later I would remember this incident when Senator Lyndon Baines Johnson persuasively made the same distinction. Although he addressed me as "boy," I sensed immediately that the word had a different meaning than if it were used by a southerner. "Boy," the sheriff had said, "what am I going to do with you, trying to shoot up that train?"

Of course I was powerless and I could think of no placatory response. After a few seconds, he suddenly smiled, and relief flooded me. "There are some of your folks camped down by the railroad station," he beamed. "Why don't you stay with them until we get this thing straightened out?" This was all right with me, although I hadn't the faintest clue who my "folks" were. As it turned out, he took me to a contingent of Black troops, I believe from the U.S. 5th Cavalry. The friendly sheriff made the introductions, and with these men I had a wonderful time for some seven days. Then my sheriff showed up and informed me that there were no charges against me and that I was to report to the Pullman offices in Los Angeles for pay and passage to New York. Two days later, as I left the Pullman offices, I heard ringing of bells and tooting of horns; in the streets people were dancing. "What is going on?" I asked a passerby. "Don't you know? Don't you know?" he replied excitedly. "The war is over."

For millions of people around the world, November 11, 1918 must have been a day of heartfelt relief from the fear of oppression, likely death, and the savageries of war. I, too, standing on the street in Los Angeles, shared the moment. I was free of the prospect of boot camp, and caught up in the celebration of war's end, I felt that I was free of an uncertain future. I was in a country full of vigor and celebratory confidence, and I knew that I was at the right place at the right time.

When I arrived in New York City a few days later, Harlem was in a festive mood. People waited expectantly for the return of the celebrated 369th Infantry Regiment, the Black regiment had the best fighting record in the U.S. Army. There was enthusiastic talk of Marcus Garvey and the U.N.I.A., new opportunities at work, new and better places to live, new cafes, new everything, even the "New Negro." In early 1919 I understood little of all this and I certainly did not know I would soon be living through the era now known as the Harlem Renaissance and the Jazz Age. But I sensed that there were opportunities here for a level-headed immigrant, and all I need to do was to study, develop a sound philosophy, and get to work. All this I was determined to do. Never again would I be threatened with the life of a shoemaker.

Chapter 2

The Call to Politics and a Change of Philosophy

HARLEM, and for that matter New York City after World War I, provided a veritable feast of ideologies, movements, and countermovements. The war had transformed the social atmosphere in the United States and the returning Black veterans expected a better life for their courage and dedication in the war in Europe. One Black leader in Texas had stated that the war would be the source of Black people's second emancipation so great was his certainty of the American people's gratitude. But this was not to be. In the very next year, 1919, more than seventy-five Black people were lynched; and in East St. Louis, Detroit, and other places there were race riots, by one count twenty-five in all. Things were looking worse, not better.

In Harlem, the response to the ambivalent treatment of Black soldiers in Europe and to the unequivocally racist and discriminatory practices at home, caused a political reaction that was as varied as it was unprecedented. Movements and ideologies all vigorously vied for the attention and support of New Yorkers.

At the crossroads of the main thoroughfares, Muslims, or people purporting to be Muslims, could be seen on one corner, invoking Allah as the saviour of colored people. On the corner opposite one might find Chandler Owen, A. Phillip Randolph, or the elder Hubert Harrison laying down in certain and magisterial tones the emancipatory laws of socialism. Somewhere nearby, Cyril Briggs of the African Blood Brotherhood would hold forth on the importance of ancestry and of the blood; and in some hall not far away, the Black Communists would defiantly rise to songs of comradeship, liberty, and solidarity. This alone was exciting and heady, and generated almost an exaltation of feeling among the people of Harlem. But nothing could compare to the primal feelings of pride in race and strength in unity and the hope for posterity as when evening fell and the crossroads were vacated for the arrival of the man himself, Marcus Aurelius Garvey. Everything paled beside the dynamism, eloquence, and powerful personality of this short, stocky Jamaican immigrant. He was deadly serious and he believed profoundly in what he said. His vision was grand and the best of it transcended the boundaries of the United States. Black people felt the embrace of others in far-away Africa, Central America and the West Indies in the person of Gravey and his United Negro Improvement Association. Large numbers responded with passion and dedication.

Like so many others, I responded to Garvey's vision of the fellowship of diverse people of African ancestry. This was compelling to me for I knew something of the diversity of Black people in the Caribbean, and I knew also that a special feeling of identification among people of African ancestry throughout the world did not yet exist. I had learned from wiser men than myself of the attempts of the West Indian barrister, Henry Sylvester Williams, to forge a sense of common identification in the Pan/African Conference of 1900, and I was also aware, though vaguely, of the attempt of W.E.B. DuBois to carry on Williams' work. I was too unsophisticated at that time to fully comprehend Dr. DuBois' work; furthermore, I was not intimate with the National Association for the Advancement of Colored People and such-like organizations. The fact is that in those days organizations like the NAACP and the Urban League operated as middle-class organizations. Unlike the Garvey movement, they had little direct emotional appeal. In other words, they lacked all the ingredients of a mass movement, which the U.N.I.A. possessed in abundance. I, like many others, was more attracted to the U.N.I.A. because of its direct appeal, its willingness to seek out people any time and any place in the cause of fellowship. I responded to the possibility of a world-wide movement for racial progress by joining the movement in 1920. Although later I became a Garvey employee, and learned firsthand of the larger effects of the successes and failures of Garveyism, I did not realize its real worth until I had a bitter taste of racism in the politics of Tammany in the era of Mayor John Hylan and "Boss" Charles Murphy.

After my not joining the U.S. Army, I worked at a number of semi-laboring jobs until 1921 when I found a very good job as a labor recruiter for a Mr. Wells, who supplied manpower to a number of brick-making camps on the Hudson River. This Mr. Wells was a friend of a Mr. Banks, known in Harlem as "Chicken" Banks, the representative to the white Tammany leader from the United Colored Democracy Club of Harlem. Mr.

Banks was looking for Black election inspectors to register Blacks in Harlem for the upcoming city election of 1921. Mr. Wells recommended me for this week's work, and so began my practical political education.

For someone coming as I had from the Danish West Indies where only the elite could vote, the realization that anyone in New York 21 years old or over could vote was truly an eye-opening experience. I was even more impressed when it was explained to me that if I registered during the registration period, I, too, could vote. This was another good omen, for this was 1920 and in that year I had turned 21. The business of being a voter and an election inspector lifted my spirits. But in the end I was again very much disappointed with the outcome.

All inspectors were instructed to keep the Party's own registration books after registration ended on Saturday and return them to the club-house on the following Monday. So, on Monday, following the instructions posted on the books, I attempted to return them to the Cayuga Democratic Club, located in a limestone house in one of the better neighborhoods of Harlem. Admitted to the foyer, I was asked peremptorily by the doorkeeper:

"What do you want?"

"I want to deliver these books," I politely replied.

"This is not where you are supposed to deliver your books," the man scolded. "Take them to Banks Restaurant on 5th Avenue."

In those days I prided myself on doing things precisely, and the instructions on the books were clear. My reply, therefore, was firm:

"But the instructions say deliver them here."

"Never mind what the instructions say," he said loudly. "Do as I tell you to. This club is not for coloreds. Chicken Banks' is the club for coloreds."

What followed had by now become simple reflex action. Throwing the books in his face, I yelled, "You can deliver them yourself," and left.

I knew immediately that I would have to keep a low profile for some time if I were to keep this connection with the Democratic Party going. I wanted to do so, because such a connection seemed as if it had possibilities for me and for my friends. But as I thought about the rebuff by the doorman, I came to the conclusion that I knew little about the basis on which the doorman and his employers had built their confident hauteur. The origins and basis for their profound disregard for Black people, regardless of manners, character, and education, began to intrigue and annoy me as I grew older. I resolved to study this hateful business so that one day I could assist in hastening its disappearance.

It was a fortunate coincidence that my political "consciousness raising," as it would be called today, came at a time when so much was happening in New York City. In Harlem, there was so much being written of the

"New Negro," and such a mighty outpouring of literary and art works, that people soon began to characterize it as an "artistic renaissance." I was not an intellectual, so I could not judge, but I read the papers and learned that our people were doing good work. I was pleased with this development and felt proud that as a people we seemed to be emerging from a hesitant phase to a more assertive and assured one.

But somewhere in my own soul, I now knew that I, too, desired to make a contribution. Exactly how was not clear. One thing was certain, I knew too little of America, and, more important, too little of my immediate environment. I decided to observe carefully everything politic, social, and economic around me, to try to make sense of it all. One day I expected I would find a way to put the fruits of my personal study to good use.

In my "walks of discovery," as I called them, around Harlem, I saw parts of all that has been written about the Harlem Renaissance. I noted that few Black New Yorkers found difficulty in getting a job, but as my friend, the journalist Ray Stannard Baker, noted in his book, *Following the Color Line,*[1] very few of these jobs were of the best quality. I noted also the proliferation of jazz clubs and of others that were such in name only. I could not miss seeing the influx of white downtowners for fun and games; long before it ended, I wondered how long it would last. All this and more I witnessed, and much of it has been chronicled in very good histories of the era and of Harlem.

What is generally not noted however, is that in World War I and throughout the 1920s, there were also the beginnings of a political renaissance. That "renaissance" was less spectacular than its literary counterpart, but it was undeniably more durable, practical, and farsighted. In fact, it never died, as has been said of its artistic twin, but built itself slowly, literally block by city block all through the 1920s, 30s, and 40s, to this day. It is a fascinating story in which I played a small role, and today I look back with a sense of accomplishment on all those years of exhausting as well as exalted struggle.

What seems to be generally unknown is that in the early twenties there was what could be called a club movement among Blacks in New York. These clubs were of all kinds—social, civic, and political. At any of these clubs, sooner or later the "progress of the race," in art, literature, or economics, would be discussed. I was not artistic and so was not "in" with the artistic and intelligentsia crowd, but I did frequent a Black Democratic political club in my district where we discussed all manner of things. We did not have the power to implement our ideas, for our community was represented by whites with little interest in the welfare of Negroes, least of all in the ideas of young men such as myself. In fact, my club and others like it were merely weak buffers between the Black population and the white political parties. Far more powerful, by the way, were the Republican clubs at that time. But when New York Governor Franklin D. Roosevelt was elected President of the United States in 1932 and Black people began a dramatic shift away from the party of Lincoln, the Black Democratic clubs fared better.

My association with the Democrats between 1920 and 1925 was merely one of expediency. I was not yet so politically sophisticated as to be able to make a clear philosophical choice between Republicans and Democrats. I think now that I merely gravitated towards the Democrats because at that time in New York, Tammany held power and, more important, they appeared to have the stamina and skill to remain in power for a very long time. Actually, I was more a Garveyite in this period than a Democrat. This was not unusual, for it was a time of political flux in Harlem and shifting and overlapping political allegiances were common.

I became a member of the Universal Negro Improvement Association around 1920. Since the word "improvement" was in its title and since I needed improvement, I decided that involvement would be worth my while. It was not long before I met a powerful man in the movement, Ulysses Simpson Poston, who was then Garvey's Minister of Labor and Industry. In this post, U. S. Poston controlled all of the business ventures of the U.N.I.A., with the exception of the Black Star Line and a few small ventures.

In 1919, among the businesses were two restaurants, one of which was located in the U.N.I.A.'s Liberty Hall in Harlem. That one did a thriving and profitable business, but the other one lost money. There were also three grocery stores and a wet-wash laundry. These were unprofitable, too, when I met Poston. Since, as Minister of Labor and Industry, Poston had to travel a great deal, I suggested that perhaps I could be of some help. He accepted the suggestion immediately and promptly made me his assistant. The restaurants, laundry, and stores became my responsibility.

I was delighted to have this job, because I had ideas about how to turn the ventures around and had very much wanted the chance to test my ideas and prove myself. Although this was my primary motive, apart from the desire to help the organization, there was a secondary, although almost as compelling reason. This came in part from the atmosphere of the times and in part from the assessment of my own potential and possibilities after the war. In the so-called Jazz Age, the business of America was indeed business. I saw that and reasoned that without a college degree, the best chance I had of proving myself, with no profession, was to get involved in business wherever and at whatever level. This then was my chance to learn about business, even as I learned about the business of politics after work at our little club.

It did not take me long to solve the problem of the stores. I did this simply by establishing a procedure of greater bulk buying for the stores and restaurants, insisting on bulk discounts and establishing a central storage at Liberty Hall. This was all that was necessary in this case because service was good and patronage was adequate and steady.

The laundry was another problem entirely. It was not new, and its old equipment placed it at a disadvantage with the newer ones. Competition was fierce too, because there were quite a few laundries about. When I took over, the laundry served one apartment house and had one wagon route. It was painfully obvious to me that drastic changes had to be made. By winning support from customers, we were able to develop another route, but this now meant, at least to me, that the horse and wagon which we did not even own, had to go. In its stead, I bought a used Model T truck.

I am embarrassed to recall, even now, my first encounter with that truck. One day the driver did not show up and I decided I would carry on for the day. I had never driven a truck, or a car for that matter, but I knew in theory how these things worked and thought it would be a simple matter. The truck had to be cranked to start, so while I sat and majestically held the steering wheel, a young assistant cranked away. It must have been that I had not properly depressed the clutch, for the next thing I knew I had zoomed across the street, climbed the sidewalk and was almost through the door of the building across from our laundry. I retired as driver immediately, for if I hadn't, my young assistant, who just barely escaped with his life, would have made me. As it turned out, we prospered eventually, my confidence soared, and I began to believe that I had some talent for business.

I would argue at this point that the complete history of the Garvey Movement is not yet written, for nowhere has anyone told of the opportunities given to men and women like me to learn the art of business within the movement, or, more important, of the experience of Black people working for and with other Black people in successful Black enterprises. What is generally bandied about is the failure of the Black Star Line. This, I think, is a biased and unfair picture of Garvey's influence and of his entrepreneurial activities.

I recall, for instance, the time when U. S. Poston began to talk about the importance of agricultural commerce to Black farmers in the South. Within a short time a number of these farmers asked to send us products to sell directly in the New York and New Jersey markets. One staple I recall vividly were very big yellow-red yams; in a little while New York sidewalk vendors began selling hot roasted sweet yams. As I recall, they did well. The Black farmers' idea was to bypass the white middlemen who cheated them with impunity. We started with a small group of suppliers and retailers, but in time we found ourselves with demand on both sides, more farmers who wanted to deal with us and more vendors who wanted yams and other southern products. This double demand taxed our ingenuity and stretched our management skills, adolescent as they were. We ran into trouble when one of the shipments froze in a railroad car over in Jersey. This disaster taught us a lesson, that in the business of perishable items, margins were slim, and one did not take chances with the vagaries of weather.

As we developed expertise and some commercial success in one area we found ourselves moving almost involuntarily into other markets. Within months after mastering the yam business, we found ourselves in the Florida orange and grapefruit business. The initial trouble here is that the fruit would be sent to us in boxes, but all sizes and shapes were included. This created obvious problems, so we now had no choice but to behave as middlemen. In this role, we developed a system of sizing and grading before we passed the produce on. This, of course, increased costs, but our contractors did well, and we learned another lesson in the art of management.

For me this experience was invaluable, and since my circumstance prevented me from getting a Master of Business Administration, a degree that began to assume importance at this time, my textbook was the *Journal of Commerce*. I studied it carefully and read avidly what passed then for the business pages in the newspapers.

As my knowledge expanded from reading and practice, my thoughts turned to the West Indies. Certainly there were products there for importation, and in due time, we became factors for Caribbean limes. I used the word "factors" because, although we were acting as middlemen, all transactions were on consignment. We did not buy from our sources and then sell at a profit. We merely received goods in trust and sold them at a profit for our sources for a small fee. In retrospect, the entire experience was awe-inspiring. These farmers trusted us because we were the U.N.I.A., and they knew that we would not cheat them.

Our success caused us trouble eventually, with none other than our esteemed leader. Mr. Garvey, indeed, had little business sense. Great economic ideas for human upliftment, yes, but business practice, sadly, no. Garvey believed, for example, that all the gross proceeds from the business ventures should go to the U.N.I.A.. When Poston and I suggested twenty percent to the Association, in order to have money for expansion and a cash reserve, his answer was an emphatic, "No!"

In one incident, we had agreed to sell in New York two rail tank cars of cane molasses for two people in Georgia. By this time, my "bible," the

Journal of Commerce, had taught me all I needed to know about cane molasses, including the grade price ratio, and current market price. I knew enough, also, to contact the American Molasses Company on Wall Street to make a quick deal. The price they offered was a good one and I picked up the check myself. In this deal, as in the others, the idea was to deduct our usual expenses with the net going to our shippers in Georgia. When I returned to headquarters, I realized that my superior, Ulysses S. Poston, was out of town. On an impulse, I suppose to impress the great man, I decided to show Garvey the check. His secretary showed me in and I was quizzed on the whole operation. Garvey seemed pleased and I left the check with him. That was a serious mistake, for later Poston and I had the devil of a time retrieving the money to pay the people in Georgia. Was this a case of exploitation of funds? Certainly not. The man was simply naive about the basic fundamentals of doing business.

It is seldom mentioned, but it was clear to me in 1925 and it has remained so to this day that Garvey created a giant movement that finally overwhelmed him, and us. In other words, despite his obvious defects, he was too successful too soon. As assistant to U. S. Poston, I witnessed the moving pleas made to us by poor tenant farmers in the South. Did we have the necessary trained personnel? Of course not, and so we failed there, not from ignorance of what should be done but from the lack of trained people to do the job.

It should be remembered, too, that it was from the demand for business deals that the idea for a shipping line developed. I was not involved in this, and I do not know if U. S. Poston was. I do know that Garvey did not simply decide to trade with the African countries, so the idea of a steamship line was born. On the contrary, it was Africans in various colonies who implored us to do business with them. Blacks from several African areas suggested trade in skins, and those in Ghana suggested trade in cocoa beans. At a time when white firms were making exorbitant profits in the import and export of goods to and from Africa, the Black Star Line was not a far-fetched idea. Indeed, it was well-known at the time that the Cocoa Trade Board, located in Great Britain, controlled the Ghanaians' cocoa trade, and the Trade Board was virtually owned by the Bank of England. Knowing this, we saw the Ghanaian overture as a chance to break the British monopoly. If in this we could be successful and make a profit for the Ghanaians and the U.N.I.A., then we would have had the best of all worlds. Unfortunately, for reasons now well known, we never had a chance to test these possibilities, for our steamship line never got off the ground, so to speak. With proper organization and advance work in the laws of maritime trade as well as a sound knowledge of steamships, the Black Star Line could have been profitable. Its failure only proves that the organization lacked expertise for everyday large-scale business, but not that the idea was unfeasible.

Though the business connection with Africa failed, the U.N.I.A. became by the mid-twenties a driving force for African emancipation. As early as 1921, as Jomo Kenyatta has written, the Garvey dreams and ideas were a valuable source of inspiration, for Africans were "hungry for some doctrine which lifted them from the servile consciousness in which Africans lived."[2]

I was privy to a great deal of the correspondence directed to the U.N.I.A. Ministry of Labor and Commerce. I saw firsthand the opportunities revealed and made possible among Black people here in the United States, in Central America and the Caribbean, and in the African countries, and between the Black and white populations. As I learned more about the business of business, I came close to despair on a number of occasions when I realized that we were woefully, even tragically, short on the expertise needed to capitalize on all the obvious opportunities illuminated by our movement.

It is impossible to say what would have happened had Marcus Garvey not been laid low in 1925. Perhaps we would have hired white expertise, although I think the odds would have been against it. Maybe we could have bought time to train our own people, since, except for the Black Star Line and Mrs. Garvey's clothing factory, all our enterprises were profitable. In any event, the fall of Garvey, engineered by the U.S. Department of Justice, immediately generated a "crisis of confidence" in the entire movement, which quickly affected the business end in negative ways. Within a short while, the whole structure fell apart and various managers formed independent companies from the segments they had managed for the U.N.I.A.. U. S. Poston, for example, formed his own company to trade in produce, and Captain E. L. Gaines, former member of the Executive Council of the U.N.I.A., formed an export-import company based on the contacts we had established. I decided to go with Gaines, but I felt little of the excitement of earlier years, for we all knew in 1925 that for us in the movement, a joyous and uplifting era was quietly passing away.

Nearly all historians who write of Garvey and the U.N.I.A., ultimately render negative verdicts of the man and his mission. A great deal of the material used to arrive at these evaluations is gleaned from the speeches of Garvey and from the views of his contemporaries, quite a few of whom took a dim view of Garvey. This is most unfortunate because, despite Garvey's misunderstanding of the social and political stratification of Negroes in the United States by relating it to color, he was, as strange as it may sound, within the American mainstream.

No one can argue that Garvey was not fully within the parameters of "democracy." Indeed, the structure of his organization testifies to that. Some people regard him as a demagogue. This view, I believe, comes from people who do not and will not even appreciate a truly charismatic figure, which if nothing else, Marcus Garvey was. It is instructive to remember that at one point, the Reverend Dr. Martin Luther King was talked about in the same way.

But if one disagrees with this, then certainly at least, it has to be admitted that Garvey was a capitalist. Apart from his purely political posture, it was this facet of Garvey's program which made him attractive to American Blacks. None of the other contending leaders and movements were so unabashedly capitalistic. The combination of political capitalism and social and political uplift which Garvey preached was a powerfully persuasive force among Black people.

Prior to the establishment of the U.N.I.A., it was difficult to get Black people to raise capital for entrepreneurial pursuits. Somewhere between slavery and the twentieth century the system of capital formation, called *esusu*, characteristic of West African societies and always extant in West Indian societies, was lost among Negroes in the United States.[3]

In the case of the Black yam producers, for example, Poston and I knew that all these people were defying the conventions of their recent history and of the South to send us their produce. To do so in the 1920s was a very courageous step, with consequences of economic reprisals at best and physical horror at worst. These people risked such dangers, however, not only because they had faith in Garvey and the U.N.I.A., but also because what we were doing as well was engaging them in an endeavor that was familiar to them—ordinary business enterprise.

In this regard, the U.N.I.A. was in no way radical. It was thoroughly American, more so than Eugene V. Debs and the Socialist Party, which was looked upon with less disfavor. If anything, the Department of Justice should have been pleased with Garveyism, because if one considers the trading and political connections the U.N.I.A. had established with the Caribbean and Africa by 1924, it could be argued that, given a chance, the bonds between the United States and the countries of these two areas would have eventually been stronger than they are today. It is no secret that healthy trading links among countries promote political understanding. I believe therefore, that if we had been allowed to progress in our young trade with Africa and the Caribbean, the great distrust of the United States in so many of these countries today might not have developed. The Grenada invasion might not have occurred.

In any case, our efforts in the U.N.I.A. were not encouraged. To the ordinary white American government official and to the southerner, the bonds of solidarity and fraternity felt by Garveyites all over the country were frightening. In the South and Midwest especially, Black supporters of the U.N.I.A. were seen as losing their fear of white people considered necessary for white social and economic control. If being a Garveyite erased Black people's fear of white reprisals, then the outcome could only be bad. It would mean that Black people would soon demand, at least equality of competition in the marketplace. Even though Garveyites were not demanding "social equality," the greatest fear of whites in the 1920s, the mere possibility of equal competition in the marketplace, was seen as a threat throughout white America.

There was no mystery to this sense of dread, for simply stated, most whites in the twenties knew that if they competed freely with Black people they would lose as much as they won, and their illusion of superiority would vanish all too swiftly. Worse, the economic status of Black people would inexorably rise and unless there was a uniform rising tide, then thousands of white people would soon find themselves in the lower economic strata recently vacated by Blacks. To any white person already in a marginal position and maintained at an artificially elevated level only by the color of his skin, the mere thought of displacement caused violent reactions. It is no wonder that our people were attacked all over the country! Malcolm X's father, for instance, a staunch recruiter for the U.N.I.A., was killed for this audacity in Lansing, Michigan, and his body thrown on the railroad tracks. There are people alive today who faced death in those days for the cause.

The legacy of Garvey and the U.N.I.A. to this day remains to be unbiasedly assessed, for he was, indeed, a great force in the development of Black people in Africa, the Caribbean, and the United States in asserting a belief in themselves, in reasserting their claim to the equal worth of their ancestry, and, for me, as a prophet for the possibilities of achievement if one is willing to fight injustice and work in the interest of one's community. The composition of my constituencies changed with time, but for me Garvey's fundamental rules have remained constant to this day.

In New York, the decline of the U.N.I.A. coincided with the decision of the Tammany organization's decision to drop two-term mayor "Honest John" Francis Hylan from the mayoral ticket. A majority of Tammany leaders had become disenchanted with the mayor's well-developed sense of his importance and with his poor relations with the press, which ridiculed him for building the Bronx Market, which they called "Hylan's Follies." Besides, the popular Democratic Governor, "The Happy Warrior," Al Smith, couldn't stand the mayor, so Hylan had to go.

The man Tammany anointed to be Hylan's successor was dapper State Senator and songwriter, Jimmy Walker, the author of the smash hit song, "Will You Love Me in December as You Did in May?" But Hylan, stubborn as usual, had decided that his job would not be had for a song, and aided by the Democratic leadership in Brooklyn, Queens, and Richmond counties, prepared for a primary fight. Hylan named as campaign manager Police Commissioner Freuhauf, who quickly chose the retention of the 5-cent subway fare as the campaign's big issue. This was, indeed, an issue that one could work with in Harlem. So Ulysses Posten, the leader of our little club, contacted the Hylan campaign headquarters and set up a meeting with Commissioner Freuhauf. The upshot was the "Hylan 5 Cent Fare Club" of Harlem.

The formation of this club and participation in this campaign greatly advanced my education in practical politics. I quickly learned that politics did not merely involve presentation of the issues in speeches in the attempt to persuade the voters, but also included a knowledge of the myriad complex levers of power, as well as skill in their use.

In the Hylan–Walker primary campaign, charges had been made that a tie-in existed between Jimmy Walker and Gerhard M. Dahl, Chairman of the Board of the Brooklyn-Manhattan Transit Corporation. If this could be proved, then a great deal of political mileage would be gained for Hylan's campaign. For a while nothing could be found, until one day a gentleman I knew, Oscar Waters, a perennial politician, came in to our club and announced that he had been Gerry Dahl's butler.[4] He said he had a package that would connect Walker with Dahl and Olvany, Tammany's new leader. I believed his story, accepted his package, and hurried down to City Hall, hoping to score some points for our campaign. The package was taken in, and I was asked to wait outside the mayor's office. About half an hour later, Oscar Waters and a police captain from Harlem walked by me and went into the mayor's office. They stayed there so long that I finally left and returned to the club. I later learned that the package did indeed contain documents of meetings between Dahl and the leader of Tammany, and the *New York Times* carried the story.[5]

Sometime later, Oscar called me and invited me to the grand opening of his new "club" in another district. My first reaction was, "Why do we need a new club?" Of course, Oscar's club was in a different district; however, in my naïveté, I had considered the 5 Cent Fare Club *the* Harlem club. I was a bit disturbed and feared that I had perhaps made some mistake. These fears were confirmed when I walked into Oscar's club. In one room a crap game was in progress, in another, poker was the game, and in another, blackjack. I realized then what the payoff had been, and Oscar confirmed this by patting me on the back and saying, "Son, we haven't got too long, but we got to make the most of it for the time we have."[6] Oscar's fatherly advice was well meant and I am sure he expected me to be pleased; however, this was not the reward I had expected. I had thought that by working in the campaign, the recognition of our efforts would have translated itself into a dialogue about raising the level of Black political participation in Harlem, or something of that nature. A "license" to operate a gambling and drinking parlor had not been part of my expectations.

I didn't have the heart to behave uncivilly in the face of Oscar Waters' genuine pleasure. He was of a tribe that was foreign to me, and I resolved there and then that if I were to ever gain any prominence in New York politics, I would never consider this kind of reward. Years later, as I grew wiser from reading and experience, I found that what I thought was a random payoff to Oscar Walters was routine. During the famous investigation of Tammany by Judge Samuel Seabury in the early thirties, what I had objected to in the mid-twenties was found to be still going strong, and worse, it was pervasive. Herbert Mitgang, whose book on Seabury's investigation was published the year I became Leader of Tammany Hall, had this to say:

Sub rosa licensing in the 1920s was a lucrative source of income for the district leaders and Tammany Hall. The fees charged by the city's Department of Licenses for legal licenses were petty compared to the amounts that were charged unofficially for certain illegal licenses. Jimmy Hines, a West Side leader, "licensed" Arthur (Dutch Schultz) Flegenheimer's policy racket. Big Tim Sullivan "licensed" Arnold Rothstein's gambling places. The "license" frequently stipulated payment of a percentage of the income in return for immunity from police raids. Occasionally a token arrest was made for the record, but overeager policemen soon found themselves pounding night beats on Staten Island.[7]

What Oscar had received from Freuhauf was a "license," and his remark to me was prophetic, for although Hylan won in Harlem, he lost by 100,000 votes to Jimmy Walker in the rest of New York City. Whether Oscar's place survived after the election, I do not recall, but I imagine it did, since Walker proved eventually to be Hylan's philosophical bedfellow. Mitgang recounts that some time after the election, Walker appointed the former mayor to a judgeship in the Children's Court in Queens. When Alva Johnson, a reporter, asked about this questionable appointment, the new mayor replied, "Alva, the appointment of Judge Hylan means the children now can be tried by their peer."[8] In this loose laissez-faire atmosphere, Oscar may have survived the twenties, but I doubt very much if he survived the onslaught of Judge Seabury. After all, Mayor Walker didn't.

In the brief primary campaign, I had glimpsed how the patronage system worked. I had been able to get an inside look at the Democratic Party's attitude toward Harlem and Black people. I also had been able to assess in a very superficial way the future of the Republican Party in New York City and saw little hope there for Black people. Although I did not like their uninhibited style, I determined then to stick with the Democrats. In fact, I had no place else to go, for my appetite was now whetted for political work. I was aware that I could accomplish only modest things at that time, but I was convinced, as had been Garvey, that in Harlem there was a great yearning for change and that I would be able to effect some useful change if this yearning, this new mood, could be politically harnessed. Lofty as these thoughts were, I had a more basic problem. I had no job. As was the custom, I went to see Police Commissioner Freuhauf to see if anything could be done for me, and was quickly offered a job as policeman. I simply could not see myself as a cop, so the mayor's office came to my aid and I was sent with a letter to Mr. William Eagan, the stationmaster at the Pennsylvania Railroad, to be considered for a Red Cap's job. I took this job, and stayed at Penn Station until I started my own ice business.

For anyone unfamiliar with the economic history of Black people, it will come as a surprise that in the Jazz Age, a Red Cap's job was a very good one in any northern city. In fact, a Red Cap was ranked with a Pullman porter, who was just a shade beneath the professionals such as medical doctors, professors, and such. It was not that a Red Cap was learned or possessed any power, but if he were a serious individual, his job was usually secure and his income was very good. In my case, I had one small advantage: I was, though not the only one, a political appointee of sorts. As such, I was a part of the Democratic organization, but not yet on the inside.

It is important to note at this point that the 5 Cent Fare Club died immediately after the Hylan–Walker campaign. The questions now were: "What could be done to increase Black control in Harlem?" "How do we increase the power of those of us who wish to lead?" At Penn Station, there were several other men, who, like me, were "political appointees," and during slack periods we, along with the others, would talk politics and economics continuously.

We considered ourselves as mavericks because we were not part of the United Colored Democracy, in the late 1920s headed by Ferdinand Q. Morton. Morton was a sort of extraterritorial leader, which means that he was not a bona fide district leader. He had been appointed head of the Civil Service Commission by Walker, which gave him patronage powers, and thus, he maintained his status. The real district leaders in Harlem at the time were for the most part Irish, and Morton had to work with them as a kind of grand representative for a number of Harlem assembly districts. To "The Penn Station Gang," as we called ourselves, this situation was intolerable. We wanted to become real district leaders so that we would have a say in the framing of policy, control patronage, and select candidates for office.

In New York City, then as now, the basic representative unit relating to the state was the Assembly District. If one became the leader of an A.D., one essentially chose the State Assembly candidate. If Blacks controlled two contiguous districts, the two Assembly District Leaders chose the candidate for the State Senate. The control of two or three districts gave the leaders the power to select the candidate for the U.S. Congress.

The power to select candidates was not the only benefit derived from district control. A host of other things became possible, from the placement of people in government offices to exercising control in the placement of public housing. A number of districts working together could make beneficial deals. For example, if there were three district leaders working together, they could go to the mayor and say, "Mr. Mayor, you have X millions of dollars deposited in Y bank. Now we have this little bank in our area, and it would be a good thing if you were to deposit a million or so in our local bank." It would be a foolish mayor indeed, who wouldn't listen to such a plea. These, then, were the kind of beneficial things that my colleagues and I wanted to do in Harlem. But this could not happen unless the people who lived in the districts were in political control and sat at the tables of the policymakers.

The trouble with implementing all this was that one simply could not go out into the streets of New York and tell the people to do this and do that. People are not moved that way, and especially by unknown "Young Turks." For us who saw ourselves as "New Democrats," that is, unaffiliated with the United Colored Democracy, our desire to develop a broad-based and active political entity was stymied by the fact that most of the Black voting population before 1934 were Lincolnian Republicans. Even when these Republicans were added to those who voted under the auspices of the U.C.D., the simple truth emerged that most Black people did not have any serious party affiliation, and, more disturbing, did not vote.

This is not to say they did not argue about politics. In fact, political argumentation was a favorite pastime, but that was what it remained, a pastime. This condition was not surprising, for indigenous northern Blacks had, for the most part, become disenchanted with politics by World War I. The situation worsened when large numbers of southern Blacks, who were even more disillusioned by the political process, came north. "Why should I vote?", I remember them asking. "What has politics done for me?", they would ask in righteous indignation as they slammed the door in my face. The answer lay in what politics *could* do, but by this time most New York City Blacks had developed a near-contemptuous attitude toward politicians. To this day, I have not been able to determine how or why I knew it then, but after the Hylan–Walker primary elections, I sensed that the posture of Harlemites towards politics would soon undergo drastic change.

Perhaps because I was an immigrant I saw it more clearly, but several things were obvious after 1925, all of which I thought would affect Harlem directly, and which would demand swift and sure responses from those of us who desired to be political leaders.

In the first place, I became acutely aware that all of New York City was in a state of flux. Immigrants, including Black ones, had been coming into the city in large numbers since World War I. Although in 1925 a severe immigration bill had been passed which greatly limited immigration of West Indians and other peoples of color, the influx of Caribbean people into the city was already so high that cultural heterogeneity was now the rule, rather than the exception. There were also southern Blacks, mostly of the laboring class, but there was also a good percentage of the educated. There were small business people from Chicago, Kansas City, Memphis and St. Louis, people with a fair amount of money that had been in their families since Emancipation. There were also the intellectuals, mostly from northern states, who clustered around the NAACP and the Urban League.

Since by 1927 Garvey was gone, and since none of the other movements promised much hope for Black people, and that included the United Colored Democracy, I must have concluded that the future lay with the Democrats, who despite their rough and ready if not rowdy ways always seemed more genuinely "political" than the Republicans. I perhaps decided unconsciously that all the other movements in Harlem would soon give in from sheer fatigue, and that people would have nowhere to go but back to the two major parties. This movement I knew would not be automatic and would involve a great deal of publicity, public relations, and even propaganda. I sensed that there would soon be a great deal of political fermentation throughout the city and that Harlem, with its volatile mix of desires, wants and yearnings, would soon be ready for pragmatic mainstream politics. It was my intention, therefore, to "infiltrate" the Democratic Party, build a base with my friends in Harlem, and wait for "the times and the manners" to change.

As I thought about these possibilities and waited for the changes I expected to occur, I continued to earn my living as a "political Red Cap." I knew it was not the best job in the world, but when one is young, full of good health and heady dreams, the most menial job is seen as temporary—a mere stepping stone, and certainly not a situation to dampen enthusiasm. Surrounded by a group of people with similar views, full of ribald camaraderie and good spirits, a better future always seemed ever-nearer, and the present was easily discounted: that was my situation. My state of mind was also constantly buoyed by the knowledge that "Chief" Robinson, our boss, a very impressive looking six-foot two Negro, thought highly of me and placed me in various positions of trust. Besides, the job itself was not overly demanding and paid relatively well. At least I was not cooped in a factory all day, learning little and perhaps dying slowly from toxic fumes. Besides, I was able to meet all kinds of people in the station, in all kinds of ridiculous situations. This added to one's education and certainly to one's enjoyment.

I remember one day my squad was "on the tracks" to meet the trains. As I stood by the baggage ramp, a dapper young white man, wearing spats and with razor creases in his pants, motioned me over, and with a silver-headed walking stick, pointed to a bag and said, "That one, porter."

For some reason his entire manner rubbed me wrong, and in anger I grabbed the handle of his bag and jerked it off the ramp. Anger was quickly replaced by shock when the bag tore open and out tumbled an array of liquor bottles, some of which broke and spilled their contents over my customer's pants. This was during Prohibition! To this day I do not remember exactly what happened next, but I know that I beat a very hasty retreat and gave myself another, by now standard, lecture on the need to curb my temper. No punishment evolved from this adventure and in due time, I became the leader of a squad. This was a helpful promotion, for it gave me more time to think of the future and lessened my exposure to bootlegging young blades.

I have no idea of how today's Red Cap or Sky Cap regards himself, but in my day, despite the position of Black people in America, our group at Penn Station maintained its dignity, and for the most part were treated with courtesy. Perhaps we were a unique bunch, for we had similar ambitions. We discussed our individual and collective goals endlessly and I know that we all eventually did well. We all went to school while we worked. Some of us graduated from the Penn Station Political Academy, as we called it, went to college and got law degrees. There was a fellow by the name of Brown who soon became a police lieutenant. Another fellow, Redman, also became a policeman and later a very successful businessman. There were others I met again over the years, whose names I do not recall, all of whom have kept the faith and have prospered.

In my case, I had always kept an eye open for a business I could enter on my own or in equal partnership. This opportunity came through an advertisement in the *Amsterdam News*, the Negro newspaper, announcing that a large block of apartments, the Dunbar, would soon be available for Black occupancy. The people living at the Dunbar would be of middle-class means; therefore, I decided to implement an idea I had discussed with my friend and fellow Red Cap, Chick Jones. We thought we should try the ice delivery business, beginning at the Dunbar, so we went to see Roscoe Conkling Bruce, the apartment manager. When he seemed to applaud the idea, we got started. Imagine our surprise when we found out at the apartment opening that Mr. Bruce had reneged and had given the contract to the Knickerbocker Ice Company, the largest ice company in New York! We immediately protested, but Bruce's response, worthy of Calvin Coolidge, was, "Business is business." Our response was straight-forward. We simply hired some City College students, dressed them in shirts advertising Jones Bros. Ice Company, instructing them to meet the moving vans as they came to the apartment building, and solicit the new tenants on our behalf. As it turned out, the residents, impressed with the students and with what we were attempting, ignored the Knickerbocker Company, and we secured the concession for the whole building.

It was from this venture that Chick and I got the idea that since we knew all the people at the Dunbar, it would be a pragmatic step to join the local Democratic Club, and begin the work of becoming district captains. After all, the large Dunbar apartments were our natural constituency. Our ulti-mate ambition, of course, was to one day become Assembly District Lead-ers in Harlem. We did not contemplate achieving district leadership in the 22nd Assembly District in 1928, for our leader was a powerful Irishman, James J. McCormick, who was also a Deputy City Clerk in charge of marriage licenses. As such, he commanded patronage and could fix more than traffic tickets. In many ways, he epitomized the kind of Irishman that Tammany's boss at the time, George Olvany, had in mind when he de-clared that:

The Irish are natural leaders. The strain of limerick keeps them at the top. . . . Even the Jewish districts have Irish leaders. The Jews want to be ruled by them.[9]

Superficially, that statement seemed true in the twenties, because Irish leadership was pervasive. I knew, however, that in Harlem the social complexion of the place was changing swiftly, and soon, also, would the leadership.

In the meantime, our little group of U. S. Poston, Captain Gaines, Chick Jones, and I, along with a few other Blacks prominent in business and the professions, united to press for our own municipal judges in Harlem. But why should our own municipal judges be so important at this time? There were two main reasons. In the first place, the population of Harlem had increased noticeably in the decade between World War I and the Great Crash of 1929, and with the increase in the population, housing problems multiplied. The ultimate arbiter of housing conflicts then, as now, was the municipal judge. But in the 1920s Harlem did not have a municipal judge of its own.

However, in 1930 the State Legislature and the governor, then Frank-lin D. Roosevelt, decided to award four new municipal judgeships to Manhattan, two of which were to be in Harlem. This legislation was a compromise, in fact, for when Roosevelt signed the bill it was generally understood that the judges elected in Harlem would be Republicans and perhaps Black, while the other two elsewhere would be Democrats. This view resulted from the continued belief among political experts of the 1920s that Negroes were still inexorably wedded to the party of Lincoln.

However, we, the new Democrats, made up in great part by West Indian immigrants, had no such allegiance and could work, secondly, for the election of Black judges. When we were able to cooperate with the United Colored Democracy, made up mainly of indigenous Negroes, our influence increased and our earlier demands for Black representation could be pressed. The realization by 1930 that this cooperative Democratic effort was possible and politically promising was the second reason for focussing on capturing the municipal judgeship. It should be stressed that originally all of us in Harlem merely wanted judges in our district, preferably Black, but by 1930, any astute observer could see that Blacks were getting fed up with the Republicans. Certainly, with the State Legislature, the Governor, and the City Board of Aldermen predominantly Democratic, the already minimal advantage of being a Republican had been further seriously reduced.

We the Harlem Democrats realized the bind the Republicans were in, but we had a problem of our own, and it had to do with who the candidates should be. In my group there were enough young lawyers from which the two candidates could be drawn, but they were all West Indian immigrants. I had not even thought of this as a problem until it was quietly pointed out to me by more sagacious heads. It immediately suggested the necessity of a mixed ticket. Our group decided to back James S. Watson, leaving to the other factions to select the other candidate. The person they settled on was Charles Toney, an indigenous Negro and an associate of the leader of the United Colored Democracy, Ferdinand Q. Morton. Toney was a lawyer, as was Morton, and they belonged to the same law firm. Both of our candidates were therefore well-educated men, articulate and savvy. Because of their skills, both men prevailed in the elections and the expected Republican victory never materialized. For our little group of Poston, Gaines, Chick Jones, and I, all refugees from the U.N.I.A., the election of Toney and Watson in 1930 was a significant event, a sign of the times as it were, for not only did we have our own municipal judges, but three other realities became clear to us, as well.

First, the election proved that our group, we could call it the New Democrats, could work with the old United Colored Democracy in the larger interest of Harlem. This development was gratifying to us since so many in our group, including myself, were immigrants. Second, it became apparent that the old United Colored Democracy was dying and the future would belong to us, the New Democrats. It is necessary to stress how important this realization was to us. It wasn't that we were antagonistic to Morton and the U.C.D., but it was that our group believed that the time had come to let Tammany Hall know that we expected to be treated as equals. If Tammany could be made to understand this, then there would be no need for a "Colored Democracy" and the stigma attached to that designation. Our attitude in 1930 might have struck some as premature. I am certain, as later events proved, that the Tammany leadership did not take us seriously, but we were serious, and made up as we were of Garvey-ites, West Indian immigrants, and militant native Blacks, we were an eclectic crew, ruled by no white-appointed leader, and circumscribed by no burdensome traditions. Our goal was to make Harlem a place for Harlemites and a place in which the people felt they had a stake with representatives of their own.

Third, the election of Watson and Toney with the full support of Tammany leadership did not mean that much had changed at the district level. This was illustrated by the case of Sybil Bryan Poston. Mrs. Poston was the wife of our acknowledged chief, U. S. Poston. After the election of Judge Watson, Mrs. Poston indicated her desire to be Watson's secretary, a patronage position, in which the secretary actually served as an administrative aide. The salary was also far above that of a secretary, and what with generous vacation time and other little perquisities, it was a job to be desired. My colleagues and I, now that we quickly learned how the system worked, felt it was only fair to U. S. Poston to support his wife for the job, and at the suggestion of Judge Watson, I headed a delegation to see our district leader, Mr. McCormick, about the matter.

The meeting was unsuccessful. McCormick's reply was that if he were given the authority to choose the secretary, it would go to someone who had supported him all these years. What he meant was that the position would go to a white person, and so it became clear that James J. McCormick was blind to the changes taking place in his district. We resolved then and there to begin work on his removal. We did not labor very long, for in 1932, Judge Samuel Seabury finally caught up with James J. and his gang. Mitgang described his operation:

When a couple came to this municipal chapel, two dollars went to the city—and "tips" of ten or twenty dollars went into his own pocket. These were not exactly voluntary contributions from eager bridegrooms. All through the ceremonies, his top desk drawer was left open conspicuously—and he indicated that bridegrooms could put their tips there. An anxious couple could get to the head of the line by crossing the clerk's palm. . . . McCormick admitted taking tips . . . but said he had only one regret: "I'll get it at home for holding out." McCormick's wife had not known how much other people's marriages had enriched theirs. [10]

Fate, it seemed, had conspired to aid our own cause. As a result of these revelations, McCormick was forced to resign and was replaced by another Irishman, John Kelly, who saw that the era of undisputed Irish leadership so fulsomely celebrated by George Olvany was on the wane. He worked diligently with us until inevitably the changing neighborhood and the legacy of racial leadership led to his replacement.

Chapter 3

The Beginning of the End of the Old Tammany and The Rise of Black Democracy in New York City *(1932–1940)*

THE INAUGURATION OF President Franklin D. Roosevelt in 1933 began an era of hope for most Americans. By March, Herbert Hoover was gone, and though the Depression grew deeper, we Blacks in New York politics felt a subtle lift in our spirits. In part, this changed mood came from the renewed perception that the rapid demographic change in New York City since World War I had now created political possibilities in a number of assembly districts. Changing numbers were of interest to us, but so too was the composition of the new population.

It is usually stated that the large migration of Blacks to northern cities in the 1920s came from the south. It is seldom noted that a large number of West Indians also migrated to the United States in this period, and while not all settled in northern cities, by far the largest contingent ended their journey in New York City. This was an interesting development because, as a result of the immigration law of 1917 which insured that all immigrants had to be literate, these West Indians were, for the most part, English-speaking and highly literate. A large percentage also possessed marketable skills and many were professionals. The mix of migrants and immigrants proved useful for the emerging politics of the early thirties, which required literate minds and new insights. These new arrivals further hastened the departure of whites from certain Harlem districts. This departure, however, was never a frantic exodus; rather, it was more of a cautious withdrawal, with no similar intention to withdraw indicated by the white leadership in their changing districts of Harlem. But we New Democrats were determined that the leadership should reflect the complexion of the people. By contemporary standards, such a view would be seen as impolitic; however, in the years before the civil rights revolution, hardly any white person voted for a Black candidate. Therefore, Black political power came only from predominantly Black constituents. To be in charge of our own neighborhoods and to have influence within the Democratic Party required the removal of the leadership of the Irish Old Guard in Harlem.

We knew that in time the changing population would aid in this endeavor, but the process would not be very swift. Another problem was that our group of political activists, as we regarded ourselves, were not as experienced as we needed to be in the ways of everyday politicking. We also lacked connections beyond Harlem and the rest of Manhattan—a definite drawback. Fortunately, the Roosevelt campaign of 1932 came to our aid.

It is common knowledge nowadays that Franklin D. Roosevelt put together a new ethnic and labor coalition during the New Deal years. In our case, however, no one came seeking us to be part of this coalition, because if the Democratic Party solicited Black support too strongly, then Southern Democrats would certainly take offense. That is why until he died in 1945, FDR cannot be said to have wholeheartedly included and welcomed Black people into this much-written-about coalition. That was left to Harry Truman in 1948. The fact is, we were the ones who, so to speak, "included ourselves in," and U. S. Poston was the initiator. As soon as the 1932 presidential campaign was under way, Poston convinced Vincent Daley, the New York State Democratic Chairman, that Black votes, which until then were by and large Republican, could, with some work, be converted to the Democratic cause. As a result, Daley gave U. S. Poston permission to create in Harlem a Democratic club which came to be called the Vin Dale Club. From this base, we did serious work during the campaign for the Democratic ticket throughout the state. Perhaps our efforts on behalf of the ticket were not as great as we thought then, but there was no question that in New York a greater number of Black people voted for the democratic ticket than ever before. No doubt the Depression and FDR's homey style played a great role, but Black voters needed to see Black people working for the Party as regular personnel, and that's how we conducted ourselves in New York. We were certainly ahead of the rest of the country, for it was not until 1936 that Blacks across the nation voted overwhelmingly for the Democrats.

The participation in the campaign brought unexpected rewards. The Vin Dale Club was designated as the official Democratic Club for the U. S.

postal service. At first I was unaware of the significance of this, and it took a few weeks to educate myself. The full extent I never learned, nor needed to, but I learned that prior to the Democratic victory, a similar Republican club existed in Washington Heights, and that that club had been the official Post Office Department club. Our club, therefore, was simply inheriting the Republican legacy now that Democrats controlled the Post Office Department. It was from these revelations that I began to understand how the State and Federal Patronage system worked. I was indeed learning.

I should perhaps note at this point that the Vin Dale Club was not part of the Tammany organization, and its connection with the postal service caused it to operate in a far different way from the ordinary political clubs. It was, in fact, a hybrid employment agency and local court of appeals for the Post Office Department employees. Within the postal service most clerks, mailmen and other employees were subject to demerits for any infraction of rules. These demerits were issued by the local postmaster and could vary from a day's suspension without pay to outright dismissal, if a certain number of demerits were exceeded. The "Court of Appeals" for these demerits was the Vin Dale Club. Except in the most egregious cases, the judge and jury in these appeals was the club leader, at this time, U. S. Poston. The club, in order to fairly adjudicate these cases, had a "price list" on the demerits, and "X" number of demerits equalled "Y" number of dollars. In this way, discipline and good employee behavior were maintained at work, and money was made for the club and the party. The system worked well because the postmaster knew our club and knew it was under the protection of the State Party Chairman. The club prospered because in those days the postal service paid its employees very well. Furthermore, the onset of the Depression aided its popularity because Post Office jobs were safe. One only had to be watchful of one's demerits!

The windfall for the Vin Dale club was encouraging, and our association with it certainly stimulated our imagination and whetted our appetite for greater things. Our group was better off economically than most of the Harlem population, for we had jobs and we were already well-connected with the State Democratic leadership and Tammany enough to feel somewhat secure. We knew, however, that for the ordinary New Yorker and Harlemite in 1932 things were on the decline. We decided to go with FDR's message by preaching to the Harlemites the importance of understanding the economic dynamic surrounding them, and the importance of political participation in the scheme of things. Of course, we did not put it that way. That kind of talk we left to the Republicans who, for the most part, were college-educated. We took our standard of communication from Charlie Payne, one of our group whose favorite word was "beefstew-ology."

Charlie had started out with Ferdinand Q. Morton in the United Colored Democracy, the group we were trying to displace. In the late twenties and into the thirties he would ride around in back of a truck exhorting people to join the U. C. D. with catch words like these: "You can have all the '—ologies'—sociology, psychology and the rest—but all I am interested in for us is beefstew-ology!" In the twenties this drew good-natured laughter, but after 1930, Charlie Payne was taken a lot more seriously.

It became clear to us by 1933 that the onset of the Depression had made Harlemites a great deal more serious about politics. Perhaps I should say they became more aware of the relationship among politics, government, and their own welfare. There was no question that more people expressed interest in the Vin Dale Club than ever before and our little meetings here and there generated a great deal more interest than ever. My group came to the conclusion that it was time to make a move for district leadership wherever feasible. Unfortunately for me, I resided in the 22nd Assembly District, headed now by that politically astute Irishman, John J. Kelly. In this district Blacks comprised about twenty percent of the population, so I saw no possibility of taking over there. This, fortunately, was not the case in the contiguous 21st District in which Blacks were the majority. In that district the ruling Democratic Club was the Chicopee Club, and Henry Shields, a Black lawyer, was a member. After careful review, our group, the core of which was the Penn Station Intellectual Gang, decided that Shields should run for District Leader.

Prior to 1938, the year of the "Reformation," an Assembly District Leader could be elected and removed only by a vote of the County Committee. To understand the importance of this and the necessity for the "reform" of 1938, a brief description of Tammany's pre- and post 1938 structure and voting procedure is necessary. The basic unit in the hierarchy has remained the Assembly District, from which representatives were elected to the State Assembly. For Tammany's purposes, each Assembly District has a District Leader, usually a male, and a co-leader, a female. Sometimes if the district is large, then as already indicated it is split in two, East and West or North and South, as appropriate. Each Assembly District (A. D.) is divided into election districts and each of these election districts (E. D.) has a captain responsible for liaison with the District Leader, and for getting out the vote on Election Day. At present, within each E. D. the number of individuals elected to form this Assembly District's county committee are proportioned to its number of registered party members. If, for example, there are forty election districts in an A. D., and if each E. D. has ten county representatives to the A. D. committee, there would be 400 county committee members in the A. D., and they along with committee members from the other A. D.'s form the New York County Democratic Committee which *is* Manhattan, with a Chair who is second in command to the County Leader. At present, the Assembly District Leader is elected by popular vote of registered Democrats, and together these District Leaders form the Executive Committee of New York County over which the County Leader or "Tammany Chief" presides.

But prior to the "Reformation," there were two important differences from the present norm, both designed to prevent insurrection. In the first instance, the Assembly District's committee was *not* elected proportionally to the number of registered Democratic voters in that election district. In fact the election rules stated that, "The County committee shall consist of two enrolled in each election district, and as many others as the Executive Committee designates." This Executive committee was made up of the county's Assembly District Leaders; therefore in that setup the District Leader through his influence in the Executive committee could stack his district's County Committee. After 1938, county committee members were elected by popular vote and their numbers were proportional to the enrolled Democratic voters of the election districts. In addition, prior to 1938, District Leaders were not elected by popular vote, but by the captains within the election districts. If, for example, there were 40 E. D.'s in an Assembly District, each with an average of ten district committee members, there were then 400 district committee members and they elected their District Leader. Since these District Leaders elected the County Chairman, the "Boss of Tammany Hall," if he could provide favors for enough of the District Leaders, he was able to control the County Executive Committee, and through it any single district leader, and to an extent the captains within the district. Later in 1949 a number of colleagues and I initiated a change in the Party's rules so that the District Leader would be elected by popular vote rather than be selected by the district committee controlled by the captains. But in 1933 the prospects for Shields to be chosen Leader in the 21st Assembly District seemed very good.

We knew, too, that the Democratic organization had noticed the demographic shift taking place in New York, and we counted on sensible people reading properly the signs of the times. So we ran Shields, and he won. The local district leadership, headed by Houlihan, was upset, but recovered speedily by making a deal with Shields in which Houlihan remained the District Leader for another two years. But why would Henry Shields make such a deal? The answer was that Shields was a criminal lawyer, and he depended to a great extent on case assignments from judges for a livelihood. In this arrangement, Houlihan, with long-standing connections, could be of great help. Viewed in this light, some sympathy could be felt for Shields, but none was forthcoming from Herbert L. Bruce, who had been Shield's primary financial backer. Bruce was especially angry with Shields because in the campaign to unseat Houlihan, Bruce and Shields had joined forces to form a Black club, the Beaver Club. When Shields made his deal with Houlihan, Bruce took over the leadership of the Beaver Club and secured Shields' suspension for 99 years!

The reaction of the Black members of the Chicopee Club to the formation of the Beavers was a clear indication that the political pulse of Black leadership in Harlem was quickening. As soon as the Beaver Club was formed, another Black contingent in the Chicopee Club defected to form the Ramapo Democratic Club. Two things accounted for this development. First, the new Ramapo group did not like the idea of the upstart Bruce and his Beavers taking over their district; and, second, since they saw the reign of Houlihan and the Chicopee Club coming to an end, they desired to fill that vacuum. Within two years, the issue was resolved when, in the primaries, none of the candidates of the three contending clubs had a clear majority. This impasse forced a compromise between the Beavers and the Ramapos in the 21st A. D., for the election of Herbert L. Bruce as the first Black Tammany District Leader in New York City; this marked the beginning of the end of Irish leadership in Harlem.

In this development, I had played a small role. I had assisted in setting up the Beavers, and, more important, had supervised the handling of their petition. The eventual election of Bruce was, therefore, very satisfying to me, for he and I had been undergraduates, so to speak, at the Pennsylvania Station Red Cap Political College. His election in 1935 meant that the dreams we had dreamt at Penn Station were not so farfetched, that they were indeed possible, and that perhaps soon our group would be admitted to the inner sanctum of the Democratic Party as equal and fully participating members. In the larger sphere, I reasoned that as Harlemites and other Black New Yorkers watched our progress, increasing numbers would be induced to become active in politics. I expected that as soon as the population shifted further, there would be additional districts we Blacks could control.

This control was important to us because we needed it to provide Blacks with political and other job opportunities. For example, the Consolidated Edison Corporation was, in the twenties and thirties, one of New York City's largest employers. Being a utility, it had to work hand in glove with the city leadership. Because of this, Tammany literally controlled the jobs at Con Ed. We knew this and wanted some of those jobs if not downtown, then at least in Harlem.

There were, in addition, other benefits to be derived from this control. We expected that local political power would assist us in raising Black self-esteem, in demonstrating that Black people had the brains and energy to conduct political and economic affairs with skill and prudence, and could, eventually, represent all people. But before any of this could happen, we had to control our home bases.

I should note that at this time I had left Penn Station and now held another political appointment, at the Board of Elections. This job was pivotal and a most important one in my career. It gave me an opportunity to learn the election laws, but it soon became clear to me that mere knowledge was not enough, since court interpretations could differ significantly from the apparent meanings of the statutes. It was, therefore, necessary for me, as an ambitious young man in a hurry, to study the court rulings with great care. From this labor I learned a great deal that served me very well later. I learned, for example, that the Board of Elections was a creature of the two major parties. Since this was so, third parties and independents had a very tough row to hoe before they could get on the ballot.

Let us suppose that someone wished to run for the State Assembly who was not a regular party choice; he would have to get together a petition to be on the ballot. The election laws specified the color of the paper on which a petition must be drawn. It specifies how it must be drawn. It specifies an affidavit. Rules abound as to how the voter signing the affidavit is to be identified, not only by name and address, but also by his Election and Assembly District numbers. All of this is supposedly for the purpose of checking the authenticity of the petition, how the petition should be numbered in filing, etc. Various sections of the election law covered these procedures, and every one of these sections was a booby trap for the uninitiated. When a petition is filed with the Board of Elections, it is assigned to a team of a Democrat and a Republican, who go through the petition with the enrollment book, and check everything.

Of course, this team is never very meticulous about the regular organizations' petitions, because each Assembly District has a law committee with a chair. If, for example, there are 120 A. D.'s in New York County, there will be 120 chairs, and probably a minimum of three or four lawyers on each, who are in effect apprentices in election law. The chair of the entire New York County organization also chairs the County Committee's Law Committee governing all other law committees, and it is he who is the organization's advocate to the Board of Elections, the defender of organizations' petitions before the courts, and the challenger to any opposition's petition. Since he, if a Democrat, does not usually challenge the Republicans, he is usually supported by them. Almost all attempts by those outside the regular parties were quashed in this way because of booby traps in the election laws.

Of course, the laws provided for appeals from the Board of Elections, but they also stipulated that an appeal to review the actions of the Board of Elections must be filed in the State Supreme Court at least fourteen days before the pending election. This was not a well-advertised fact. Let us say, for example, that Sam Smith, an independent, wishes to run for the State Assembly against Jim Jones, a Democrat. His election petitions come to the Board of Elections, where the Republican inspector and I, his Democratic counterpart, already know that Smith's must be dealt with last. About three days before the election, we submit a report on Smith to the Commissioner of Elections. This report could be positive or negative. All during this period Sam Smith is in agony, not knowing whether or not he is a viable candidate. In contrast, his Republican and Democratic opponents already know their fate. In this situation, Smith may have neglected to file an automatic appeal to the Board of Elections. If our report states that Mr. Smith has not complied with the election laws, because of some little mistake, and if the Commissioner accepts our report, which he usually does, then in this instance Sam Smith is out of luck.

There were, at times, wily characters who knew the ropes, and who, expecting the squeeze, would be ready in court by the time a negative report came out. Having taken the precaution, such an individual would feel reassured. Such a feeling was most often premature. Why? Because the presiding judge cannot alter the "facts" of the case. This is an important point, because many people, knowing that in the majority of cases the judge (or judges) was nominated, supported, and elected by Democrats, would argue that such judges were biased against non-Democrats. This, of course, has always been untrue, for in fact, the judge had no need to be prejudiced. The situation was already taken care of before it came to court. Since the "facts" will be presented by the election inspectors, and since the Commissioner is supposed to have reviewed the "facts," all the judge has to do is to allow these "facts" to be shown as "true" in open court. In this exercise, the Chairman of the County Law Committee, a learned and influential figure, would be in court on the side of the Commissioner and inspectors. And as in the case of Sam Smith, our new insurgent is a goner.

It is important to remember that hardly any petition came before the Board without some little defect. Therefore, when we clerks found one that was good in most of its particulars, there was still another weapon handy, that sweeping declaration that it was "permeated with fraud." This declaration can be made if, for example, the petition is signed by one person for two persons in a home. This appears to be a minor matter, but it was and is against the law. One such occurrence plus any other minor defect and the petition could be deemed by us to have "permeated." This procedure was very simple and very legal, and in this way socialists,

Communists, irregular Democrats, Blacks, and others were kept out of the political process in New York City prior to 1938. Although I learned a lot during my stay at the Board of Elections, I never deluded myself that I knew everything. The process of implementing and interpreting these laws was so mine-filled that unpleasant surprises were not uncommon, even for the most wary. Soon, I too would learn a valuable lesson.

I have noted that during the 1935 campaign to elect Herbert L. Bruce as District Leader in the 21st Assembly District, I remained in the 22nd. This was simply a home base from which I could assist my friends in the other districts in which Negroes were becoming the majority. My expertise lay in organizing, a good knowledge of the election laws generally, and particularly in the gathering of petitions.

The use of this expertise was urgently demanded in 1939 in the case of the reelection of Judge James Watson. Early in that year, rumors were widespread that Watson would not be supported for reelection in the fall. Herbert Bruce, as District Leader of the 21st Assembly District, and the rest of us were outraged at the idea of dropping Watson from the ticket. We saw in such a move a disregard for the desires of our group as well as for the changing political realities in Harlem. Something had to be done.

Bruce, whose Assembly District formed a small part of Watson's municipal court district, argued that I was the only one who had the ability to organize the 19th A. D., which encompassed the largest part of the court district. At this time the 19th covered central Harlem, and by now had the largest proportion of Negroes. The objective of the proposed organizing effort would be to displace the District Leader, Harry C. Perry, who was the half- brother of the Tammany boss. In this effort, Drs. P. M. H. Savory and Clilan B. Powell, co-owners of the Black newspaper, the *Amsterdam News*, joined Watson, Bruce, and me, and promised financing for the project. The result was the Dahoga Democratic Club, from which J. Raymond Jones would run for District Leader. But in our first outing, we ran afoul of Section 135 of the election laws.

Section 135 specified that all petitions should be bound and numbered *consecutively*. Daniel Flynn, my petitions assistant, and I interpreted this to mean consecutively in order of sheets as they were collected. Since we were insurgent Democrats trying to unseat Tammany's ticket, our petitions, though bound, numbered, notarized and filed, were challenged and found to be numbered incorrectly. This was mystifying since we thought we knew the law. But the Board ruled that if there were fifty petitions in district one, then the first petition in district two should be number fifty-one. Never had I or Flynn ever heard of such an interpretation, and we communicated our skepticism to Dr. Savory, our financial sponsor. Dr. Savory wasted no time in appealing. When the case *In re Savory* reached the Appellate Court some months later, it ruled that, "This matter is now academic," and further contended that no useful purpose would be served by rendering a decision. Later we learned that our appeal had fallen under the jurisdiction of the First Department of the Appellate Court, which had a five-judge panel, on which sat two pairs of opposing judges and a "swing" judge. It was this judge whom the Tammany organization convinced that J. Raymond Jones was undesirable as District Leader. Once again, my petitions were thrown out.

I have said that in 1939 I did not think I knew all there was to know of the possibilities for sharp practice around the election laws, but I had been confident that our little group had taken all the precautions and that we were safe. There was now nothing we could do, but I, for one, felt that these rulings were simply an exercise of superior power rather than impartial law. Given the changing times and manners, as I perceived them, it would not be long before my group and I would be able to exercise similar power.

Ruled out of the race by the courts, I was left with no alternative but to support someone else. Since my cause was now hopeless, I decided to support Jimmy Ravenal, a veteran of the "Steel Helmets," the famous 369th Colored Regiment of World War I. Ravenal, a long-time member of the old United Colored Democracy, was certainly qualified, but his association with me made him unwelcome to the Tammany crowd, led in this instance by Clarence Neal. But all this maneuvering had sent a message to the Democratic leadership: no longer could a white man lead the 19th. If not Jones, then it had to be some other Black person. In the end, they chose Daniel Burrows, a realtor, and with the Board of Elections' blessing, they railroaded him through.

I had lost my bid for District Leader, but this was not important. The objective was to replace the leadership, which we did, and to reelect Judge Watson, which we also did. In the process, I learned another lesson in practical politics, and satisfied with the results and my contribution, I went back to the 22nd A. D.

John Kelly, the leader in the 22nd District and a U. S. Marshal, had designated me a Deputy U. S. Marshal after the defeat of McCormick. It was a promotion from being a clerk at the Board of Elections, and I took it for several reasons. The salary was better, for one thing, and for another, I would be able to travel and maintain a car. A per diem allowance, although small, was not forgotten either.

As a Deputy U. S. Marshal, one of my jobs was to take Federal prisoners from New York to other states and sometimes vice versa. For this job I was assigned an assistant. He, too, was a political appointee. In this instance, my assistant was white, and I must say that travelling outside New York State in the late thirties, even as a Deputy U. S. Marshal, was for me a reeducation.

My assistant, Henry House, a former boxer, was a fine fellow, able, loyal, and smart. In those days I stood about 6 feet and weighed around 190 pounds. I was not small and neither was my aide. We made a good team. I carried a gun, but he didn't. He carried the prisoner's papers and, if not needed, the handcuffs. We had many adventures; I will always remember House as a fellow with great presence of mind.

On one of our first trips, to Milan, Michigan, we went by way of southern Pennsylvania. Outside of Harrisburg we stopped at a roadside diner for breakfast. We all sat on the stools in this diner—the white prisoner, the white guard, and I. The waiter took the order from both the prisoner and the guard and completely ignored me. When we brought it to his attention I was shocked to hear him reply. "We don't serve Negroes here." This was just outside the capital in the great state of Pennsylvania. For a moment I was nonplussed. I had to control my immediate reaction. Here I was, an officer of the Department of Justice, armed and taking a prisoner by automobile with permission of the U. S. Marshal, being denied service. This was a new experience for me. How do I respond? Do I cause a scene? Do I react in such a manner that it would reach the papers, embarrass myself, embarrass the U. S. Marshal's office, and probably set up a lasting block against the appointment of other Black men as Deputy United States Marshals? These were the questions that hurried through my mind, but Henry House, the guard, came to my assistance. He spoke up and said to the waiter, "That's all right, the Marshall will wait. Bring our food," and he put his hand on my shoulder and looked at me very sternly. I kept quiet. The waiter went away, came back and served us. Henry House then got up from the stool and said "Marshal, this is your breakfast," and stood beside me. I then opened my coat, displayed my gun lying on my right hip and the badge on the left lapel of my coat. I never said a word, but ate, while Henry House stared down everybody in the place. Not one person raised a voice one way or the other. We ate and walked out. This was my first experience of this kind in a northern state, and it was very definitely an education. We avoided that route in the future, taking the more frequently travelled truck routes 22 and 30, where we encountered no problems.

On another occasion, I picked up a prisoner, a swindler, who was wanted in Norfolk, Virginia. This time we went by rail to Cape Charles, Virginia, where we boarded a ferry to Norfolk. The prisoner, though depressed, was very dapperly dressed. We went to the main deck and sat down. Nobody said anything to us until the ferry pulled out, and then I was alerted by a

Black man in a white coat timidly coming up from the lower deck to the main deck where everybody was seated. I don't recall whether he was a steward. But he came over and very sheepishly and somewhat surreptiously leaned over and said to me, "You can't sit here. You have to go downstairs." I looked at Henry and Henry looked at me and said, "Oh well, another one." I ignored the steward. This was the attitude I had adopted. I paid no attention to him. But he kept talking, and I kept looking off into the blue yonder, admiring the scenery. Soon he decided he wasn't getting anywhere and departed.

Shortly after, another rose from the gangway, followed by epaulets, indicating an officer. He would have to be—He was white! He came over accompanied by the Black man and asked, "What's the trouble, Sam?" Sam told his tale, and the officer politely informed me that he, too, saw things Sam's way. The situation was now getting serious. Henry House always carried a big envelope with United States Department of Justice United States Marshal insignia on it. He carried this envelope with the leg irons and handcuffs, which we seldom used because our prisoners were actually not the desperate, violent kind. So I said, "Henry, you'd better use them." Henry promptly took out the leg irons and cuffed the prisoner to himself, and I opened my coat, displayed the gun and badge and just looked up at the officer. Henry was smiling and he whispered, "We are in the service of the government of the United States, U. S. Department of Justice. We are doing our job and we are molesting no one. Might I suggest that you leave us alone?" That was enough. The officer got red, turned around, and walked away.

This story, however, did not end here. On landing we removed the cuffs and irons from the prisoner and walked to the Marshal's office nearby. He had been telegraphed to expect us, so he was ready. As we walked in, this United States Marshal, who was a man as big as Marshal Dillon in the movies, walked right up, extended his hand to the prisoner and said, "Welcome Marshal, how was the trip?" I'm standing there, and House is standing there, and I am trying my best not to laugh. But House begins to explain, and the Marshal and the prisoner are standing there, both their hands half extended. They never touched because the prisoner was reluctant to put his hand out further and the Marshal is reaching for it, and Henry is explaining, and I'm just smiling and saying, "Marshal, here are the commitment papers as a result of your warrant." Well, that guy could have slapped me down if he could have gotten away with it. He was so embarrassed it was not even funny. Once Henry and I were out of earshot we had to sit down and laugh.

I also recall an incident at the Waldorf-Astoria in 1938. I was given a subpoena to serve on a prominent California movie star staying at the

Waldorf. I walked to the elevator and found my entry blocked by a white starter, so resplendent in uniform he would make a field marshal weep with envy. He asked me where I was going and I told him. "Go around the corner," he said, "and you'll find the freight elevator. It will take you up." I looked at him and said, "Oh no, it won't. You are going to take me up. This is New York City. This is my hometown." No response. I said, "That's the manager's desk over there isn't it?" He said, "Yes." I walked over, showed the fellow my credentials and explained. He said, "Well, what's your objection to using the service elevator?" I said, "My objection is based on one fact. Answer me this question. If I were white would you stop me?" "Well," he said, "service is service." And I said, "Well, unless you want a hell of a lot of problems, I am going upstairs in a regular elevator. And I will report to the Federal Judge, who sent me here to serve these papers, what is happening." In the next instant he was out from behind the desk, personally escorting me to the "field marshal" who promptly took me up.

In 1987, I find this very amusing, because in 1962, after I had played a role in the reelection of Mayor Robert Wagner and a year prior to my becoming the first Black Leader of Tammany Hall, the mayor held a dinner party in my honor. More than 1,200 people, Black and white, Jews and Gentiles, Catholics and Protestants, were in attendance. And where were we? In the grand ballroom of the Waldorf-Astoria. I marvelled then, as I do now, how the times and the manners have changed, for the field marshal was not at his post in 1962 and neither was his ghost.

Chapter 4

New Beginnings in Black
Politics *(1941–1953)*

WAR BROKE OUT in Europe in 1939, and we in the United States hoped that we would never have to become involved as we had in World War I. But by 1941 anyone with any political sense knew that the odds against our noninvolvement were great. For the unsubtle observer, it appeared as if the war had no relationship to politics, but I felt instinctively that the war would profoundly affect the relationship between Blacks and whites both in New York City and in the rest of the country. A politically uninitiated youngster during World War I, I had learned a thing or two by 1940, and I knew that Blacks had profited from the spoils of World War I. I knew that if we participated in World War II, despite the fact that a number of Black men and women would die, once again at home the political complexion of the face of the United States would swiftly change. 1941 then, was a critical year.

In that year Negroes in all five boroughs of New York and in the rest of the state gathered under the leadership of A. Philip Randolph to inform President Franklin Delano Roosevelt of our awareness of the rampant discrimination and segregation in the defense industries that the United States, as a consequence of Lend-Lease, had geared up to help the British. While the United States aided its allies abroad in the fight against bigotry, we made it clear that we would no longer tolerate bigotry at home. Randolph and his organization, which came to be called the "March on Washington Movement", or MOWM, threatened to take ten thousand marchers down to Washington, D.C., to march around the White House and the Capitol in a display of disapproval of the continued discrimination by corporations doing business with the government. As soon as Randolph announced the protest, the President's aides made a series of calls to him pretending at first only a mild concern, and assuming that the expression of the President's disapproval was sufficient to deter Randolph and his people. Randolph, however, had wide support in New York from Blacks, and whites as well, particularly the leaders of a large number of liberal labor organizations that supported the Harlem Negro Labor Committee headed by the West Indian immigrant, Frank Crosswaith. Such widespread support as well as Randolph's obvious determination to carry on, caused the President to reconsider.

Apart from the anticipated disruption of business the demonstration would cause, the President had another consideration. The MOWM argument that certain aspects of United States social life were not any better than Nazi Germany, where Jews by this time were being exterminated merely for being Jews, had a telling effect upon the White House. At no time did FDR or the U.S. State Department want the international community to regard America as even faintly comparable to the Fascists of Europe. Furthermore, we had treated the Japanese disdainfully since the Russo-Japanese War to a great extent because they were racially different, and now the Japanese were staring at Hawaii with interest. The President and his advisors knew they would welcome news of racism in the United States for propaganda. He also knew that Blacks had fought valiantly in the Spanish-American War, even saving the life of his cousin, Theodore. Blacks who had distinguished themselves in Europe in World War I had been cited by the French government and were now part of the March on Washington Movement. Consequently, the President arranged a meeting between Randolph and his lieutenants at the White House in an attempt to solve this dilemma, for under no circumstances should 10,000 Negroes be allowed to march on Washington.

President Roosevelt, as history has documented, was a peculiar fellow. Distinguished historians argue that he believed that through face-to-face diplomacy, he could change the opinion of any political opponent and persuade him to see the wisdom of his view. For this, historians have castigated him about his relationship with Joseph Stalin, Charles De Gaulle, and others. He was no different with Philip Randolph.

As the story goes, the first thing the President tried to do was to charm the group. Randolph, a very courteous, well-bred, well-spoken, articulate man had a voice, it is said, like the sound of a pipe organ at the hands of E. Power Biggs. Not only that, he spoke with a clipped oxfordian accent, more representative of a member of the Barbadian upper class than the son of Black middle-class parents from Jacksonville, Florida. So when Roosevelt made the case that perhaps the march should be called off, and then he would see what he could do, Randolph responded that the priority should be the other way around—the President should do something he had the authority to do, and then the march would be called off. Randolph spoke in such mellifluous tones, with such authority and exquisiteness of syntax, that his performance completely flabbergasted the President. Stunned, and delighted, Roosevelt turned to Randolph, who was flanked by a number of Black graduates of Harvard, the President's alma mater, and said, "Tell me, Mr. Randolph, what year were you at Harvard?" To which Randolph replied, "Mr. President, I have never been at Harvard." No one knows the President's thoughts at this discombobulating moment, because he went on to more serious matters. But perhaps he might have thought that within the Negro population there were many like Randolph who need not have gone to Harvard to meet the President on equal terms and to show all the qualities of what he may have considered to be the superior Harvard man. In the end, the President had no choice, and within a few days he issued Executive Order 8802, forbidding discrimination for racial reasons by any corporation doing business with the government of the United States.

To implement this order, the President created also by Executive Order the Fair Employment Practices Commission, known as the FEPC, under the jurisdiction of the Justice Department, to handle all reports of discrimination and prosecute violators. The FEPC turned out to be a weak instrument, but it was enough at this time, because Negroes knew that backed by the Executive Order they could fight battles locally with vigor and determination on a legal foundation. It was a small but significant step forward, one of many laying the foundation for the 1960s' civil rights explosion.

I was not personally involved in the March on Washington Movement, but I gave my support through my colleague, Richard C. Thomas. The import of an Executive Order was not lost on me. It was a political plus, as well as an economic one; a positive sign of the times for what we were attempting to do in New York City. The war and rumors of war, the March on Washington Movement and the issuance of the Executive Order 8802, the formation of the FEPC, and the new migration of Blacks from the West side and middle parts of Manhattan into Harlem as well as migration from the Southern states to New York, all portended significant Black political progress and activity in New York in 1941.

No longer a young man, I approached middle age with confidence, enthusiasm, and optimism, thanks to fortuitous events. The time seemed right for another attempt to change the political complexion of things in Manhattan. In 1939, I left the 22nd A.D. to run against Harry C. Perry, a white leader in the 19th Assembly District. I lost, making it possible for Daniel L. Burrows to become the 22nd District Leader. I found on my return to my club—the white club of John Kelly, U.S. Marshall—that Kelly, after encouraging me to make a run in the 19th Assembly District, had made a deal behind my back with the judges to insure that I would lose by their ruling my petitions incomplete. Soon John Kelly called me in and tried to chastise me for having gone into the 19th to run, when in fact he had earlier encouraged me to do so. I let him know that I knew that he was the one who had sabotaged my petitions and made it impossible for me to win in the 19th Assembly District. I realized also that he was concerned that others might know that he had encouraged me, so that now he was trying to blame me. I thought this behavior very irrational and with my age and secure self-confidence, I refused to allow myself to be bawled out by an insecure and vascillating politician. I vowed then and there that the time would come when I would take the leadership of the 22nd away from him.

In 1941 the 22nd Assembly District was essentially white and had been ever since I had joined in the 1920s. I had the impression that it would soon be possible to have Black leadership in this neighborhood even if the numbers of Black people were small. As it turned out, this happened very soon and herein lies what we might call a fortuitous and serendipitous story.

The 22nd Assembly District was one of the most powerful in New York City. The district boasted such members as Assemblyman Daniel Flynn, U.S. Representative James Gavagan, John Kelly, himself a Federal Marshal, and of course, J. Raymond Jones, though I was nowhere near the league of these three gentlemen. It must be remembered that in 1941, Tammany Hall was not in power in New York City. The Mayor was still Fiorella LaGuardia, who had come in with Roosevelt and eventually was to go out with him in 1945. LaGuardia owed much of his political clout to Roosevelt, although technically, as a Democrat, he was a fusion candidate supported by the American Labor Party, the Liberal Party, and to some extent, Republican votes. But since Roosevelt was somewhat put out with Tammany leadership all during the 1930s and into the 1940s, he tried from Washington through the Postmaster General, James J. Farley, and Sidney Hillman labor leader and prominent Roosevelt supporter, to control politics in New York City, as well as in New York State. The 22nd Assembly District knew that Roosevelt wanted to make some changes and that Farley was about to do something about it.

The contemplated change was to get rid of John Kelly for reasons that were unclear to me. I was not opposed, because his double-crossing in 1939 still rankled in 1941, and not only that, I aspired to take over the district. And so it happened that in the election year for the leadership, I knew it was time to support the Roosevelt and Farley candidate, whoever he may be, against John Kelly. As it turned out, the choice was not difficult, because they chose Congressman Joseph Gavagan to run against Kelly; we did all we could to ensure Gavagan's victory.

Politics, of course, is a system of friendships, a matrix of loyalties—or disloyalties for that matter—and the election of Gavagan had certain interesting consequences. One consequence was the election of Michael Kennedy as leader in the Hell's Kitchen district, as a result, in part, of support from Daniel Flynn and myself. For our support, Flynn was promised a judgeship, but when it became available, Gavagan took it for himself. This was not kosher and at the state convention when Flynn called Gavagan certain Irish names, much to the surprise of bystanders, fisticuffs very nearly ensued. Another more positive result of my interventions were two jobs for my people in the Internal Revenue Service; one went to Richard Thomas and the other to Enoch Clark. In fact, Gavagan had received three slots in the I.R.S. from FDR and that third slot went to Bucky Wilder, a Gavagan man, who had been my body guard for a while when I was Deputy U.S. Marshal. These development were excellent for me, but not for my friend Dan Flynn, who had lost out. Six years later, after the Wagner election in 1947, I remembered what had happened to Danny regarding that judgeship, and when a magistrate's position opened that I could offer him, I did. He refused it as being too low, and so I gave it to a Black person. In this way, another Black man was put on the Magistrate's Court.

John Kelly's removal and Gavagan's election had personal rewards for me also. At the same time Gavagan was elected District Leader, I was elected the chairman of the 22nd District Country Committee. Towards the end of the year I was reasonably content with my accomplishments and surveying the scene, I was fairly satisfied with Black accomplishments in the Democratic Party. But by December, the feeling I'd had earlier in the summer that events would quickly accelerate had become even stronger. Late in the evening of December 7, 1941, my telephone rang: there on the line was none other than Congressman Joseph A. Gavagan. Calling from Washington, he yelled in my ear: "My God, my God, we are in a war! The Japanese have bombed Pearl Harbor and destroyed the place." My feeling, of course, was deep sorrow for the men that had been killed; like any other normal person I despised and disliked wars, but I knew that in a war a nation cannot afford to be as divided and bigoted as it is in peacetime, and so I felt somehow that ironically in this war effort, whites would have to come to regard Blacks with greater respect, if not with camaraderie.

By 1943, it had become clear to me that because of the racial mix, it would take too long for me to achieve leadership in the 22nd A.D., and on the suggestion of Adam Clayton Powell, my friend at the time and a City Councilman, we decided that I ought to make a run for the 21st Assembly District leadership, then headed by Herbert L. Bruce. Bruce, an immigrant from the West Indies, was Black, and there was no intention of starting an internal feud, but there were certain developments in the wind which made Bruce's removal necessary. Adam had decided to resign as City Councilman in order to run for the new Congressional District in 1944 encompassing mostly all of Harlem. Adam had the best chance of winning because he was well-known as a City Councilman and, with my help, would be unlikely to lose. As soon as Adams announced his candidacy, Bruce, entrenched in the 21st A.D., came out against him. We could not risk someone of such power in Harlem not supporting Adam, so we decided to try to take over Bruce's district in order to ensure Adam's chances. But there was more to it than that, for Herbert Bruce was a friend of the Tammany Hall leader, Michael J. Kennedy, and, although I supported Kennedy, it seemed to me that his friendship with Bruce would somehow prevent his support for Adam in 1944. Nevertheless, I supported Kennedy, while I campaigned against Herbert Bruce, and this campaign against Bruce in the 21st A.D. brought me some temporary allies, notably among them Clarence Neal, District Leader of a neighboring district, and Burt Stand, Secretary of the County Committee.

While all this was going on, Adam Clayton Powell asked my support for a member of his own club, Fred Dickens, who opposed Daniel Burrows, the successful compromise candidate in 1939 in the 19th A.D. Because I was supporting Adam for his run for the Congressional seat from Harlem, I supported his candidate Dickens, who handily defeated Burrows. The support of Powell, Dickens, and the rest, however, was of no help to me in the 21st. Bruce's defenses were too great, and Adam was not yet powerful enough to assist me as he might have in later contests. Consequently, I lost to Bruce once again and returned to the 22nd.

Despite my loss to Herbert Bruce, my position was strong and my standing good; but I was still not a leader. Nevertheless, Adam Powell and myself had our own man now in the 19th Assembly District; and Bruce, at least knew that he would have to behave.

After the Bruce campaign, I went back to the 22nd Assembly District. It seemed in 1944, even with the war still on, that fortune smiled on my efforts. Gavagan, as District Leader of the 22nd, had supported Congressman Michael Kennedy in his run for Tammany Leader in 1942; therefore, when in 1944 an opening appeared in the State Supreme Court, Kennedy had a say in the matter and nominated Gavagan for the seat. This was in January, and since Daniel Flynn had left for the Navy, Gavagan's resignation left me virtually in control of the 22nd Assembly District for the first time. Since I was the chairman of the county committee of my Assembly District, it meant I was responsible for overseeing the election of a new District Leader. In this capacity I decided that I should become a candidate. This I knew was not going to be easy because of the ethnic antagonisms already apparent in the district. At this time the district was divided almost evenly among Jews, Blacks, and Irish with a few marginal Puerto Ricans and Italians. It soon became apparent that the Jews and Irish would not support Jones, but if an Irishman were a candidate, the Blacks and Jews would not support him, and so on. It was a very interesting political situation, one which did not bode well for me.

My problem was complicated by the animosity of Tammany Leader Michael Kennedy. The previous year, 1943, Kennedy had come under pressure to resign as Tammany Chief in favor of Edward V. Loughlin. Kennedy had been able to repulse this pressure until January 1944 because Joseph Gavagan, a member of the New York County Committee, that is, Tammany Hall, had been his staunch supporter. With Gavagan gone, Michael Kennedy threw his support, not to me, but to Judge "Forty" McQuade.[1] He utilized the indirect approach. First, Kennedy talked with Joseph Gavagan and asked him to talk to me. Kennedy suggested that I go along with this gentleman, this judge that he wanted to place ahead of me. When I decided that I would not go along wit it, he tried another ploy. He tried to have Burt Stand, a secretary to the New York County Committee, and Clarence Neal, the Irishman known as the "three-fingered wonder" and the Chairman of the County Committee, work on me.

It should be noted here that the Chairman of the County Committee was almost a Deputy Tammany Leader, and the Secretary of the County Committee was an assistant to the Deputy Leader. In most instances, even when the New York County Leader was changed, the Chairman remained unless he himself succeeded to the County Leadership or was removed by the Leader, and so did the Secretary. So in many ways, these two men were most powerful, because they insured the continuity of the organization when changes took place, and in time they built up an enormous amount of influence and persuasive power. The two incumbents, luckily, were my friends, and did not go along with Kennedy's scheme to prevent me from becoming the 22nd A.D. Leader. Thwarted by his supposed cohorts, Kennedy then threatened to go through the courts to prevent me from becoming District Leader through some technicality.

Kennedy had no idea that while trying to get rid of me he was seriously undermining his position. In a very impolitic move he asked Stand and Neal to set up a meeting between him and me. It was one that I shall never forget.

It was set at the New York Athletic Club, which at that time was very Irish Catholic. Important Irishmen from as far away as Buffalo came to this club when in New York to pay their respects. The huge building had two entrances, one on 59th Street, and the other on 58th Street. Neal was unable to come, but Burt Stand accompanied me to the Club, and took me in through the servant's entrance into the lower hall. Stand left me there on a bench beside the elevators, while he went upstairs to talk to Kennedy. After about 20 to 25 minutes, Stand and Kennedy came down and Kennedy talked to me about his good friend, Judge McQuade, and how I should agree. I listened to his story and finally said, "Mike, I'm sorry. I won't go along with it." I had already decided that Kennedy was a most insensitive person, for he seemed totally unaware that the longer he talked the more my resentment mounted. Not only did I resent his trying to pressure me to go along with something that would not have been attempted if I were white, but I felt also that I had labored long enough, my turn had come, and I was not going to allow myself to be pressured out of a post for which I had worked so long and so hard. Furthermore, I knew that if I had been white, I would not have been brought through the servant's entrance. It seemed to me that if Kennedy had had any brains at all, he would have insisted that I come through the front door, which would not have raised an eyebrow at that time anyway, and arranged for me to go through the conference room to meet him rather than coming to the basement level to meet me.

As I understood it later, Kennedy had given the word that I should enter through the back, and of course, Stand did not try to talk him out of it, because he knew I would be annoyed. And it was in Stand and Neal's interest that I not go along with the blandishments of Michael Kennedy. When we left, Burt Stand said to me, "Well, how do you like that?", and I knew exactly what he was talking about. Kennedy did not know it, but the die was cast.

Dissatisfied with my response, Kennedy took the case to court. But here again, he got caught in the middle, because Stand and Neal saw to it that the case went to the "wrong" judge. The judged ruled that the rules of the County Committee were set, and they gave power to the Chairman of the District County Committee, who would sit until removed by the County Committee. In other words, I was temporarily the leader of the 22nd A.D. by virtue of my chairmanship of the district's County Committee.

County Leader Kennedy did not welcome the judge's ruling on my behalf. Being stubborn and tenacious, he made his last move against me at the next meeting of the 22nd A.D. County Committee. This was an important meeting because on the agenda was the district's sentiment on the County Leader question. Knowing what was at issue, Michael Kennedy sent his two most prominent Harlem supporters, Herbert L. Bruce and Fred Dickens, to "observe" our meeting. Neither of the men was in my district so they had no business being "observers." I had, however, anticipated interference from some source, and had obtained a court order, banning anyone not a member of our club from the meeting.

Since the meeting was being held upstairs at our club, I had stationed our official gendarme downstairs, a very large Irishman, a captain from the 30th precinct. He was told not to let any unauthorized persons upstairs. Soon after the meeting convened, we heard loud voices downstairs, and I knew that trouble was afoot. Signalling my own guards, about ten men, I descended the stairs. There was the captain staring down Dickens and Bruce, both of whom displayed revolvers on their hips. The captain and I knew that, being restauranteurs, they had licenses to carry guns, but their gangster demeanor so infuriated me that I temporarily lost my self-control. Turning to the captain I said, "I have here a judge's order barring outsiders. Now get these guys with their guns out of here. If not, we will take those guns and stick them up their------." At this point Bruce and Dickens, smart boys that they were, knew the game was up and made for the exit.

In retrospect, I am ashamed of that outburst, because regardless of one's age, a person tries to maintain a good image. In my case, profane or crude language had always offended me. This, of course, was due to the influence of my mother, but the sight of those boys with guns did something to me and the phrase came out involuntarily.

It also may be that in 1944 with the war on that a looser atmosphere prevailed in New York and that I too had become crude. I had noticed that since 1941 the whole New York scene had changed. There seemed to be more criminals, more liberties taken with impunity, an almost devil-may-care roughness which offended me. I didn't want to be part of politics by intimidation. Deals, yes, thuggery, no.

So although I was thoroughly unhappy after that meeting, I consoled myself with the belief that I had done the right thing. Given my goals, I put the incident behind me and decided to carry on. The Bruce/Dickens visitation did not help Michael Kennedy at all. Indeed, it sealed his fate in our district, for we threw our support to Edward V. Loughlin and by the end of January, Michael Kennedy was gone.

My support for Loughlin, and Stand and Neal's support came in very handy a few months later, because immediately after the vote the Assembly Districts were reduced by reapportionment in Manhattan's New York County. Until early 1944 there had been twenty-three Assembly Districts in New York County, but after the reapportionment, only sixteen remained. The 22nd A.D. of which I was now Leader was redrawn into a larger district, now called the 13th. The redrawing of these boundaries created a very interesting situation. The western half was predominantly white and the eastern half was, by a small majority, Black. The district was therefore divided into east and west, and I found myself Leader of the 13th A.D. East, with Angelo Simmonetti Leader of the 13th A.D. West.

1944 also was a year of Congressional and Presidential elections, and indeed it was a good year for Democrats everywhere, because that was the year in which Franklin D. Roosevelt won again, for an unprecedented fourth term. By then it was clear that under Roosevelt's leadership, we were not only winning the war but also winning friends and allies all over the world because of the valiant way our troops fought, and the way the President, by himself and through his wife's efforts, conducted a humane administration at home. The President carried on his coat-tails quite a few Democrats in local elections.

One candidate running in 1944 who did not need Franklin Roosevelt was Adam Clayton Powell. When Powell announced in 1943 that he would not run again for the City Council, it was understood that I would assist in his campaign for the new 22nd Congressional District seat. This campaign was a political stroll down the avenue, for Adam was already famous in Harlem, and a spellbinding orator. It did not hurt that his district was eighty percent Black.

After the campaign, my relationship with Adam Clayton Powell became an on and off, up an down one. From the beginning I knew that he was a mercurial man, most sincere at any moment, but prone to forget the importance of his commitments once the moment had passed. Powell had come to my attention, not as the Assistant Minister of the Abyssinian Baptist Church from 1930 to 1936, but as a writer for the *Amsterdam News* beginning in 1936 in a column he called "The Soapbox". I read this column from time to time, but it never occurred to me that someone obviously so well taken care of by an indulgent father and a large and mothering congregation would ever think of offering himself to the hurly-burly of politics. But in 1938 Powell formed the Greater New York Coordinating Committee for Employment, and the next thing anyone knew he was picketing, with signs "Don't Buy Where You Can't Work," sundry establishments that discriminated against Negroes.

This picketing was enormously successful, and corporations such as the New York Telephone Company began to hire more Negroes. He even took his picketing to the World's Fair of 1939–1940, where the fear of the disruption of something so international encouraged a compromise, and a number of Black people were hired. Although Powell's successes in ensuring employment for Negroes was not what might have been called spectacular today, the fact is that in those days persuading a New York bus company to hire Black drivers made for jubilation in Harlem.

I had watched Powell's activities before 1940 expectantly and with a great deal of admiration because what I was trying to do within the Democratic Party was certainly not sufficient for Harlem. I can say with all honesty that at no time in my career did I want to be a czar in Harlem, and the record shows that I had always tried to cooperate with activists who intended to alleviate the conditions of Black people. Consequently, the greater the number of organizations for self-help—political, economic, or cultural—the greater I thought would become the general standards of living in Harlem and New York City. Powell's group was not unique. many other groups were fighting to assist in bettering conditions for Negroes in Harlem, among them the Communists, the Negro Labor Committee, a loose association of labor unions, and others. All these were welcome.

In the 1930s, the number of jobs usually held by young Blacks were being eliminated, and Black people in New York City felt the grip of the Depression, in my opinion, far more painfully than any other groups. Black employment within New York diminished as lower-level jobs that white had once scorned went to needy whites instead of Blacks. And as technology raced on, elevator operators, for example, were replaced by automatic elevators. Young Black unemployment increased, and it was into this milieu that Adam stepped with confidence.

Powell's base was the Abyssinian Baptist Church, pastored by his father, Adam Clayton Powell, Sr. When he first appeared on the scene in 1936, he identified with all the splinter groups conducting their particular campaigns to alleviate conditions in their areas. With the force of his personality and the power of his presence, he melded these groups into one solid group, the Greater New York Coordinating Council. His biggest push to control the masses was to denigrate the Black middle and upper classes who comprised the Black intelligensia. Walter White, Secretary of the National Association for the Advancement of Colored People, thought Adam was more detrimental than helpful and saw him as a demagogue. Frankly, in many ways he was right. At that time there were not too many Blacks on Sugar Hill and Strivers Row, but Adam made light of those who were. Yet the church people were upwardly mobile, and, ironically but understandably, his strength weakened among his strongest supporters in the church who lived in Sugar Hill and were moving on to Long Island.

But Adam was a great orator, and a very attractive man. (Women all thought him most handsome, with a great personality.) Picking up on the ambiance of Roosevelt's New Deal that the responsibility of the government is to assist its citizens needing social services, Powell launched out on this theme to see what he could do.

I think that Adams was really a child of the New Deal more so than of the church, and his decision to run for the City Council in 1941 had come from his belief that the New York City Council could do more for Black-people than private philanthropy or the Church. His success as a council-man bolstered his belief that others could do the work on the City Council while he went on to larger and more important arenas. In his early days, Powell genuinely desired to bring about improved welfare for the citizens of Harlem. That is not to say he did not bask in the attention his efforts brought him—he certainly boasted a proud ego—but undoubtedly, in the early stages, he worked indefatigably and somewhat thanklessly. He had not yet developed that cynical contempt for his own people which in my opinion, he displayed so blatantly in the later years of his life.

By 1943 Powell was one of the outstanding men in Harlem, along with people like A. Philip Randolph and Channing Tobias, a very popular leader of the YMCA. Tobias was well-known in social work circles, and Randolph, a national hero for having forced President Roosevelt to issue Executive Order 8802, the successful developer of the Brotherhood of Sleeping Car Porters, Workers and Maids, and the successful publisher and editor of the *Harlem Messenger* between 1921 and 1928. But somehow it seemed more logical in 1943 that Adam Clayton Powell would be the man to run for Congress.

After Randolph met with President Roosevelt at the White House and successfully negotiated Executive Order 8802 and the establishment of the FEPC, the March on Washington Movement continued, strategizing to insure adherence to 8802. In 1943 Randolph made the mistake of inviting Adam Clayton Powell to speak at a Madison Square Garden rally. Powell got such a tremendous response that he chose the moment to announce that he would run for Congress the next year, rather than seek reelection to the City Council. Whatever plans Randolph had for running for public office—and there had been rumors—were eclipsed that evening.

Since 1935 when we elected Herbert Bruce the first Black District Leader, Bruce, Hulan Jack, and I with others had been working strenu-ously to integrate swiftly as many Black people as possible into the Dem-ocratic Party. We operated strictly within the confines of the Tammany machinery, hoping to elect Blacks to the State Assembly and Senate, City Council, and the rest. We also tried very hard to elect District Leaders in the hope that one day we would elect a Borough President, a Tammany Leader, and so on, and had been moderately successful even before 1944. But what Powell brought to our struggle for Black political leadership in Harlem was a revolutionary approach we were not capable of, being com-mitted to the normal processes of the Democratic Party machinery. In fact, Adam had built a popular organization along revolutionary lines outside the Tammany and the Republican organizations, although he made the occa-sional insouciant bow towards the Democratic Party when it suited his purposes. Adam Powell did not need the Democratic Party; if anything, it needed him. Furthermore, his timing was perfect because we now had a few district leaders, a few magistrates here and there, and an assemblyman or two. But what we needed was to make a big push of strength and vigor, to take advantage of the social and political ferment caused by the ongoing war. Powell's timing and the bold manner of his attack could not have been better designed.

But there were problems. Within the Democratic organization and within Powell's own group, the question now became, "Is Adam's popular coalition going to attempt a takeover of the community that we, the political group, had been carefully building all these years?" This question was not unusual, for naturally professional politicians resented the incursion of radical candidates for public office, and although we secretly lauded Adam Powell's rhetoric, he made us uneasy from time to time by his extremes which we considered unnecessary. The Black Democratic politicians in Harlem, me included, feared Adam, because his entire thrust was to the radical left, some of whom were Communists, like Vito Marcantonio. For a while Adam put us in a quandary.

For myself, I decided very soon that our political group should work with what I called the popular group, that is, Powell's. People thought members of the political group worked solely and specifically for their own interests rather than for the general population. While this was not true, it seemed credible on the face of it, because party workers and friends received priority in the distribution of patronage. I thought that a combination of the politicians and what we might call the popular or civil rights group would have an encompassing appeal to the people of Harlem and other parts of New York because such an umbrella would deal with what may be called their "daily living needs."

Thus, I saw no reason at all for the local Democratic leaders to oppose Adam Clayton Powell, and I lost no time in telling them that we ought to support the man. Without waiting for others to join me, I informed Mr. Powell that I would support him for his candidacy in 1944, which I did. I continued to support him for quite a while, until he became, in my opinion, undependable. It could be that I supported Adam for much too long, but if I erred on this side of indiscretion, it was for the following reason.

I had noticed that in the Congress of the United States, as elsewhere, longevity is synonymous with seniority. I had watched with great dismay as I grew more sophisticated in politics, how Southern senators and representatives returned year after year after year, and although there were no greater numbers of them in the Congress than Northerners, with regularity they became chairmen of the various powerful committees because they had been there longer. Although technically a chairman of a committee in

Congress is not supposed to have any more votes than anybody else, these chairmen enjoyed a certain deference that made their vote somewhat weightier than those of their supposedly equal colleagues.

It occurred to me then that after 1944, with only two Black representatives in the Congress, that is Powell and William Dawson from Chicago, it was important to send these men back to Congress again and again. Seniority would give them leadership of important committees, to the benefit, not only of their immediate constituencies, but of the Black constituency throughout the country. As it happened, despite criticisms throughout his Congressional tenure, Powell eventually became the chairman of the House Education and Labor Committee in January 1961. For a long while, until his troubles began in 1966, the majority of Congressmen, excluding bigots, and Presidents Kennedy and Johnson lauded him as a very hard-working, brilliant, astute, and effective leader.

Although Adam Clayton Powell was supposedly a Democrat, he was not a Democrat of the kind that I was. I was part of the "machine" and I worked from the inside out. Powell worked from the outside in. My fights in the Democratic Party took place behind closed doors, seldom out in the open, and since I was not a public officeholder as Powell, I obtained jobs for various Black people through the city government, and saw to it that Black workers benefitted in the dispensation of patronage. In addition, at the clubhouse, I attended to the needs of people in their everyday lives. For example: "My son is in jail, can you help?" "I am being harassed by the police, can you help?" "The rats are biting my baby, can you do something?". All these complaints had to be taken care of in the normal and traditional way.

Powell, on the other hand, as an outside figure, brought pressure through the media, and kept the party's political feet to the fire, so to speak. It could be said that every negative move by the Democratic Party, or by the Republican Party for that matter, was a positive one for Adam. Every time he was attacked by the *New York Times*, Adam claimed it an attack on all Black people. In this way he gained the support and the adulation of the Black masses in New York and the rest of the country. Of course, with this unique individual in our midst, really a human catalyst, Black political leaders in New York had to chart a careful course between him and the community. Since he made things happen and created new realities out of old ones, he had to be handled with care: like all catalysts, chemically speaking, there was a tendency at times for him to over-accelerate his action on his substrate.

But Powell, as a man of such potential, was not easily understood. From time to time, particularly after Carmine DeSapio became Tammany leader, certain Harlem leaders tried to do Powell in. They tried in 1958, and I came out of early retirement to run his campaign, a story to which I will return later.

The O'Dwyer Campaign of 1945

In 1945 Fiorello La Guardia had been Mayor of New York City for three full terms; he announced that he had decided not to run again after his term ended that year. Interestingly, his decision coincided with the end of the war, the death of FDR, and with the return of several former politicians who had gone to fight abroad. Many of them did this with a genuine feeling of patriotism, but some in a calculated effort to win one distinction that could be parlayed into political currency at the war's end. Two such men were William O'Dwyer and his friend, John M. Murtagh. I had known Murtagh before the war from the Mayopac Club, and through him I came to know O'Dwyer when he decided to make a second run for mayor. I had played a small role in 1941 when he had run for mayor against the popular La Guardia and garnered 42% of the vote. When O'Dwyer ran for Kings County District Attorney in Brooklyn, the second time, he was in fact away at war having achieved the rank of colonel. Yet he won with the greatest of ease, since he was endorsed by all parties, including the American Labor Party, the party of La Guardia, the man he had tried to unseat as mayor in 1941. I felt certain from the beginning that O'Dwyer would be a formidable candidate. I noted this, because a number of people in the Democratic Party had begun to make plans to jump on the O'Dwyer bandwagon in 1945. I made no overtures to O'Dwyer. I had concluded in 1941 that, although most people thought La Guardia was simply unbeatable in 1941, there was more to that puzzle.

I believed then that O'Dwyer's problem was Manhattan. Although he had done well in all counties, two things seem clear to me. In the first place, I knew that in Manhattan he was still seen as a Brooklyn politician. I believed that if he had been from New York County, the odds would have been better. If my first assumption was correct, then a logical assumption could be made that every effort would have been made to increase the vote in New York County. If that turned out to be true, then Harlem would be pivotal. If O'Dwyer saw all this, that Manhattan would be the key, then sooner or later we would hear from him. For by 1945 the Negro vote had become so powerful that no one could win in the Democratic Party without it. Unless you were as bigoted and insensitive as Michael Kennedy, it was obvious that something had to be done to garner the Negro vote. William

O'Dwyer, referred to as "The General," was not a fool, and so he sought advice when he returned from the war as to how to attempt to insure the Negro vote. Old friends advised him that Dr. Channing Tobias should head his campaign to get the Black vote in Harlem and elsewhere because he was the big gun among intellectuals, and was a powerful presence in the NAACP. Yet, others advised him that things had changed since the war began, that between 1941 and 1942, there arrived on the scene a bigger mouth in Harlem, none other than my friend, Congressman Adam Clayton Powell. Although O'Dwyer knew of Channing Tobias before he left for war, he did not know this new fellow, Powell, and the Abyssinian Baptist Church meant nothing to him. Furthermore, reports about Powell certainly were controversial and conflicting. So O'Dwyer was caught between two personalities, Channing Tobias and Adam Clayton Powell, without either of them knowing it. The question was, who would be the best campaign manager to insure the Negro vote and to avoid conflict between Powell and Tobias?

At this point, my old friend, John M. Murtagh, stepped in to arrange for the services of what we call in international diplomacy the "third party." And so it was that one day I was at the Carver Club when in walked Murtagh, still in his army uniform, asking to please speak to me. He told me that the General was having a problem choosing between Powell and Tobias, and wanted to know if I would come down and talk to him about it. I replied I would and in due time, I went down to headquarters, and agreed to try to resolve the problem. I told O'Dwyer that it would take me a few days to arrange everything, and that when it was all set, I would report.

What I did was very simple: I went to see Dr. Tobias, told him of the problem and assured him that I knew he did not want to get involved in a political crossfire. But since he had considerable influence in the Negro community, while we wanted to have Powell's support, and because I was committed anyway and would throw my influence behind O'Dwyer, I suggested that, to remove any possibility of conflicts of ego that might damage the campaign, we ask a respected member of the Black community to be nominal campaign manager. The best choice was Col. Vernon C. Riddick, who had returned from the war and was a Colonel in the National Guard. We would all work under Col. Riddick, and since Tobias held such an exalted standing in the community, I suggested that he accept the position as honorary chairman of the campaign. This way, in conversation with his friends, his rank would be very high. Dr. Tobias, who was not a man of overweening ego anyway, accepted this, and I went on to deal with a more prickly problem, that of Powell, now full of vim and vigor in his first term as Congressman from New York.

My story for Powell differed slightly from what I told Tobias. In effect I said, "Look, we want you to be the honorary co-chairman of the campaign with Dr. Channing Tobias. We know you are very busy in Congress, and we don't want to disturb you, so Riddick and I will do all the work." To Adam, already full of himself, this was fine, as long as he was not called upon to do work beneath his dignity. Furthermore, he knew it was in his interest to have Bill O'Dwyer, who would most certainly become Mayor of New York, if not his friend, then certainly not his enemy.

The secretary of my club, Corliss Crocker, and I did most of the work; however, we took a back seat as far as credit was concerned. Politics is matter of image as well as work, so ostensibly I was to only advise O'Dwyer as to the best way of garner the Negro vote. But by 1945 I was beyond that, and the candidate gratefully accepted my suggestions for handling Powell and the citywide campaign. The election itself was never in doubt, for Fiorello, that unsurpassed vote-getter, was gone.

I firmly impressed upon O'Dwyer that Powell was a fine politician and as such, O'Dwyer had to make some definite commitments that Powell could use in press releases as reasons for his support of O'Dwyer. I reminded Bill that Harlem would need a magistrate, so he promised Powell that the first magistrate position would go to a Negro. Knowing Powell would no doubt exaggerate his own role, O'Dwyer went along and off I went to meet with Powell to assure him I had no reservations. After our meeting, Powell announced he would be honorary co-chair with Riddick as campaign manager and Corliss Crocker as assistant manager.

My decision to mediate between Tobias and Powell and to act as a third-party liaison in garnering Negro votes was not at all unusual. This was the business of politics, and as I used to say in those days, "Nobody does anything for nothing." My intervention in this case, however, was not politics as usual, because Powell, Tobias, and Riddick, with their high standing among Negroes not only in Manhattan but in Queens, Bronx, and Brooklyn, were influential symbols. O'Dwyer needed their support to influence Black votes in the other boroughs. Because of the high stakes involved, it was understood from the outset that the rewards would have to be visible and substantial, and Mayor O'Dwyer, a man of his word, an officer and a gentleman, played fair. The next year Vernon Riddick, a lawyer by training, was appointed the first Black magistrate, a position he had desired for some time.

My Job in the Department of Housing and Buildings

In my case the wait for a substantial post was a longer one. Immediately after O'Dwyer's election, the mayor appointed me his personal secretary, and his "eyes and ears" in Harlem as some newspaper saw it. In 1947, I moved over to Secretary to the Board of Elections, an instructive and desirable patronage post. It was while I was laboring there that I received a call to present myself at the Mayor's office. I had no inkling of what was planned, so I was nonplussed upon arriving at the mayor's office to find Robert Wagner, Jr., there.

O'Dwyer began: "Ray, you know Bob Wagner, don't you?" I answered yes and Wagner nodded in agreement. Then the Mayor said, "I want to know something from you. Can you say no?" I looked over at Robert Wagner, who was grinning and who seemed to be very pleased with himself. Quickly, I reasoned that whatever was going on was good, for Wagner was already the city's Tax Commissioner, and I got the feeling he had just been promoted to something. Having sorted all this out, I replied, "Hell, yes, I can say no."

"All right," said the Mayor. "I am going to announce that Bob Wagner is the new Commissioner of Housing and Buildings, and you, as Deputy Commissioner, will take over the Housing Department."

I was genuinely surprised. It wasn't that I was overwhelmed by the importance of the job, although it dawned on me a few hours later that I was now the highest ranking Black official in the city. Neither was I overly impressed by the $6,500 yearly salary. I was surprised by my good luck, and why not? The fact is that for years I had been complaining to the mayor, party, commissioner, whoever I thought could help change the poor state of housing for Blacks. Nothing much had been done. But here I was now in a position to hear the complaints and do something about them.

Late that evening I finally figured out why I had been chosen for the job. In a somewhat oblique way, I had been chosen because of Mayor La-Guardia, although he was already a year out of office. LaGuardia, a well-meaning but very impulsive person, had demolished all over New York a large number of tenements that he thought substandard, quite a number of them in Harlem. The Mayor never levelled an entire city block; rather he razed a house here, an old apartment building there, and so on throughout the community. This activity came under the heading of "slum clearance," and I am sure La Guardia had every intention of finding some means through some city agency to replace these buildings. However, in the majority of cases in Harlem, the lots were left open and eventually became health hazards. The buildings had been razed to the ground, and onto the uncleared lots, the residents of adjoining buildings dumped their garbage, attracting rats and other vermin, making the area odoriferous, and unhealthy, and in general creating a very bad atmosphere.

After O'Dwyer became mayor and I became his personal secretary, as well his "eyes and ears in Harlem", Hugo Rogers was elected Borough

President of Manhattan, and I became chief investigator in the office of the Borough President. One might well ask, "What has all this got to do with my selection of Deputy Commissioner of Housing in 1947?" Well, within the Borough President's office was the Borough Superintendent for Housing and Buildings. Through this fellow I worked to make my complaints heard and have a few changes made in Harlem. Because of these complaints and changes, I became well-known in the field. The relationship between the Borough President, the Borough Superintendent for Housing and Buildings, and the City Department of Housing and Buildings is best explained by Herbert Kaufman and Wallace S. Sayre in their excellent book, *Governing New York City*, first published in 1960. In speaking of the development of the Department of Buildings, Kaufman and Sayre explained its complicated evolution:

The troubled evolution of the Department as an organization, is itself testimony to the uncertainties of purpose and method which have accompanied the functions of the agency. When the change of 1901 was adopted, the regulation of buildings was left with the five Borough Presidents, in recognition of the many "local" forces which demanded accommodation in the application of the Building Code and other regulatory controls. However, when the social reformers of half-a-century ago won a victory in their battle against the "tenements," they preferred to entrust enforcement of the Multiple Dwelling Law not to Borough President, but to a new city department—The Tenement House Department. Thus matters stood until 1938, when the new charter established a Department of Housing and Buildings, transferring the functions of the Borough Presidents in this field, as well as the functions of regulating multiple dwellings, to the new department [renamed the Department of Buildings in 1957].[2]

So far everything is pretty straightforward. But Kaufman and Sayre continue:

Moreover, the Commissioner of Housing and Buildings does not find it easy to establish his leadership or control over the internal organization of his department. Until 1957, the charter required that there be "in each borough a branch office and a borough superintendent." The Borough Superintendent was made, for all practical purposes, an autonomous official, his actions being subject to review only by the Board of Standards and Appeals—not by the Commissioner. This concession to borough autonomy, and to the interest groups accustomed to that arrangement, was also accompanied by a comment that there should be a Division of Housing within the Department, its head to be one of the deputy commissioners.[3]

It is important to note, that prior to my being made Deputy Commissioner for Housing in 1947, a post mandated by law in 1938, I had worked in 1945 through the Manhattan Borough Superintendent, whose peculiar position and strange autonomy has just been so well described by Kaufman and Sayre. The Borough Superintendent, it can be seen, was essentially a political figure. Although his actions were subject to review only by the Board of Standards and Appeals, it was understood that he worked out of the Borough President's office and that the Borough President's dissatisfaction with his work could easily cause his removal. Thus the Borough Superintendent knew that he was a creature of the political system. As I was a Tammany Leader and had some influence throughout the entire borough, the Borough Superintendent knew that it was in his interest to assist me whenever reasonable.

Through the Borough Superintendent's office, therefore, I made most of my complaints, and through this agency also I persuaded the Borough President's office to clear up an empty lot, or provide a bit of fencing here, a bit of asphalt there, and so on. In this manner, I created a few small playgrounds, which made me something of a hero in my district. It was not until the City Comptroller raised the question of the city's liability in case a child should get hurt on one of these playgrounds that I had to curtail my perfectly legal but ad hoc operations.

All this I had been able to do between 1946 and 1947, and so as I reflected on what I had done in the year since William O'Dwyer had been mayor, it finally became obvious that someone, probably the Borough Superintendent, had informed the Mayor of my activities and he had decided it was in both our interests to promote me to this official position.

Leaving the Borough President's office to become Deputy Commissioner of Housing was, on the surface, a promotion. Taken at face value I could do much more for the entire city and could use my influence to improve those areas that were most in need of housing improvement, particularly my own constituency of Harlem. I soon found out, however, that things were not as easy as they appeared. Indeed, I had more fun when I operated free-lance, so-to-speak, through the Borough Superintendent. The problem at the outset had to do with the structure of the Department of Housing and Buildings. I refer again to Kaufman and Sayre, who describe the structure and its problems so well:

The Commissioner of Buildings and his two deputies, accordingly, administered an agency which has two quite distinctive assignments: first, the issuance of permits and certificates for all buildings and structures in the city under the terms of the city's Building Code, the State Labor Law, the rules and regulations of the city's Board of Standards and Appeals, and other related statutes and rules; second, the enforcement of safety and sanitary standards in multiple dwellings under the terms of the state Multiple Dwelling Law, the more stringent city Multiple Dwelling Code, and other related statutes and rules. These two main tasks of the Department have some common elements, but they also bring to the Commissioner the difficulties of working under two quite separate set of rules, dealing with two sets of constituencies, and competing or cooperating with two groups of other governmental agencies. One assignment does not strengthen his hand in performing the other.[4]

About the Department of Buildings, which Housing and Buildings came to be called after 1957 when the Commissioner of Buildings brought the Borough Superintendents under his control, and essentially took that element of his department out of the Borough Presidents' office, Kaufman and Sayre noted that

The Commissioner has no great assets when he deals with the other agencies of the city government. The organized groups in his constituency are in such matters more often more hostile than helpful to him. His leverage with the Bureau of the Budget is according to slight, as it is also with the Personnel Department. He cannot often command high priority with the Law Department, upon whose staff he depends for assistance in the prosecution of housing violations. . . . In short, the Commissioner is not a favorable situated bargainer when he deals with the other agencies of the city government.[5]

Similar dynamics applied essentially, and probably even more so, to the period prior to 1957. This I found out soon after my appointment. In my first year I immersed myself in the study of the department's records. I was particularly concerned with the clear pattern of constant complaints from certain sections of the city throughout the years, which had never been addressed. I soon realized that the organization of the Department was not conducive to rapid change in any area in housing generally or, for that matter, in specific buildings. Since mine was an inspection and enforcement agency charged with enforcing safety and sanity regulations, and since there were always people trying to cut corners in order to maximize their incomes and profits, there was never a day that I was not at war with some builder, landlord, or group of investors. Certain agencies like the Real Estate Board of New York, the Buildings Congress, and various other builder's associations were always opposed to some regulation or other. At times too, the department was at odds even with individual house owners. Take for example, fire escapes. In the 1940s, a fire ladder was hooked on to the top of the roof by iron bolts, and in some instances, these fire escapes had been so loosely attached, and in other instances had so rusted away and had not been inspected or replaced, that in times of fire they would give way, and people would die. This was my responsibility, and whenever someone was killed as a consequence of this, the District Attorney would call me before a grand jury to explain why.

It is unfortunate but true that many landlords were not too concerned about fire escapes and safety because they knew that in case of catastrophe blame could legally be shifted from them to the department for not having inspections and subsequently informing them of the necessity to make repairs. After all, it was known that there were two types of inspections the department was supposed to carry out: one, a mandatory, statutory inspection, and two, inspections resulting from complaints from tenants and other individuals. If the mandatory inspection was not done and some injury took place as a consequence, then the city was liable, and many of the landlords knew this. Fire escapes, one of our responsibilities, were very important items because live could be lost if they were not secure. Since we were understaffed, we were a harried group because of potential litigation.

Let us take another example, that of exits. I was never able to understand why exits were part of the Housing Division's jurisdiction. It seemed to me that it should have been under the Division of Buildings, but for some obscure reason, we in Housing were supposed to administer exits. The regulation governing "entrance and egress," that is, entrances and exits, came under the Multiple Dwelling Law, which covered assemblage. This referred to apartment houses, dance halls, nightclubs, movies, and the like. The law provided in the 1940s that there should be two means of egress for each building, and that the Department of Housing was to inspect buildings, certifying that at least two exits were accessible for quick exit. In most cases, as far as dance halls and public places were concerned, we had minimal problems. But we also had to inspect exits to fire escapes, which in most cases were windows.

Problems arise when people living near the fire escapes would bolt their windows or put bars over them to deter entry of thieves and other unsavory characters. But the law said that the exit to a fire escape must be free to be easily opened and must not be "encumbered" in any way. Attempts to enforce this law in the interests in the houseowner or apartment dweller were vigorously opposed, and in many instances our efforts were condemned, by the very people whose safety we were trying to insure.

I soon learned that a sense of humor was an absolute necessity if I were to maintain my sanity and do a good job. Some of the complaints that came into our department were, in modern parlance, absolutely weird. There were two types of complainers. In the first group were what we called the "occasionals," random complainants from all over the city who ran the gamut from reasonable to extreme. In the second group were the "perennials." In time I developed an affection for the "perennials" because they were predictable, for the most part harmless, and certainly not as extreme in their demands and language as were the "occasionals." For example, there was one whom we called the "toilet seat lady." Although she was listed with the perennials, in actuality she came in twice a year, usually at around the same time. Insistent and combative, she would not talk to inspectors. Neither would she deign to talk to chief inspectors (my chief assistant was beneath her dignity). She always insisted on seeing me, the commissioner. No attempt, no ploys, no strategies would prevent her from seeing me. She would sit in the outer office until the lights went out if necessary. Once I saw her, she would present me with this toilet seat which was broken right down the middle and she's ask, "What are you going to do about this?"

Then there was a lady who every year brought in a bag of roaches. With her I was most solicitous, because under no circumstances did I want this lady opening her bag of roaches in my office. Roaches and rats were the bane of my existence. There were innumerable complaints about them, and although we worked hard in this area, when I left the office in 1950 I was convinced that despite all the work we had done, we had merely accomplished a stand-off.

As Kaufman and Sayre have pointed out, our office was not a very popular one, politically or otherwise, since we had so many other departments to answer to and so many oversight institutions. Our money actually came from one source, the Mayor and the Board of Estimate, but here too we had problems. On the day I took the job in January 1947, I informed the Mayor that because of my previous association with the Borough Superintendent, I knew the problems and limitations of the department, and in order for me to do a worthwhile job there had to be more money allocated. Of course, O'Dwyer breezily promised he would assist me in any way he could, but very soon it became obvious that there would be no increases, and problems became worse. The time had come, I decided, to do something dramatic. Matters came to a head one day when one of my "occasionals" brought in a bag of rats and deposited them on my desk, screaming that she was tired of complaining and I could have her rats. I was very upset by this development and decided that it was time the mayor shared my misery.

In those days, a number of us would from time to time visit Gracie Mansion early in the mornings for breakfast. Since the Mayor was a bachelor at that time, he apparently liked the camaraderie of a number of his aides around him, usually a shifting group, to talk about matters before he went down to his office. So I called and told him that I would be coming down the next morning for breakfast. As usual he was affable, said he would be glad to see me, and so I went. The Mayor was all smiles. "How about a cup of coffee and Danish." he says. "I've already had breakfast." "Fine," I said. Then he turned to me and said, "Now, what's all the trouble about?" So, holding in my hand the bag of rats the lady had given me the day before, I launched into my usual speech about health hazards, the fact that the number of complaints were increasing, and the rest. I could see that his eyes were glazing over and that he was losing interest. "Well, I told you . . . " he began, and before he could finish, I reached down and opened my bag on his desk. He leapt out of his chair and literally screamed words I will not repeat right now. I, too, was fed up and so I said,

"These rates were loosed on my desk yesterday, and I want you to see what I am going through." When he had calmed down he said, "All right, all right! Let us call the secretary! Call a meeting of the Board of Health this afternoon in City Hall." "Fine," I said, "That's a good move." And then he looked at me and we both laughed.

It will be noticed that the Mayor said here to call in the Board of Health and not the Commissioner of Health. This is an important distinction, because we were dealing with a sanitation problem, and it should be understood that the Board of Health was essentially a semi-autonomous body in city government. Although the chairman of the Board of Health is actually the Commissioner of Health, appointed by the mayor, the Board itself is a creature of the State Legislature and of the City Charter, and is responsible for the creation of the City's Sanitary Code. It writes regulations that make up the Sanitary Code and are, in effect, city laws. These sanitary laws are enforced by the Department of Health under the direction of its Commissioner. The Commissioner, however, cannot tell the Board of Health what to do; he is merely its chairman; although he has power in his own Department of Health, he has very little with the Board. On the Board of Health were four other members besides the Commissioner, and the law stipulated that at least two of them must be medical doctors. Since the Board of Health makes the rules and the Department of Health is supposed to enforce them, and since the Board of Health is responsible for disease prevention and with the larger problems of public health, it could declare a health emergency at any time in New York City.

Now, with regard to the lady with the rats, we had come to the conclusion that there had been a near epidemic of rats in New York City because of all those uncleared lots and buildings where they proliferated, not only in Manhattan, but in the rest of the city. But as Commissioner of the Department of Housing I knew there were laws that prevented me from clearing these lots officially. Because these lots were private property, it was unlawful the for Commissioner of Housing to enter and clear them out, even if they were health hazards, since the city's authority does not extend beyond the sidewalk. In the case of a health emergency, however, I could. So the meeting with the Board of Health was called, and a health emergency declared. Once that was done, the Department of Health, over which the Commissioner of Health presided, was now able to cooperate with the Deputy Commissioner of Housing, myself. It was in this manner that we began clearing those problem lots, closely inspecting a large number of dwellings, and thereby fending off serious health problems. In the evenings as I walked home with New Yorkers brushing by in their inimitable style, I was struck time and time again that almost no one on the streets had the faintest clue of how difficult and complex the process of clearing those lots had been, and how close parts of the city had come to an epidemic of rodents.

Although I accepted the job as Deputy Commissioner of Housing in 1947, being around City Hall as long as I had, and having worked at the Borough President's office before that, I had no illusions whatsoever that I would be having a wonderful time. I have said that in the first year of my tenure I spent most of my time coping with day-to-day emergencies and studying what would be done to improve the performance of the department. On the first anniversary of my appointment, I felt that I had learned enough of the new job, so that certain changes could be instituted. I had several meetings with the Board of Health, the new Commissioner of Housing and Buildings (Robert Wagner had become Chairman of the City Planning Commission), and the Chief City Magistrate, Edgar Bromberger. As a consequence of these meetings, we presented Mayor O'Dwyer with a plan that placed responsibility for the safety and sanitation of their houses and apartment buildings on the landlords. The Mayor was very pleased with this because it meant that the city would no longer be liable as it had been under previous regulations. The plan passed close legal scrutiny in June of 1948 and we were able to go to the press with the announcement that in part read as follows:

From July 1, 1948, the greater part of the responsibility and burden of obtaining the speedy removal of violations reported by our inspectors is shifting from the department to the landlord, where, under the provisions of law, it belongs. This simply means that the landlord receiving official notice of violation is required not only to comply with it at once, but also to notify the department within thirty days that he has done so, otherwise legal process will be put into operation which will result in his appearance in a Magistrate's Court.

The department is assured that the magistrates will continue their cooperation in effectuating this program which is designed to eliminate all fire hazards, and unsanitary and unsafe conditions as expeditiously and speedily as possible. The Chief City magistrate will advise the magistrates of the new departmental policy and posture, and emphasize the necessity for a speedy disposition of court cases, a minimum number of adjournments, and the imposition of a graduated scale of fines consistent with the department's efforts to effect enforcement. . . .

When a fine is imposed in a case where all items of violation are not compiled with, the department will request the magistrate to inform the owner (in court) that the responsibility rests upon him not only to comply with the violations, but also to notify the department within the time stipulated by the court. Otherwise the owner or agent who has not removed all items of violation within this stipulated time will be again subject to court action and penalized much more heavily as a second offender.[6]

To make sure that everybody understood that we were serious, we outlined in our press release how we would check on violators.

At the present time each housing complaint is required under law to be docketed and its dispositions to be indicated. This complaint docket will be continued, but in order to make sure of the effectiveness of the new procedure, the department will use, after July 1, 1948, a new system of docketing violations. After our inspectors have reported a violation it will be docketed in chronological as well as numerical order, and in addition the department will use a newly devised system of ticklers. Two ticklers will be put into operation in each borough office: one central tickler in the violation section of the Division of Housing and one "legal bureau tickler" in each borough office of the department.[7]

All this may not sound very important, but indeed it was. It had taken me all year to iron out the legal ramifications and to get down a procedure understandable to all members of the department, particularly the inspectors. Furthermore, the regulation had to be easily understood by tenants and landlords.

In addition to making sure that violations would be treated automatically, and that safety and sanitary hazards would be removed, I had calculated that our new system would not only more effectively protect the lives and health of the tenants (of which at that time there were more than one and half million), but would also take some pressure off the department, still woefully understaffed. I thought, in addition, that the system we had devised would bring in needed revenue through fines. Although these fines would go to the general treasury, I had every intention of reminding the Board of Estimate of our contribution, so that additional inspectors could be hired.

Our system, which went into effect on July 1, 1948, worked wonderfully. Within the first quarter, there was an observable decrease in the number of violations and an improvement in safety an health precautions. This is not to say that a satisfactory level was ever reached, because despite improvement, the department never was able to make the thorough inspections, and issue all necessary notifications to reduce violations to what may be called "normal" levels. But it was a more efficient way of doing things; and in addition, the new plan had one added bonus: it improved morale for inspectors, chief inspectors, and other members of the Housing Department.

Harlem

Since I was now in a position of authority in the Department of Housing and Buildings, many expected me to do something for Harlem. I knew that as the Housing Commissioner I could not play favorites with any area of New York City. I knew New York and its governance, however, and I was thoroughly aware of the unofficial ways in which Harlem could be assisted, and also of what may be called the "official unofficial" ways. I reasoned that if I were to do everything strictly by the book, precious little would be done for Harlem, and God knew that, more than any place else, Harlem needed assistance.

What I did was very simple. in discussion with the people in the Carver Club, I expressed the wish that while I was Deputy Commissioner for Housing, some means could be found between the department and responsible citizens of Harlem to clean up the streets, rubbish-strewn lots, and the backyards and interiors of the buildings in the neighborhood. From these discussions, Harold A. Stevens, a State Assemblyman at that time, put together a group that came to be called "The Lot Playground Association, Incorporated." Stevens got together with various church organizations, the YMCA, and a number of other civic groups, and proposed a plan to the Borough President's office (not to the Department of Housing, because that would have been too direct and would lead to misunderstanding by the public): the owners of certain unused lots would be given tax-exempt status by the city for permission to use their lots as recreational areas. In addition, the Borough President through the Borough Superintendent would authorize the installation of "temporary surfaces" on these lots so that they could be used as playgrounds. At that time the Borough President was Hugo Rogers.

The timing of the presentation of this proposal was fortuitous for him, because Rogers wanted to be Tammany Chief and he knew that support for the plan would win political points in Manhattan. In fact he characterized the initiative as "an outstanding example of what neighborhood groups could do to handle their own community problems."[8] Within a few months he became Tammany Leader; but within a year the Italians, led by Carmine DeSapio, unseated him.

And so the group was set up with Mrs. Viola Austin as president and myself as Chairman of the Executive Committee. In this way quite a number of formerly rubbish-strewn, vermin-infested areas were cleaned up, and more than fifty new playgrounds were added to the Harlem community. Some playgrounds, though temporary, still remained in 1951 when I left the Department of Housing and Buildings. This initiative marked an unusual cooperation between the Department of Housing and Buildings, the Borough President's office, and local civic organizations in the Harlem area.

The cleaning up of vacant lots was one step. I also determined that the citizens of Harlem could do more to clean up their backyards and the interior of their buildings, which had deteriorated to an alarming extent because of overcrowding. This problem resulted from the subdivision of houses that should not have been subdivided at all, and crammed with new immigrants and migrants, began to deteriorate conditions. Earlier, in the Borough President's office, I observed that people do not spend very much time and energy taking care of their dwellings when they believe they are being taken advantage of by landlords. As a result, an alarming number of multiple dwellings in Harlem were in violation of the building codes, and were fire and health hazards. With overcrowding it meant that there was a need for increased sanitation services. The sheer number of people in these houses generated garbage in high volume. Because it was illegal to put garbage out on the streets before the designated time, many people now just threw it in the backyard, "forgetting"to take it out on the sidewalk on collection days. The people also used the vacant lots that we had not yet converted into playgrounds. As a result of our playground initiative, the People's Civic and Welfare Association of Harlem led by its chairman, Glester Hines, decided that it too would participate in the clean-up of Harlem. Hines, who knew how government worked, sought to bring pressure to bear up on residents by asking the Commissioner of Health to order the cleanup of all backyards and interiors immediately. In this he obtained the support of Mayor O'Dwyer and the Borough President's office. I became a member of this group too, and the Department of Housing began issuing warnings and summonses for violations of the sanitary codes in the interior of buildings. We were less successful in this approach, because the Commissioner of Health chose persuasion rather than coercion, but some progress was made.

In 1951 when I left office I had to content myself with the understanding that one can only do so much unless one has dictatorial powers. Of course that was an impossibility as well as a method of which I could not have subscribed, even if it were possible.

Chapter 5

"The Fox"

I DO NOT KNOW WHEN it was that peo-
ple began to call me "the Fox of Harlem", but it must have been sometime
after the O'Dwyer campaign. I have always been at a loss to explain how
it came about. Perhaps such a perception resulted from my participation in
the Mayor's election in 1945 which resulted in a magistrate's job for Riddick; or soon after when Daniel Flynn, who returning from the wars had
been elected as 13th District Assemblyman, decided to run for Congress,
providing an opening in the State Assembly that I engineered for a member of my own club, Harold Stevens. Then again, it may have been because the Mayor was telling everybody that I was his "eyes and ears" in
Harlem, or because in January of 1947 he made a big to-do about appointing me as Deputy Commissioner of Housing at a salary of some $6,500 a
year, in those days, quite a bit of money. Perhaps, though, by 1948 it was
something else, that this true story, which made the rounds in Harlem,
might illustrate.

The Case of the Assistant Welfare Commissioner

Throughout the 1930s and 40s responsibility for the Department of Welfare was constantly being shifted among the federal, state, and municipal
governments. When Bill O'Dwyer was Mayor, to head up one segment of
the Welfare Department he appointed a fellow, whose name I forget, but
who, as I soon found out, was a member of the American Labor Party. As
I moved about City Hall immediately after that appointment, I learned that
the Deputy Mayor and the Assistant Mayor both objected to the appoint-

ment. This was interesting news to me because the appointee not only was a member of the American Labor Party, but he had also talked to certain members of my club, the Carver, and offered one of them a job in the Welfare Department without consulting with me. I was thoroughly annoyed also that this city employee had dared to come into my neighborhood and tried to steal one of my men. The Deputy Mayor and the Assistant Mayor, being appointees of the Mayor, could not do very much about their objections to this man because their jobs depended upon the goodwill of the Mayor. But there was not much that O'Dwyer could do with me. I was a District Leader; I had some power in New York, and technically I was independent of O'Dwyer.

The Deputy Mayor and the Assistant Mayor came to me and suggested that I should request that the Mayor do something about his new appointee. The Deputy Mayor informed O'Dwyer that I was very annoyed and I needed to talk with him—I was taking their case to the Mayor without mentioning their names. I met with Mayor O'Dwyer and told him that as a District Leader, I thought it was my job to build up the Democratic Party, not the American Labor Party. What he had done would undermine my efforts as a District Leader, and those of all District Leaders in the county. If he wanted to operate this way, I told him, that was his perogative and I could only express my displeasure, but what I objected to was this man giving a job to one of my boys. In addition, I was a trifle annoyed with my own man for having accepted the job in the first place. So the Mayor said, "What do you want me to do, fire him?" and I said, "Yes, that's what I want you to do. This will teach both of them a lesson."

About two weeks later I was at Gracie Mansion for a private meeting with the Mayor; a call came in from one of his assistants complaining that the press was raising the issue as to why no work had started in that particular segment of the Welfare Department where the man who was just fired had worked. The Mayor said, "Ray Jones is here," and turned to me so that his assistant could hear over the phone., "What do we do now, Ray?" My answer was, "Rehire the man. Put him back to work." Of course the Mayor was astonished at this and so must his aide have been, but that's what was done.

Apparently, the department head had aided O'Dwyer during his campaign in 1945 and the Mayor thought he owed him something, which was understandable, but it seemed on the other hand, that this individual felt that because he had gotten this job through the Mayor, he had carte blanche to run roughshod over Democratic District Leaders. This was something he had to understand he could not do, not in my area anyway. As for the man from my own Club, I had no problems with him being rehired: I made sure he knew he had been fired for not being astute, and was rehired because I thought he had learned his lesson. Besides, I knew he was a very competent person, someone I would have recommended myself if I had been consulted.

This story, I understood, made the rounds, mostly with embellishments. I hasten to add here in my defense that it wasn't that I was the boss of anything, I was merely the leader of one Democratic Club in Harlem—a very good club indeed, I thought— and if it were to retain its high standing, we could not have people raiding it for men who might not be ready for high office. Such a situation would reflect very poorly on my Club, and I did not want any such negative associations.

The case of the $10,000 check

But perhaps my reputation as "The Fox" had to do more with the case of the $10,000 check. This all started in one of those transitional periods in the leadership of Tammany Hall, in 1947, when Frank Sampson, the remaining Irishman, was the New York County Leader. In late 1947, the Italian-Black alliance in Tammany Hall was getting strong, the Italians wanting to make their move for the leadership of Tammany. They could not accomplish this alone, and so had decided to develop an alliance with Black leaders, since many of the Italian districts adjoined Harlem. For example, right next door to me was Angelo Simonetti in the 13th Assembly District West. The manner of the take-over attempt was very interesting.

The County Executive Committee was made up of District Leaders. Each district had a leader and a co-leader. At that time, I believe, there were 21 districts. Some districts were divided into two parts, A and B, or East and West, or North and South, as the case may be. In those districts where there were two sections, leader and co-leader of each half had a quarter of a vote, since the full district was splitting one vote on the Executive Committee. Some districts were divided into three parts, and in those districts each of them had one-sixth of a vote. These Italian groups tried to set up a number of committees on the County Committee, appointing chairmen loyal to them. They pushed through a resolution allowing each chairman one full vote. This move was really an extension of a tradition by which the Tammany Leader always had one full vote, as did the chairman of the County Committee. One full vote also went to the chairman of the Rules Committee. This was 1948, and since I was the chairman of the Rules Committee, I had that vote, plus one quarter of a vote as District Leader in the 13th A.D. East. Usually my co-leader voted with me, so I had in effect one and a half votes. This new development ensured that any one of these chairmen could outvote four District Leaders in a two-section A.D.! But before the battle for the leadership could take place, and the eventual election of Carmine DeSapio, the question of judgeships and of head of the Civil Service Commission came up.

These two stories well illustrate how tricky nonelectoral politics were and are, and how careful one has to be in order to survive. I am not so sure that I survived because of any superior intelligence, or cunning—as I've been accused of—but I think because I was careful. Mere survival in these tricky waters, I suspect, added to the myth of "the Fox."

In 1947, the same year in which I became Deputy Commissioner of Housing, Ferdinand Q. Morton, the black leader, resigned as Commissioner on the Civil Service Commission, a job he had held since 1922. This was an important position and since Morton had been there so long, we felt that this position should continue to be held by a Black person. But so often as happened, the Harlem District Leaders found it difficult to unite quickly behind any one person. In my Club, the man I had in mind was Professor Benjamin E. Dyette, a former Law Professor at Howard University who had practiced law in New York for quite a few years. By 1947, although somewhat advanced in age, he had a very high standing in both the white and Black communities, an honorable man, and quite distinguished-looking. He was my choice, but he certainly was not the choice of Joseph Pinckney, Joseph Ford, or Mark Shavers, all local leaders and allies of the new Congressman, Adam Powell. On Dyette's side, though, was Cecil Carter, another local leader and an immigrant from the West Indies. He was Dyette's good friend, sharing a common British-Caribbean background.

Dyette had also been a member of a group of Black men in Harlem that had been organized by Professor Kenneth Clarke, a group that met from time to time to discuss how much influence we had, how we could move the government to help a brother or sister in trouble, and how to effect the passage of local laws in the interest of the Afro-American community. I came to know Benjamin Dyette through this group. When we called a meeting to address the opening for Commissioner, and Dyette was suggested, Joseph Ford and Joe Pinckney, as usual, spoke as one. Whenever we considered anybody for a job, those two always chirped in unison, "Is he qualified?" But the word "qualified" did not mean what it meant out on the street. "Qualified" meant how much money the prospect had, or, in other words, would he be able to finance his campaign and at the same time make a contribution to our club.

As soon as the meeting began and Cecil Carter put up Dr. Dyette's name, within seconds the question "Is he qualified?" was raised. I smiled at the question because I now thought we were going to have some fun.

Cecil Carter stood up and began reciting a long resumé for Dr. Dyette. Joseph Pinckney soon got fed up with this and said, "Aw, come on, cut it out, Ray. I mean, is he *qualified?*" Here I did something which I thought of as funny at the time, but later on almost got me into serious trouble. The clubhouse in which we were meeting at that time was the Carver Building. This was a building that I had cajoled my club into buying through a corporation I had formed called the Carver Holding Corporation. At just about the time this meeting was taking place, I had sold stock in the building to a few friends so that the building would be held by a small number of people. I had an account with the Manufacturer's Hanover Bank and Trust Company and had in my pocket a check for $10,000, made out to be deposited to the bank. And so it crossed my mind to take this check out of my pocket without the boys seeing what was written on it. Their knowing it was a check, however, would answer the questions quickly. "Of course he is qualified!", I said. "Here is $10,000, and I want nothing to do with it, but indeed he is qualified," I concluded as I returned the check to my pocket. In the twinkling of an eye, Ford and his friends all agreed that Benjamin Dyette was their candidate, and right there and then we drafted an endorsement to be sent to the County Leader.

But New York County Leader Sampson had his own ideas. This was a significant post and he wanted to put his own man on the Civil Service Commission. I did not know this and was mystified a few days later when I got a call from the Commissioner of Investigations, my old friend, John Murtagh. "Ray," he said to me, "I would like you to come to my office as soon as possible. I'm interviewing all the Harlem leaders one by one." I did not know what this implied and so was only mildly disturbed by the request. I met with Murtagh; seeing him I knew I was in for trouble. He seemed very unhappy to see me; immediately, with no preamble, he told me that it had been reported to him by the County Leader that the boys in Harlem had agreed to split $10,000 for the Welfare Commissioner's job. The fact that I was called in meant that the Mayor knew about this already; Murtagh verified my suspicions—he told me the whole thing had been reported to the Mayor by Frank Sampson. Indeed, I was not sure how it would turn out, but I told Murtagh about the prank, suggested that he call the bank where I had deposited the check at 2:30 p.m. the day before, and had signed the papers for the building. This he did. Thankfully, John Murtagh was not above appreciating the combination of prank and guile involved in the story, and so by the time I finished telling him all that had happened, he was laughing. Since he had checked with the bank, it was clear that what I said was true. He reported to the Mayor and I was out of trouble, but I soon heard this story recounted and in that version, I was all guile and sly cunning!

How to appoint a Black judge

In the spring of 1948 a seat on the Surrogate Court opened up. Despite the hierarchy that indicates the State Court of Appeals as the highest court in New York State, followed by the Supreme Court and so on, New York City views the Surrogate Court as the most powerful court in the state because it deals with wills and estates, and thus controls the greatest patronage. A judge on the Surrogate Court is a powerful figure, very important to the party with which he is affiliated. Therefore, no jurist can get to be a Surrogate Judge without the sponsorship of some party. As it happened, in 1948 County Leader Sampson decided that the man for the job was Vincent Impelliteri, President of the City Council. This was no surprise, because Sampson, before becoming County Leader, had been the District Leader of Impelliteri's Assembly District. But Carmine DeSapio and his group decided upon an opposition candidate, Francis Valente, a judge in the General Sessions Court. Justice Valente was well-connected, having, among other benefits, an uncle in the State Supreme Court, Justice Louis Valente. As I understood it then, the DeSapio group first considered Louis, but decided he was too old for the Surrogate post. If Louis Valente had considered leaving the State Supreme Court for the Surrogate Court, imagine how powerful and desired the Surrogate post was!

Frank Sampson, as County Leader, did not contact me, because I think he assumed that since I was Mayor O'Dwyer's man, I would go along with anything the Mayor said. By the time the choice was made, however, no one from the County Leader's office had contacted me, although Carmine DeSapio had sent Angelo Simonetti, my counterpart in the 13th Assembly District West, to see me about this matter. Until then I had stayed away from this issue because of certain obligations to the Mayor, and although I did not like his County Leader, I was not in a hurry to take sides with the Italian group, particularly because they had not so far done me any special favors. In addition, when I heard about the decision against Louis Valente, I counted the possible votes should a confrontation arise between DeSapio and Frank Sampson, and realized it would have been a stand-off in the Executive Committee—that is, without my vote. As it was, as I have pointed out before, I had a full vote as Chairman of the Rules Committee, and I also had half a vote if I voted with my co-leader, who usually supported me on these issues. So I was in the enviable position of having the tie-breaking vote if my calculation proved correct. Eventually Angelo Simonetti sought my support, and since I had received no instructions from the Mayor, I decided the time had come to make a move that would mark some progress for the Black community and reflect some credit on my Political skills.

The Italians hadn't decided on Judge Francis Valente, but if he were successful in getting the Surrogate position, there would be an opening in the Court of General Sessions. Until now, there had never been a Black in the Court of General Sessions. We had other judges and magistrates, but no one in the highest criminal court. It would be a highly visible position for a Black person and I thought that if I supported this Judge Valente, a Black man could then be placed for the first time in the Court of General Sessions. So, having thought about this matter before meeting with Simonetti and rethinking it as he sat in front of me, I said, "I will give you my pledge on my work of honor to back your Valente for the Surrogate position if you can arrange a meeting during which every member of your group pledges to support a Black candidate for the judgeship in the Court of General Sessions as long as he is qualified." Simonetti, of course had to check with his group, but soon he called and assured me that we had a deal.

Of course, word got out to the newspapers almost immediately and most of them, including the *New York Times*, were opposed. The Mayor himself, who had been on vacation and as I have said had given me no instructions, was annoyed. He was piqued that I had voted against his man Sampson, and so when the Commission of Investigations called me and told me the Mayor wanted to see me, I knew I was in for it. I knew, because when the Mayor wanted to talk to me about normal business, somebody from his office would call me up, but when he was displeased he would ask some other office to call me, in this case John Murtagh. So because I knew this was a big affair and I was determined not to back off because it was important to have a Black man in the Court of General Sessions, I immediately wrote out my resignation, put it in my pocket, and went to see the Mayor. It was a brief meeting, for the Mayor accepted my resignation conditionally. And so it was that I stayed away for six weeks while the Mayor appointed my assistant, Mrs. Ruth W. Whaley, in my place.

My resignation did not particularly disturb me. By this time I had other things to do and I knew already that before the end of the Mayor's term, if he wished to be successful in a second run in 1949, he would need me somewhere along the line.

I had supported Valente so that we could put a Black person in the Court of General Sessions, but since this conflict had developed when the Mayor returned, I knew we needed a larger coalition of Democrats to support Valente, for either his election would be in doubt, or he would drastically split the party. So although I had resigned from the Housing Department, I was part of a team to work out this impasse. In the end, believe it or not, Valente did not get the nomination because, in the interest of harmony and solidarity, the party substituted Judge Mullen, at the time a senior judge in the Court of General Sessions. As for me, I did not care one way or the other at that point whether it was Francis Valente, Louis Valente, Mullen or Mullet, because none of these men had been my own choice nor my real concern. I therefore voted for Judge Mullen, because his absence would mean a vacancy in the Court of General Sessions that my man could fill.

This compromise satisfied the Mayor and, in fact, he was downright happy because he had won his fight against Carmine DeSapio and the Italian group. Since Judge Mullen was really nobody's man, a neutral, Sampson was happy. Carmine DeSapio may not have been entirely happy but he was satisfied. And Ray Jones was absolutely, positively happy because his purpose was achieved—securing a place on the Court of General Sessions for a Black individual.

After District Attorney Frank Hogan investigated rumors of bribery for the nomination of Valente and found nothing, and after I had participated in the compromise to nominate Judge Mullen without rancor, the Mayor now decided that he wanted Ray Jones to return as Commissioner. The announcement came in August, when he deftly moved Mrs. Whaley over to be the Executive Assistant to Raymond M. Hilliard, the City's Welfare Commissioner. [1] The man I had in mind all along for the next vacancy in the General Sessions Court was Harold Stevens, a member of my own Club. And so it was that the next year Stevens became the first Black Judge of General Sessions. Some years later we were able to move him up to the State Supreme Court.

The manner in which I had been able to negotiate the appointment of Harold Stevens to the Court of General Sessions was not lost on the citizens of Harlem, nor on the rest of the Black population in New York. All this, too, contributed to the pseudonym that always made me uneasy, the "Fox."

The Truman campaign

In his *New York Times Magazine* article of February 19, 1967, Anthony Hiss quotes a story that, if true, shows that my reputation for political cunning had reached even the White House. Unfortunately it gave President Harry Truman pause, as Hiss notes.

One anecdote that is still making the rounds tells about how Harry Truman had Jones vetted back in the nineteen-forties, and calling a knowing Negro newspaperman from New York. "Tell me," said the President, "Is Ray honest? Is there any open scandal adhering to his name?" "Well, Mr. President," said the reporter, "I can tell you one thing. If Ray Jones stole the Brooklyn Bridge, no one would ever find out."[2]

I was unaware of President Truman's interest in me at the time, but I was very much interested in what *he* was doing. Watching him with great care since his ascendance to the Presidency after the death of FDR in 1945, I liked the fact that he had surrounded himself with a number of progressive and liberal-minded people. In addition, since he had kept on his staff Judge Samuel I. Rosenman, a strong civil rights advocate and former speech writer for President Roosevelt, I felt that Truman, despite his Southern origins, was somebody on whom the Black population could depend. His action on December 5, 1946, reinforced my view, when he appointed a committee of distinguished Black and white Americans, the President's Committee on Civil Rights, to investigate civil rights and recommend improvements. One year later, the committee issued its findings in a report, *To Secure These Rights*. This document and its enumeration of Civil Rights goals impressed me greatly because of its consistency with the goals I sought to achieve in New York City.

In 1947, I was still Deputy Commissioner of Housing, and the man in the Mayor's chair was my friend. I had his ear. Since I was thought to be his "ears and eyes" in Harlem, I was respected as such in the entire New York community. Despite the normal ups and downs of politics, I felt that a President such as Truman, seemingly predisposed to our civil rights goals in Manhattan, would encourage and advance our crusade if I could gain his support. It was fortunate for me that President Truman was interested in me at that time, for I was very interested in him.

The Democratic Convention held in Philadelphia the next year encouraged my plans for Mr. Truman, for there he told the world what he intended to do about civil rights and urged Southerners themselves to do something about the problem. Some took him at his word it seems, because it was then that Strom Thurmond, who is alive and well today and voting on Supreme Court Justices, walked out of the convention with his group of Dixiecrats. His campaign to defeat Truman went nowhere and eventually Thurmond became a Republican. Then, as now, I say good riddance! After the convention I decided the time had come to do all I could to aid Truman's election in my part of the world.

Back in New York I gathered my people together, chief of whom was Dr. J. Dayton Brooks, my Executive Secretary, and drew up a plan. We discussed our plans with Herbert L. Bruce and decided to finance our efforts for Truman ourselves. Bruce was extremely helpful in planning, but for some reason he preferred our efforts to be regarded not as a crusade, as I wanted, but as an ordinary political campaign from which political rewards would be expected. Normally, I would not have anything against this, but personally, I felt our efforts should be beyond the bounds of normal politics. Somehow the image of Truman, that small man who reminded one of a fighting rooster at the convention as he stood up in front of bigots from the South, had touched me deeply. As a Black man, I instantly recognized what he was in for in the campaign, and I felt as if Truman and I were one. Later on, in 1967, I was pleased to discover that during that same period we were both thinking of each other, though hundreds of miles apart.

Ultimately, my idea of a crusade for civil rights won out over Bruce and the rest of my team. But to do this properly, I needed the cooperation of all the Harlem leaders. I spoke to Joseph Ford, Adam Clayton Powell's right hand man, but he could not care less, because Adam was not interested. Furthermore, Adam had called Mrs. Truman the "last lady of the land", and thus, to put it mildly, did not hold Truman's favor. My friends in the Interdenominational Ministers' Conference, however, were receptive. I told them that my people and I would do all the work, but we would turn over the entire pageant to them. To insure their cooperation I saved the best part for the last. When I assured them that my group would do all the financing, good cheer could be felt from everyone.

Having secured their support, I went to see Mayor O'Dwyer, and as obliquely as I could, hinted that he had a problem with the President of the United States which needed resolution. The problem was that Bill O'Dwyer had, in 1947, joined others in exploring whether General Dwight D. Eisenhower would accept the Democratic nomination in 1948. This he had done, knowing very well that Truman, a lifelong Democrat, desired the nomination. The Mayor, of course, knew where I was leading, and he knew it was in his best interest to cooperate with me, so he consented to lend himself to the "Truman Crusade." The question then became, what role should he play? I suggested that he could benefit by inviting Truman to town sometime during the campaign and declare that day a day in honor of the Truman 1946 civil rights report *To Secure These Rights*. He found this approach very appealing and left it to me to plan the whole affair.

I decided that this would be an open air event, held as soon as the weather was good. We selected a Harlem school with an excellent facade to serve as a backdrop for the dais and a choir. I wanted the sound thrown forward by the building, but I did not want anybody in the building that day. We needed a secure and controllable space for the President, as well as a space that would look good in the photographs. But we had a problem. The school had to be closed, since the event was scheduled for a weekday, so I asked the Mayor to close off the street and declare a Harlem holiday to clear the school. Of course, I figured we would get some flack, but that was all right. This was a Harlem community, certain to support such an effort, and I knew the students at least would support me on the holiday issue.

Most of the ministers of the Interdenominational Conference had small congregations, so we brought together the leaders whose unified congregations amounted to quite a nice group. We organized a combination choir, and while not overwhelming, it was a very good choir indeed. When the Mayor gave his consent to close off that entire block, and to provide police patrols for the entire affair, the most serious problems were resolved.

We sent invitations to the leaders of the NAACP, the Urban League, and various and sundry Black leaders in the northeast, but not a single one showed up except Dr. Channing Tobias of the executive board of the NAACP, a member of Dr. Kenneth Clark's leadership group and a New York resident. Why were they not there? Most of all, these people, like most white Americans, felt in the fall of 1948 that Harry S. Truman, after his courageous and moral stand on the issue of civil rights at the Philadelphia Convention, did not have a chance to win the Presidency. They placed their bets on Governor Thomas E. Dewey, that mustachioed New Yorker with the slick style, to be the next President of the United States. Everybody assumed that Dewey would win. The *New York Times* thought so, and the *Chicago Daily Tribune* actually printed the story on the night of the election that Dewey had won.

We had a tremendous time when Truman arrived, because the leader of our group, the Reverend Asa Pensa Johnson, the President of the Ministers Council, had the choir rehearse two scenes with the song "Go Down Moses." When the President's limousine doors opened, instead of playing "Hail to the Chief", as was customary protocol, a surge of voices greeted him with: "Go down Moses, way down to Egypt land. Tell ol' Pharaoh, let my people go!" This was Harlem; this was a crusade for a man whom the ministers and I wanted to show to our people as a modern-day Moses, beleaguered and embattled on all sides by the forces of racism and bigotry. This was Harry Truman who had stood up for Harlem in Philadelphia. And this would be Harlem's and Black people's candidate. Thomas Dewey would not become President if Black people could help it. There were tears in Mrs. Truman's eyes and the President seemed not to know what to do with himself. Escorted by Asa Pensa Johnson to the dais he gave what I think was one of the best speeches of his career. It was a beautiful ceremony. That night it was the talk of Harlem. Everyone connected with the event was pleased, including Mayor O'Dwyer, who later in the day gave me a knowing wink.

To some this might have seemed a minor event, and in the scheme of national affairs perhaps so, but to me it wasn't. Although I had not conceived of it as a political operation, I knew it would yield political rewards because we were showing the President at this time that we believed he would win; that he could count on the Negro vote in Harlem, if not in all

New York City and throughout the nation; and that I believed that in any future situation in which a Black could be appointed by the President, should he win, he would think of us. This is exactly what happened with the appointment of William Hastie to the U.S. District Court.

A year after the campaign, the President decided that a vacancy in the United States District Court should be filled by a Black person, particularly because the NAACP had been pressuring him for some time to appoint someone. Truman, probably remembering the good reception in New York, decided to appoint William Hastie, former Governor of the Virgin Islands, former Assistant to the Secretary of War, past Dean of the Howard Law School, a very distinguished man, and a Truman campaigner, to the post Federal Judge in the New York area.

This delighted the NAACP, but not me. Hastie certainly deserved the appointment, there was no question about that, but not in the Southern District of New York State. Governor Hastie had neither lived in my district nor was he a member of the district organization. Furthermore, we had our own candidate for the post. I thought it would have been better for Hastie to be appointed elsewhere on the basis of his work with the NAACP and for his campaign support of the President. We wanted to apply our own pressure on the White House to get our own person in. If the President felt grateful to us, then we should have our own appointment, and of course, were Hastie appointed elsewhere, we would then have two people in the Federal Courts, rather than just one.

I was thinking politically, but the NAACP misunderstood my opposition, and voiced its erroneous interpretation all over the country. I think, though, that the President understood what I was about, and eventually cooler heads in the NAACP came around to my view. As a result, Hastie was appointed as a Judge in the Third United States Circuit Court of Appeals in Philadelphia in 1949. It was to this same court that Thurgood Marshall went in 1961, only to resign in 1965 to become Solicitor General of the United States and later Associate Justice of the Supreme Court during the Johnson administration.

The re-election of William O'Dwyer

When Harry S. Truman assumed the Presidency of the United States in January of 1949 in his own right, I am certain he was a happy man, and so was I. My job as Deputy Commissioner of Housing and Buildings kept me busy all through early 1949, and soon the campaign to elect William O'Dwyer as Mayor of New York City for a second term began to loom large. There was nothing very different about this election, because

O'Dwyer had made a significant number of appointments from the Black community during his first term, had been to Harlem many times, and had become so identified with me that he was seen as a friend of the Black community in Harlem.

Because O'Dwyer did not want to take any chances with the Black vote citywide, however, we needed a new plan. We also needed to insure the candidacy of Robert F. Wagner, Jr., for Manhattan Borough President. In 1947 Wagner had been my superior at the Department of Housing and Buildings, but he had left in 1948 to become chairman of the City Planning Commission. These two positions were appointive, and the job he had held between 1946 and 1948 as Tax Commissioner had also been appointive. Wagner, therefore, had not run for elective office since he had left the New York State Assembly in 1941. Although his present and previous jobs had been given him a good deal of publicity, he was not as well known to the Black community of the city as was O'Dwyer. What was needed in the 1949 campaign was a strategy to enhance the Mayor's positive image and include Wagner as part of his team. As for Wagner's image in the white community, that was no problem, for we knew his father's, Senator Robert Wagner, Sr.'s, name was still worth a lot of political capital in New York and on that we would trade.

We hatched the strategy to put the entire ticket on a favorable footing in the Black community one morning at coffee at Gracie Mansion. I planned a party in Harlem to which the entire slate would be invited, including the Police Commissioner, the Commissioner of Welfare, and others whom the Black community would instantly recognize as authorities directly concerned with their everyday lives. This way there would be a lot of coverage and since all the Harlem and nearby political heavyweights would be invited, I reasoned that the event would be a success. I was thoroughly pleased with my plan, but the Mayor suggested a better approach. "Why don't we have the party at Gracie Mansion?" he asked. "That way everybody will visit the Mansion and all the cost will be on me." "Good idea," I replied, seeing the greater wisdom of the suggestion. "O.K.," he said. "Let's do it."

Within a very short time all was arranged. It was a fairly impressive, affair. I made certain that such luminaries as the president of the National Council of Churches, the management of Harlem's Blumstein's Department Store, a Catholic Monsignor, and others were invited. Nearly all invitees attended. The pivotal figure that night turned out to be Doxy Wilkenson, the editor of *The People's Voice*. Because Doxy was a Communist and a critic of the Mayor's administration, no one expected the two to get along, but before the evening was over, the two were deep in discussing among other esoteric topics, the relevance of St. Thomas Aquinas to Marx!

The Mayor had informed Doxy that he had spent some time in a seminary, and thus the discussion of Aquinas' philosophy. As both men debated everybody joined, most of us having not the foggiest idea of the abstruse points each made. Nonetheless, the whole evening was an absolute delight, made so in great part by the gracious presence of Kathleen O'Dwyer, the Mayor's sister-in-law, who served as our hostess. In the end Doxy and the Mayor parted as friends. In fact, the whole affair so pleased O'Dwyer that he decided to continue meeting with a number of key people from time to time in a social, nonofficial setting. To keep the group together the Mayor gave me $25,000 for expenses, and we remained active until O'Dwyer left office in 1950.

Many viewed preparations to reelect Mayor William O'Dwyer in 1949 as a lark. A very popular figure throughout the city and in Harlem, O'Dwyer was highly regarded in the Black community, since I had taken care of things between 1945 and 1949. People throughout Harlem knew that O'Dwyer had made me Deputy Commissioner of Housing. They also knew that O'Dwyer had endorsed Adam Clayton Powell's election in 1948. Such general knowledge meant that the Mayor and his ticket had no problems in the Harlem community. but there were other problems, the most important of which concerned the charismatic figure of City Councilman Benjamin J. Davis, Jr.

The Benjamin Davis-Earl Brown campaign of 1949

In 1949, I assessed Benjamin Davis as a very intelligent person and a brilliant lawyer. He had taken a roundabout route to New York. Born in Dawson, Georgia, he began his freshman year in college at Morehouse College but transferred to Amherst in Massachusetts, which had graduated one of the two first Negro college graduates in 1826. Tremendously gifted in the arts and in politics, Davis displayed extraordinary talents. An excellent violinist, he had led the Amherst College/Mount Holyoke College Symphony Orchestra. This was a most unusual occurrence in the twenties. But this was not enough for Ben. He played football too, and in his senior year he was All Eastern Tackle. After obtaining a Harvard Law degree, he returned to his native Georgia where, on being admitted to the Bar, he became the second Black person to do so since Reconstruction. As a practicing lawyer, he defended Angelo Herndon beginning in 1932 against charges of insurrectionary activities, after Herndon had led a number of protests against the unequal treatment of Blacks in Atlanta. The repugnance of "proper" Southerners, since Herndon was not only a Black man but also a Communist, complicated the Herndon case. Eventually the

Supreme Court acquitted Herndon, but Davis' involvement with Herndon, led him, he admitted later, to sympathy for the Communist cause. He joined the party in 1933.

Davis followed to a remarkable degree in the early footsteps of Adam Clayton Powell, because Powell, in his initial campaigns, enjoyed Communist support, breaking with them only after he was well entrenched in Congress. Powell's decision not to run for the City Council in 1943 gave Davis the opportunity to participate in electoral politics in New York City. In that year, Davis handily won a City Council seat, backed by the Communist Party, which was very popular in Harlem at that time. The Party had gone to great lengths stressing interracial harmony within its ranks, and proposing the possibility for an American future without discrimination, with Communism as the dominant ideology. A Black person could be whatever he or she wished to be. These claims were given much credence, for the Party had done a great job of propaganda with its defense of the Scottsboro Boys from 1932 on. Everybody knew of the Alabama case, and though the boys were represented by the International Legal Defense, everyone knew the Defense was an arm of the Communist Party.

In the City Council, Davis worked assiduously for his constituency. In fact, by 1947 he was already something of a folk hero, and in the same year he began to experience difficulties with the newspapers because of his Communist affiliation. Two years later he was arrested on the charge of conspiracy to overthrow the government of the United States. Although everyone knew this was a trumped up charge, the kind injudiciously thrown at known Communists in those days, the Democratic Party and the Harlem leadership had to do something. I had supported Davis in 1943 and in 1945, but in 1947 I had him change his registration to Democrat to get my support. But the situation had radically changed in 1949. Now, because of growing anti-communism, the Mayor was against him, the Governor disliked him, and even Tammany Hall had abandoned him. In this environment I, too, had to withdraw my support. The question now became, who can we run against him? Davis, a bona fide folk hero and an articulate politician, had an impeccable voting record. What was to be done?

Since by 1945 I was well entrenched in the leadership of Tammany Hall, and since next to Adam Powell I was considered one of the most powerful leaders in Harlem, the job fell to me to devise some means to defeat Davis at the polls in 1949. So into this drama I placed one of my own boys, Earl Brown. Like Davis, Brown was a Harvard man, except that Brown had attended Harvard College, and Davis, Harvard Law School. Brown, a Kentuckian, was also a southerner like Davis. After Harvard, Davis worked as a journalist for the Black newspaper, the *Amsterdam News,* and for a while as a reporter for *Life* magazine. Although I knew we would have to groom

Brown, write his speeches, coach him, do everything, I thought he had a good chance to defeat Davis.

While I was planning the campaign, the City Council made every effort to expel Davis since by then he had been convicted in the courts for conspiracy. The City Council expelled him in the early fall of 1949, but the expulsion occurred before the election, in which he still had every right to run and campaign. Republican Governor Dewey, famous former prosecutor, did not want to have what he called "the stigma of Communism" in the hallways of government, and not surprisingly so, considering that his sights were again set on the White House, even after Truman's win.

We knew Brown could not win without the backing of Republicans, so we decided to make him a sort of fusion candidate. This was not such a far-fetched idea in a situation like this because only four years before LaGuardia had left office, and he had been essentially a fusion candidate throughout his career. We discussed the question of Republican support for Earl Brown with David B. Costuma, the Republican New York County Leader, who said he had to check with Governor Dewey. He reported later that the Governor did not support the nomination of Earl Brown. He was not opposed to a fusion candidate, but he objected to Earl Brown because of Brown's constant criticism of his administration. Carmine DeSapio and I knew that Earl had criticized Governor Dewey, but we could not let the Governor's objection block Brown's election. We had to convince the Governor that he was objecting to the wrong Brown. At that time in Harlem there was another Brown, a street corner orator from Chicago, whose first name I do not recall. His very fluent and most articulate orations, along with his well-clipped goatee, earned him the name "Billy Goat Brown". Since Earl had reported in the *Amsterdam News* on Billy Goat Brown's antics we convinced Costuma that the Governor must have confused the two and thought that our Earl Brown was giving him the business. This seemed reasonable to Governor Dewey and he endorsed our man.

All seemed set, but when we began exercises to ascertain the political potential of Mr. Brown, we found that not only was he unable to write a political speech, but he was also unable to deliver one with any elan, although he was a Harvard graduate and an editor of the *Amsterdam News*. So to the brilliant writer and Carver Club member, Dr. J. Dayton Brooks, fell the responsibility of writing speeches for Earl Brown. Since it had taken us so long to get the fusion coordinated, we began our campaign rather late, some time in October. With elections in November, we had a very short, telescoped campaign.

Early in October, Earl Brown had occasion to go to California, and early one morning, around two o'clock or so, he awakened me with a call from Los Angeles. I wondered what bothered him so to call me at this hour.

Brown was incoherent and I could not make head or tail of what he was talking about, but I got the impression that he had learned that somebody had found something on him that would damage him in the campaign. He couldn't tell me what it was and left me in a quandary. "All right," I said, "when *you* know what is happening, let *me* know."

The next morning I began to worry seriously as my doubts about Earl intensified. I knew he was a compulsive gambler. I used to play cards with Edward Dudley, and a man about town in Harlem named Dick Thomas, and Brown himself, and I had noticed from time to time that Brown was not averse to playing a trick or two with the cards. I knew also that he favored the race tracks. I knew he always carried a tote sheet, bet regularly on the horses, and met the bookies in the morning before he went to the track. He was usually in debt to them. This I knew because he told us so.

That same morning I called in Dick Thomas, who always seemed to know everything, and asked him, "What is wrong with Brown?" He answered, "Ray, it's my fault. Benjamin Davis," he said, "told me that Vito Marcantonio was handling a contract with the Police Department to get Brown's record." Of course, I was stunned because I did not know what kind of problems Brown had. I didn't think they were anything really serious, but even a record of his gambling would have been enough to damage severely the campaign. Thomas told me that the police were not going to pass the information over to Vito, who was at that time the Communist Congressman from Harlem, until a better bid was made for it. I did not know what to do, so I went to see O'Dwyer and explained the problem. O'Dwyer was outraged that the Police Department was involved with this kind of nonsense, and, being a man of action, picked up the phone right then and there to call the Chief Inspector. He told him in no uncertain terms that this sort of thing was absolutely against the law, against all rules and regulations, and as nominal chief of the Police Department, he would not stand for it. Anybody found to be involved in that sort of thing would be punished immediately. He then ordered an immediate investigation.

Later I learned that one detective had accepted money to compile damaging information on Earl Brown. When he discovered we knew of his activities, he decided to make amends right away. He sensed that he was in serious trouble. He confessed to the Mayor's investigator that he had taken some money to do this job, and needed to give the money back if he was to avoid being hurt by his outside employers. We could have left it at this,. but we thought better of it, and decided it would be best if he were punished by the Police Department in the regular way. We sought the $500 for him to return to his "employers," and luckily were supported by a prominent, wealthy benefactor, eager to displace the Communists in Harlem and who had promised money to the Earl Brown campaign. All this was accomplished in a couple of days. About two days later, Brown returned from California and learned from his friend Dick Thomas that the heat was off.

In the meantime, Benjamin Davis became increasingly upset, because the information he expected to be out on Earl Brown was not forthcoming. He complained to Dick Thomas who promptly came to me and asked what I had done. Of course, I smiled and told him nothing. But Earl Brown, displaying a short memory and feeling confident, was making the rounds to collect his hard-earned campaign contributions. Inevitably, of course, he wound up on the benefactor's doorstep and was promptly told that his contribution had been given to me! That was a mistake, for Brown came raving into the Carver Club asking why I had stolen his money. I was nonplussed, but it soon became obvious that he was referring to the money that had saved his career. I should have laughed at the irony of the scene, but Brown was so angry he left no room for humor. Collis Crocker, my secretary, sensing that Brown was endangering himself, quickly grabbed him by the shoulders and hustled him out of my office. When it was all over, Crocker returned and said: "This is a situation where we should put as much distance as possible between us and that man." Brown was elected to the City Council that fall with a three-to-one majority, but as far as I was concerned he was no longer one of my people.

Brown's election in 1949 began an odd career which ended up satisfactorily for him, I suspect, but which would have caused me great psychological damage had I been in his shoes. He remained on the City Council until 1958, when he made the severe mistake of siding with the Tammany leadership of Carmine DeSapio against Adam Clayton Powell. It was this ironic development that caused my return to politics. I simply could not resist the chance to teach all of them, Brown, DeSapio and the Tammany leadership, a severe political lesson. I will return to this later.

O'Dwyer resigns: Impelliteri is Mayor

Since the Gracie Mansion party had turned out so well, Robert Wagner's candidacy became well known in Harlem. This was important, for I knew that if O'Dwyer did not attempt a third term in 1953, Wagner desired to run for Mayor that year. There was no better position from which to run in 1953 than as Borough President of Manhattan, since Manhattan was at that time the premiere borough in all of New York City. So I was satisfied with my job, and with my relations with the Mayor, and I felt that the future looked safe in that I felt that Wagner would not lose were he to run in 1953.

Farther afield, my relations were very good with the man in the White House, and so for myself, I was half a century old and on top of the world!

But already there were rumors that trouble lay ahead. I have mentioned before that there had been some investigations of certain members of the O'Dwyer Administration, and as time went on it became clear that some of them were indeed tainted with associations with underworld figures. The Mayor, of course, must have perceived that he would be somehow smeared by association, so we worked out a deal with President Truman for O'Dwyer to be made Ambassador to Mexico. In consequence, he resigned the Mayorship in 1950, and departed for Mexico. William O'Dwyer's resignation created serious problems for me, because the President of the City Council at that time was Vincent Impelliteri, a friend of Frank Sampson, the former County Leader whom O'Dwyer had gotten rid of with my blessing and replaced with Hugo E. Rogers.

Because of the Mayor's resignation, an election was called in November. By then Impelliteri had developed a following because as Acting Mayor from September to November, he had created a mayoral image for himself. It may be recalled that I had not supported Impelliteri's bid for Surrogate Judge in 1949, siding rather with Carmine DeSapio in support of Judge Francis Valente. I knew that "Impy," as we called him, would not forget this, and if he became Mayor I would be done for. By this time, Carmine DeSapio's Italian group had successfully elevated Carmine to Tammany Chief in 1949, following the one-year term of Hugo E. Rogers. Although the Tammany leadership opposed Impelliteri, he managed, with the help of the increased numbers of Reform Democrats, to defeat the Tammany candidate, Ferdinand Pecora, in the primary, and in the mayoral elections

I knew that the moment Impelliteri won there would be trouble to pay, and when he immediately hired Frank Sampson, the Tammany Chief from 1947 to 1948 and the leader in his district, to be his secretary, I knew my days at the Housing Commission were numbered. Indeed, during the campaign I had been attacked by "Impy," the acting Mayor, as the "Harlem Czar." Within a few days after his appointment on December 12, Mr. Sampson, who had tried to do me in before, telephoned my office asking for my resignation. The *New York Times*, of December 13, 1950, reported my resignation and quoted from my letter to the Mayor.

Mr. Jones, in his letter of resignation said he felt it his duty to review conditions in his department and to present recommendations for improvement. He cited figures to prove that the "backlog" of complaints and uncorrected violations had been cut down but that the staffing problem had not been solved.

"One of the chief problems," he wrote, "which hampers the efficiency of the division is the salary policy with respect to personnel acting in administrative and supervisory capacities.

"There is no marked differential in salaries between borough chief inspectors, supervising inspectors and the regular line inspectors which they direct. These inequities are so great in some instances that efficient administrators are drawing salaries lower than personnel they supervise. This practice stifles incentive, destroys morale and, as a result, affects the efficient operation of the division.

"I strongly urge that your administration study this problem with a view to correcting these inequities and thereby developing a division which continues to meet the requirements of efficient city administration.[3]

I am sure that to some my letter sounded like sour grapes. It wasn't really, for it was not directed at Mayor Impelliteri but to the Mayor's office and the citizens of New York City. If O'Dwyer had remained, he would have received the same letter, not as resignation but as recommendation, because the restructuring of pay scales and responsibilities was a project I had hoped to complete by the middle of the Mayor's second term. When it became clear that I would not have the opportunity to finish that project, I thought the best I could do was to let the public know what needed to be done. I know that in so doing I earned the gratitude of my fellow workers.

I was the third in line that Impy fired. Before me went Sylvester Cossentino, Deputy Commissioner of Marine and Aviation, and Philip Zichello, Deputy Commissioner of Hospitals. Obviously all this was not simply an Italian attempt to take over the political machinery of New York, but infighting among the Italians themselves who had successfully routed the Irish and were now busily settling their own internal disputes. It was an interesting spectacle worthy, I believe, of anthropological study. Despite their infighting, however, the Italians closed rank very swiftly when discerning a threat from outsiders. The Oresto Maresca Case is illustrative.

The Oresto Maresca case and the break with the Italians

After resigning from the Department of Housing and Buildings, I took a job as a secretary to Judge Harold Stevens of the Court of General Sessions. The pay was not overwhelming but I could manage. About this time the contest for a State Assembly nomination in my district was between an Irishman and an Italian, Oresto Maresca. Angelo Simonetti supported Maresca, and Danny Flynn, my long time associate, supported the Irish fellow. In fact, that Assembly nomination actually belonged to me, lent to Simonetti from a previous period. Since I felt that it was mine, I had no problem in supporting Flynn's candidate. Maresca, however, had bribed one of my Election District Captains, Antonio Rasmus, for his support, but although Rasmus' support carried his election district for Maresca,

Flynn eventually won. Flynn's victory upset Simonetti who complained to Tammany Leader Carmine DeSapio, that I had opposed Maresca, that I was not to be trusted, and that I had broken with the Italian-Black alliance. Implied in the complaint was the idea that I should be punished for my dastardly deeds. I believe Carmine considered ways to show his solidarity with Simonetti, but he could not fire me from the job I held with Harold Stevens, because Stevens was a judge whose appointment I had secured. Furthermore, I was now well entrenched as a District Leader, and there was very little they could do about that.

Since the job I had with Stevens was not demanding, I had time on my hands and decided to take a trip to Ghana on business for the Urban League. I mistakenly failed to prime Stevens with the possibilities of what might happen because I had not supported Maresca. When I came back, things had changed. Stevens' attitude was aloof, and suddenly the Governor appointed him to the State Supreme Court. Normally I would have rejoiced at this, for I was pleased by Stevens' elevation. But all this had been done without my cooperation and knowledge, so I knew something was up. I knew I could not go with Stevens to the Supreme Court because a Supreme Court's clerk or secretary has to be a lawyer, and I certainly did not have a law degree. I concluded that this new development was the handiwork of Tammany Chief Carmine DeSapio, Simonetti, and his Italian group, but I also knew that they were not yet powerful enough to do me any real damage. In fact, they arranged for me to take a secretaryship with Judge Gerald Culkin, which was all right with me. But although I was told this in early 1951, the appointment was not made for months and the manner in which it was done further distanced me from DeSapio.

In April 1951, I announced that I was thinking of resigning as District Leader. Part of my decision resulted from Senator Estes Kefauver's Committee investigation of the notorious gangster Frank Costello who, as rumor had it, had had dealings with a number of politicians in the Tammany leadership. Implicated was Angelo Simonetti, the neighboring District Leader and secretary to Borough President Robert F. Wagner, Jr. In hearings before the Kefauver Committee, Frank Costello testified that he knew Harry Brickman, the Deputy City Treasurer, a friend of Mayor Impelliteri. This revelation placed pressure on both the Mayor and the Borough President to investigate Brickman and Simonetti, with firings a possibility. Such developments did nothing to cheer my spirits, and furthermore, the entire scene was depressing. Politics had been fun since 1925. I had, frankly, enjoyed greatly the planning and counter-planning, the delicate intricacies of the game, but by early 1951, politics was no longer an enjoyable exercise. Situations were fast becoming ugly, and I was not of that culture. In April I announced my decision not to run for reelection as District Leader in the fall because of my general disgust with the present low public standing of the political organizations.

The *New York Times* announcement caught Angelo Simonetti and Carmine DeSapio by surprise because all this time they had been holding up the arrangements for my job as secretary to Judge Culkin. Carmine, galvanized by the announcement, immediately sent for me to discuss my plans. At this meeting I decided that Carmine was too crude for my tastes, that never the twain would meet, for DeSapio kept me waiting outside his office for two hours! Under normal circumstances I would not have objected, because, I would assume that once through with whatever pressing business he had as County Leader, he would make up for the hours I had wasted by spending time with me probably over a drink or two or discussing this or that. But this wasn't the case, as I soon found out. While I waited, he had convened a press conference in his office, and I concluded that he had kept me waiting deliberately to give me a message. I appreciated neither his tactic nor the message. When I finally saw him all he told me was to see Judge Gerald Culkin. As I had known Culkin's father as a Tammany District Leader, Culkin and I hit it off and had a wonderful time together. Indeed, we saw eye to eye and our association became so pleasant that I began to think more and more of resigning not only from my District Leadership, but from politics entirely.

While working for Judge Culkin, I continued to run the Carver Club, but my heart was no longer very much in it. As I said to the press in April, there had been what I considered a severe deterioration in the ethics and principles of the politicians with whom I was associated. I felt some of their shenanigans undignified, and many had come too close to criminality. Although I did not believe Simonetti and some of his friends were involved in criminal activity, the fact that they were associated with types like Frank Costello was certainly disturbing. I, too, could be smeared by association, no matter how far removed. Since I had never associated with gangsters in my life, I did not now want to work too closely with people involved with them, even indirectly. I did not relish the risk. I also considered resigning because in the Carver Club there were several young people who, I thought, could now assume leadership. I began to think more and more that perhaps I had accomplished enough, that it was time to step aside and let these young people try their wings. In 1958, the Antonio Rasmus affair precipitated my decision to resign.

The Rasmus affair

Rasmus, a St. Thomas immigrant, was the most ambitious person in my club at the time. An interesting fellow, he had given me no reason to believe that he was untrustworthy, and despite an intuitive uncertainty about him, I admitted him to the inner circles of the Carver Club. Shortly after his admission I began noticing that he imitated me in every way, right down to the cigar that I usually sported. Every chance he got he was under my wing. He would drive my car, and come down to talk to me at all times of the day when I was Commissioner of Housing. He would take the elevator down with me, walk across the street into the restaurant where I had lunch every day, and walk back with me, making sure that whoever was watching would see that Antonio Rasmus was a personal friend of the Deputy Commissioner of Housing. There was a method to this madness, but only later did I discover what it actually was.

I often visited the Renaissance Ballroom on 130th and 7th Avenue be-cause it attracted many of the movers and shakers in Harlem. Small's nightclub, a similar place on 125th Street, was also a meeting place I sometimes visited. I walked into Small's one evening and the headwaiter said "The boss is in the back and he would like to see you." I followed him to the back and Edward Small, a famous Harlem character from the 1940s through the 1960s, took me aside saying he wanted to tell me something. I knew this would have to be interesting, because Small's was also a hangout for shady characters in the numbers racket. So if Small had any-thing to tell me, it had to be some development concerning me, and about which he, as a friend, wanted to warn me beforehand. Small told me that Antonio Rasmus was moving into the rackets, and he thought I should be aware of this. My first thought was that if Tony were doing this, it would reflect very badly on me because of his association with the Carver Club. But as I discussed the matter with Small, I realized that Rasmus was moving into the rackets with authority because many thought I assisted him in this endeavor, and would and could protect him since I was a Commissioner. To make matters worse, Small reported that the police were already asking questions. "What is Commissioner Jones doing?" "Why is he moving into the rackets?" This was a most upsetting development, something which I could not tolerate. I told Small to tell the police that if they could catch Rasmus doing anything illegal they were to lock him up and throw away the key.

I soon found out too that Tony had misused his association with me in other ways. There was a woman who owned a restaurant on Bradhurst Avenue, directly in front of the community swimming pool where kids congregated. When the police eventually closed her down for certain in-fractions, she rented a place on 125th Street and 7th Avenue and sent her emissary to see me about getting a license to operate. I informed her messenger that I did not handle that kind of thing. But Rasmus got wind of the request and advised her, as I understood it later, that he was the man to take care of business. He tried to convince her in a very interesting way. He invited me to lunch one day, picked me up at my office, and walked with me to my usual restaurant. As we approached the restaurant I saw him signal a lady sitting on a bench outside. I thought to myself that something was up with that signal and had it checked out. Soon I learned that he was indeed indicating to the woman that I was working on the situation and it would be taken care of soon. At this juncture I decided Mr. Rasmus had gone too far, and I asked him to leave the Club. With this taken care of, I decided to retire from active leadership of the club and from my post as District Leader.

But the problem with Rasmus was not over. After being thrown out of the Carver club, he formed the "Truman Democratic Club," and began to spread all kinds of propaganda about my club, about his ability to take care of the district, the usual stuff. Of course, there were no laws to prevent him from forming a club. But in March I thought I might give him something to think about, and on the advice of the Law committee of the Carver Democratic club, we served papers on him by order of Justice Benedict D. Dineen of the New York Supreme Court, to prevent him from using such terms as "Executive Members," "Regular Democratic Club," "Organization," or "Association," and from using the Democratic party's emblem, the star. [4] We chose this time because Rasmus' Club was hosting a big ball at the Renaissance Casino on Thursday night, March 19th, and the court order, we thought, would throw a wrench in his wheels. Unfortunately, the ploy did not work. Fed up with the new politics, I resigned in June 1953 from the leadership of the district, as well as the club.

Upon my resignation, the leadership of the Carver Club passed to Lucius Butts, a lawyer. But Butts was not cut out for the new rough and tumble of New York politics. I soon noticed that he did not have the wit and sharpness of operation ot be able to withstand the onslaught of somebody like Tony Rasmus. Yet it seemed impolitic for me to hang around and interfere in his affairs. I left him alone, gave no advice, and stayed away, and in the primaries three months later, in September, he lost the leadership of the district to Antonio Rasmus. This development saddened me very much, but I had decided firmly that I was through with politics. I preferred gardening with Judge Gerald Culkin.

The first Black borough president

Officially, I resigned from politics in June 1953, but to a great extent I had begun my retirement when Vincent Impelliteri became Mayor and fired me from the Department of Housing and Buildings. I did not particularly care for Impelliteri and his group of sanctimonious reformers; neither did I feel comfortable with the new "rough politics" under the leadership of Carmine DeSapio at Tammany Hall. The former group was too holier-than-thou and the latter was, in my opinion, totally unholy. I perceived, by 1950, a party polarized on ideological grounds, tainted by scandals of graft and gangsterism and given to extremes on both sides. I knew that eventually I would have to take sides, and neither side appealed to me.

But people *were* taking sides. In Harlem the polar pull of Reform and Regular Democrats exacerbated conflicts. A case in point: the estrangement between District Leader Hulan Jack and me, and between Jack and Herbert L. Bruce. From the beginning, Jack displayed signs of subservience to the leaders of the party that I found disturbing. To Carmine DeSapio he was especially fawning. I became wary of his positions because his opinions appeared prepackaged by a DeSapio factory. I am not, by any means, suggesting that one should not respect one's County Leader, but Jack was going too far in my opinion. I finally decided that although he represented Harlem in the State Assembly and was a District Leader, the real representative was the County Leader, Carmine DeSapio. In Jack's biography, published in 1982, he corroborates my views of 1950. He writes:

The reign of Hugo Rogers as the County Leader and Chief of Tammany Hall came to an abrupt end when his term of office as Manhattan Borough President expired in January of 1949. A great and never-to-be forgotten struggle ensued over who was to replace him as the head of the party's New York organization. An individual who was then a leader in Greenwich Village, Carmine DeSapio, had attracted the attention, respect, and admiration of a great number of local leaders. Leader after leader approached DeSapio and asked him to take over Tammany Hall. We felt we could turn to no one else, and we pledged our cooperation if he would take the position we were urging upon him.

So compelling was the demand that Carmine had no choice but to accept, and in July 1949 he became the new leader of Tammany Hall. Little did we know at the time what a good choice we were making. As the years passed, it became clear that we had selected a leader who was unequaled by any Tammany Chief of the past, and who was unlikely to be surpassed by any in the future. Carmine pulled together the Democratic Party leaders of the five counties of New York into a powerful and tight-knit machine. . . .

Under Carmine's leadership, the Democratic Party's strength was formidable, and the people demonstrated their confidence in the Party's leadership capabilities and commitment by registering and voting as Democrats. The apathy that prevails in politics today did not exist then, people felt that the Democratic Party understood and represented their aspirations and hope. [5]

There is no question that Carmine's was a very influential and powerful leadership, but Jack's statement that leader after leader approached

DeSapio and asked him to take over Tammany Hall is not entirely correct. Carmine had made certain connections throughout the city and the Democratic Party, connections which created pressures on the various leaders on Carmine's behalf. It was not therefore entirely an uncoerced acceptance of Carmine as Jack would have it, but a subtle form of manipulation that resulted in Carmine's ascension to power in 1949. Behind it all was the development of a sense of Italian power that had its beginning during the LaGuardia years and continued in the years after the war. It meant the passing of the Irish hegemony in New York politics and an Italian ascendancy.

Through connections that had nothing to do with the Democratic Party in a formal way, DeSapio's influence extended to all boroughs. Within the Black community, particularly in Manhattan, he had a technique that was wonderfully simple. He made sure that a strong relationship developed between him and the Leader of any Black district. He assigned Angelo Simonetti, Leader of the 13th Assembly District West, to insure that I was kept under control. Simonetti then would meet with me from time to time to find out what was on my mind, what I intended to do, and report to Carmine. I knew what was going on and was not bothered because I intended to do what I wanted anyway regardless of what Carmine thought. As long as I thought my initiatives would be correct and within the mainstream of the Democratic Party, I did what I wanted to do and refused to take orders. That, of course, was the beginning of problems between me and the leader of Tammany Hall.

In the case of Hulan Jack and others, this was not the case. Jack was the leader of the 14th Assembly District and next door to him was the Italian District Leader, John Merli. Carmine had Merli monitor Jack, who was willing to be monitored and mentored. Hulan Jack made no moves until they were discussed with Merli and approved by DeSapio. In consequence, he maintained and improved his position in the Party among Regular Democrats and enjoyed promises of future power as long as he obeyed orders.

By 1953 Carmine had decided that, due to the increasing power of the Black vote, a very visible post had to be found for a Negro politician in Manhattan. The President of the City Council would not do, for that position was too important. A Mayor was not to be considered; besides Robert Wagner already had a lockhold on that nomination. DeSapio had to come up with something else. Lo and behold, the Borough Presidency loomed large and Hulan Jack was tapped for that position as a reward for his faithful service. I never publicly opposed Jack's nomination for the Borough Presidency, but there were others who found it distasteful. Herbert L. Bruce, for one, thought that Jack was certainly not the best candidate, and put forth one of his own. I knew I was not being considered because Hulan Jack's nomination signalled to me that, as far as Carmine and the leadership of Tammany Hall was concerned, I was finished as a force in politics in New York. But Jack was properly grateful. He saw his nomination as a favor, and in his book he recalls his nomination and Carmine's support:

> Even within the Democratic Party there are those who said you couldn't put a Negro over for Borough President. But Carmine DeSapio's determination was: "A Negro is part of this ticket. If you can elect the others and if they will be accepted, then make sure you sell the Negro candidate on the same basis that you sell the other candidates."
> This was a deep understanding and a deep statement and those who couldn't abide it would have to suffer the consequences. [6]

No one suffered any consequences really, because in 1953 it was easy to put over a Negro as Borough President since the Negro had already become a potent force in the politics of New York City. New Yorkers had come to realize that the times were changing and that people would be demanding more and more; astute politicians knew they would have to make relatively harmless concessions early on rather than have influence and power wrested from them. With Robert Wagner leading the ticket, Hulan Jack was swept into the Borough Presidency in 1954, where he remained for six years. Unfortunately he had to resign in 1960, and it is ironic that it was Mr. Jack who suffered unfortunate consequences.

The year before the mayoral election and the election of Hulan Jack to the Borough Presidency was a presidential election year. Since I was on the outs with the Democratic leadership, my participation in the conflict between Adlai Stevenson, Governor of Illinois, and General Dwight D. Eisenhower was minimal. The Stevenson campaign, though a national one, did shed a certain light on events in the Democratic Party in New York City. I think history will prove that Stevenson, notwithstanding the popularity of Eisenhower as great war hero and the rest was hindered most in New York City because he appeared to be the Reform candidate. Although I was at odds with the leadership of Tammany Hall, I knew what they were thinking; there was very little enthusiasm there for Stevenson once the Reform wing of the Party so enthusiastically endorsed him. The showing in 1952 was not what it could have been had the party been united, and matters were not enhanced in 1956 when Adam Clayton Powell endorsed Eisenhower. Powell's breaking ranks, so to speak, may have been a consequence of promises made to him by the Republican candidate, but on the other hand it might be construed that again in 1956 the candidacy of

Adlai Stevenson could not have endeared itself to Powell as long as it came under the aegis of the Reform wing in New York City.

With these schisms clearly growing wider—more than an ordinary lack of unity within the party—increased squabbling and hints of chicanery, I was happy to retire from politics in June 1953.

A severe lesson for Carmine De Sapio, Earl Brown, and the Tammany leadership

When Adam Clayton Powell came on the scene in 1941, he was more a social worker and a social agitator, more a man on the outside of political activity and political parties than a politician. In this context, he was very much ahead of his time, ahead of such people as James Farmer, who began his career in 1942 as a worker with the Congress of Racial Equality; Powell was certainly ahead of subsequent leaders like Martin Luther King. His decision to run for the City Council in 1941, his successful agitation within and without the City Council, and his bold decision to run for Congress in 1944, irritated some people within the Tammany leadership because, although he was nominally a Democrat, it was clear that the party needed him more than he needed it. From the very beginning of his career, Powell, because of his independent stance and his uncompromising posture regarding racial discrimination, made the leadership of the Democratic and the Republican parties uncomfortable.

By the 1950s, Powell, who was always returned to Congress with ease, had achieved seniority there. With a reputation of legendary proportions, he felt he did not need the Democratic Party to maintain himself politically and so, frustrated by the slow pace of change within his own party, he virtually declared his independence of it in 1956 by endorsing the Republican, Dwight D. Eisenhower for reelection as President. Powell had been fed up for some time with the Democratic Party at the national level and was thoroughly disgusted with the "wimpy" attitude of the standard bearer, Adlai Stevenson, who had run in 1952 and was running again in 1956. In 1952 Powell had been vice-chairman of a group which nominated Averill Harriman for President, but Harriman had lost to Governor Adlai Stevenson. This loss rankled, but when Stevenson chose Senator John Sparkman of Alabama as his Vice-Presidential running mate, any chance of support from Congressman Powell was lost. Four years later, totally fed up with the Democratic Party's national leadership, he was ready to defect.

At the 1956 Democratic National Convention, the Congressman was not to be found, and the party did nothing between that period and the November elections to return him to the fold. The Republicans, however, wooed him and arranged a meeting between President Eisenhower and

Powell the second week of October. After this meeting Powell said Eisenhower had promised to assist him in very concrete ways in the Congress to enforce the Supreme Court rulings on Civil Rights. Adam's defection infuriated the Tammany leadership, and a number of them told the press that they thought Adam had made a secret deal with the Republicans. I watched all this amused, because of course that's what he'd done; he had made a deal, and a perfectly legitimate one. If Democrats were going to remain bigoted on a national level despite rapidly changing times, and if Democrats continued to support racist Southerners, who showed no concern for desegregation as mandated by law, then I would not blame Adam Powell for his actions.

Even though a Congressman has certain constraints as a member of his party, everyone knew that Adam had always pursued an independent route, and in this particular instance morality pressed more than party loyalty. There was a very serious moral issue involved here, and Tammany and other Democratic leaders were not only mistreating Powell, but displaying their own narrow-minded insensitivity. The absence of any serious attempt at conciliation infuriated Adam further, and to teach them a lesson, he announced his support for Jacob Javits, then the Republican Attorney General of New York, who was running against Mayor Robert Wagner for a Senate post. This was a very shrewd move, because Javits, already a very popular figure in New York State, had a highly visible and well-propagandized life membership in the National Association for the Advancement of Colored People. Although the Democrats prevailed in New York City, Javits and Eisenhower won again with ease, and Powell, running again for Congress, won with his usual 75% of the vote.

Powell's behavior created much more than local concern, for he was now a figure of national prominence. He was no longer a mere Congressman from Harlem. He was now the Negro Representative for all Negroes in the United States of America. No doubt to lessen his influence, it was rumored that, on his return to Congress in the fall, the Democrats would strip him of his seniority because of his maverick behaviour. Such rumors only made Adam more beloved in Harlem, where the Black population and a number of liberal whites argued that he was being persecuted for taking a perfectly legal and moral stance.

The net effect of this controversy was that Adam Powell became unbeatable in his Congressional District, of which Harlem formed the largest part. The only thing the Democratic Party could do was censure him or drum him out of the party. This they could not do because so far he had done nothing to merit such action and besides, the party itself was not united in its dissatisfaction. To do anything drastic about Adam would require planning, and in 1956 DeSapio and the Tammany leadership were not ready.

Matters worsened the next year when Mayor Robert F. Wagner, Jr., ran for reelection. It was rumored that Powell would somehow undermine the campaign. It may be that DeSapio and company hoped he would, because such a move would be futile against Wagner, who was now a fairly popular Mayor. In the course of his first term he had managed, mostly through temporizing, to bring together the Reform and Regular Democrats into a strange, edgy relationship. It wouldn't last long, and it disintegrated immediately after the election, but in 1957 it was enough to insure that all factions worked for him. Congressman Powell, despite a penchant for hasty action, took no part in this campaign. In effect, he personally abstained, but his influence was felt through the people he supported in Harlem. They did the talking for the ticket while Adam Powell stayed in Washington.

For myself, I was out of politics, but certain people assumed that I would one day return, and they kept me informed of the stories behind the headlines in the newspapers. I viewed these stories as case studies in politics. Since my employer Judge Gerald Culkin was a learned man, I took the opportunity of dissecting and analyzing the more interesting cases with him. We spent many a delightful hour in this exercise, and when we exhausted politics we turned to opera or flowers, both topics dear to the heart of the judge. I learned a great deal from Justice Culkin, for I came to regard this period of my life as time to catch up on those areas of my education that were lacking. Opera, for instance, I had always liked, but only from a distance, since the details were lost on me; but Judge Culkin knew everything. At least it seemed that way to me. He would enter the building sometimes and everyone would know the Barber of Seville had arrived. Other times he would be Madame Butterfly! He was no respecter of gender. If it were opera, he would sing it. At times, in the company of this man and a few other of his aides, politics seemed as desirable as a bad case of the flu; but forces were already at work that would soon remove me from this idyllic and halcyon setting. When the messenger came, I was ready. I returned to politics not as the improvisor I had been before, but as a missionary.

I do not wish to be self-serving, but the truth is I did not have to return to politics when I did. In the first place I no longer needed politics to make a living. I had carefully invested a part of my salary, which, given the various positions I held, was more than adequate for my simple needs. I was and am a frugal person. So too was my wife Ruth, a near Ph. D. in economics, who had worked all her life. With her expertise on taxation, bonds, stocks and the rest, we did fairly well. Neither did I need the trappings of power as some people in politics clearly do. I had had all that before, albeit at a middle level, and as I recall, most of it had amounted to aggravation and long hours. But I did return and I can only hope that history will say it was worth the effort.

Congressman Adam Clayton Powell's refusal to participate in the mayoral election of 1957 only added fuel to the fire caused by his endorsement of Republican Eisenhower the previous year. The success of the Democratic ticket led by Robert Wagner apparently convinced Carmine DeSapio, the Tammany Chief, and Hulan Jack, the Black Borough President of Manhattan, and others that the time had come to teach Adam Powell a lesson and establish Tammany's, that is Carmine DeSapio's, undisputed leadership over Harlem. Since Powell would be running for reelection in 1958, DeSapio decided early in that year that Adam had to be removed. In order to do this properly he needed as much Harlem support as possible. His not-so-secret weapon would be that most visible Harlem personality, the Manhattan Borough President, Hulan Jack. Jack remembers the story this way:

When Congressman Powell endorsed the Republican candidate for President, General Dwight D. Eisenhower, in 1956, it is certain that he did so under personal pressure. Powell was entangled in legal problems over his taxes, and it is easy to imagine that a deal was consummated to give General Eisenhower the substantial campaign boost of Powell's influence over the Negro constituency nationally in exchange for an easing of pressure against the Congressman on the legal front.

Let me clear the air on this matter. Adam Clayton Powell did not endorse Eisenhower because he was dissatisfied with the attitude of the Democratic Party toward the Negroes. He had no particular fight with Tammany Hall at the time. He endorsed a Republican for personal reasons, much to the glee of the GOP campaign directors who could imagine the impact of announcing that Congressman Powell had endorsed their man as the best candidate to ensure the rights of the Negro minority.

Of course, this created a situation in which the Democrats felt that disciplinary action against Congressman Powell was necessary. It is commonly known that when a leader of a party breaks rank with the party, drastic action is often taken. So it was not unusual for the County Leader, Carmine DeSapio, to think in terms of what kind of penalty would be imposed against Congressman Powell. It would be unfair for me to say that I did not participate in such a discussion with Carmine DeSapio and the District Leaders. We were greatly chagrined by Adam's action, because we had depended on him to carry the campaign banner for the Democratic Party's candidate Adlai Stevenson. It was finally decided that Powell would be denied the party's nomination for reelection to his congressional seat.

This, then, was the setting for the major battle between Tammany Hall and Adam Clayton Powell. I endorsed the party's action, and proceeded to help set in motion the machinery by which Tammany would choose a candidate to oppose Adam in the upcoming Democratic Party primary. The candidate who was finally tapped for the nomination, after several others had refused to oppose Powell, was New York City Councilman Earl Brown. Earl Brown turned out to be a sad candidate. His campaign was so tired that it almost did not exist; what little he did do had little or no effect on the situation.

But the primary campaign overall was no quiet affair. J. Raymond Jones came out of retirement to handle Powell's petition drive, and a formidable combination accepted the challenge of Tammany Hall.

Representatives of the party machine came in for some strong attacks, and I was by no means the exception. The most common charge leveled against me was that I had failed to be aggressive in representing the Harlem community as Borough President of Manhattan. Of course the Congressman was always free with words. They flowed freely and smoothly from his tongue. Charges of "Uncle Tomism" and "plantation Negro" were made public, and made their way into the press. In fact, the media ate up the controversy. The newspapers reported Powell referring to "uptown Negroes" and "downtown whites," which gave the impression that we were a geographically defined constituency. By the time the campaign was over, I was being branded as a Negro on DeSapio's plantation!

Of course, these charges were flying in the heat of the battle, and made little sense on their own merits. I was no more on DeSapio's plantation than Adam was from time to time, for he also was a leader within Tammany Hall. As for the charges of "downtown white," I made it very clear that Harlem alone did not elect me to the office of Borough President, and I would not serve Harlem alone. My responsibility was to the entire borough of Manhattan.

We need not dwell on this situation any longer. Adam won the primary with a resounding victory, and that victory was against Tammany Hall.

Soon, our attention was turned in another direction, to the statewide convention of the Democratic Party in 1958. Sometime after the convention, and the renomination of Averell Harriman as the party's gubernatorial candidate, Carmine DeSapio, Adam Powell, and Averell Harriman reached an agreement. Adam Powell—who had called Tammany Hall every name under the sun and announced his willingness to wipe it from the very face of the earth—had found a gracious avenue by which he could make his way back onto the plantation. He once again became an active leader of Tammany Hall—as did his comrade in arms Ray Jones—and campaigned across New York State for Harriman. [7]

I have no knowledge of a deal between Adam Powell and President Eisenhower, and despite Jack's musings none has come to light so far. Where Hulan is absolutely wrong is in the assertion that Adam "had no particular fight with Tammany Hall at the time." Of course he did! Adam had become too independent of DeSapio and the Democratic Party, both Regular and Reform, to be tolerated. His independence was bad enough, but when it was considered that he was a Black man, it was intolerable. Since a great majority of Harlem leaders, with the notable exception of myself (and I had been gone since 1953) and Lloyd Dickens, were comfortable with Carmine's rule, Adam's insouciant and unrepentant independence was an insufferable irritant. It could no longer be tolerated.

The decision and announcement to dump Adam in the spring of 1958 was tactically well timed. Adam was having a number of difficulties, and Carmine and the boys knew it. Powell's right-hand man, Acey Lennon, was in jail for income tax evasion. So too was that most efficient secretary of his, Hattie F. Dodson. Hanging fire also was the business of his income tax evasion, a topic discussed in the papers daily, with a hearing imminent. The early betting was that, given the history of Lennon and Dodson, Powell himself would not escape the long arm of the law. Watching all this from a distance, I decided that Congressman Powell, perhaps for the first time in his career, was worried. It wasn't that he would lose! I am sure he felt confident, but one could not be *absolutely* sure under the circumstances. That feeling of pure certainty can be felt in politics and it is quite different from mere confidence. After musing on this interesting spectacle, I decided the time had come to return to the political arena.

Helping Adam was important, but of much more importance was the chance to rid Harlem of condescending absentee rulers. I decided early that if I ever returned to politics, one goal would be to make Harlem independent. Thus quite a few of the leaders now so subservient to De-Sapio would have to learn new lessons or leave school.

Antonio Rasmus, now a Harlem District Leader, was one of the six who sided with DeSapio. This was the same Rasmus I had asked to leave the Carver Club in 1951. His presence in the DeSapio group was symbolic, I thought, and I wondered: Who in the world will their candidate be? The answer was City Councilman Earl Brown.

The moment I heard this I was ready. The situation was irresistible, for politics has its personal aspects too. I don't believe I had ever in my career allowed personal feelings to make my decisions. But this was a situation where I could do some good and at the same time teach a lesson to a few colleagues who, in my opinion, were ascribing themselves too much importance at the expense of our community.

On the day Congressman Powell's trial began, I arranged to meet him at the courthouse. Adam seemed happy to see me, and when I told him that I thought he needed help this time, he agreed. I outlined a plan of action, suggested the themes of "plantation" and "bossism", and he concurred. I remarked that it would be best if he did the talking and I handled everything else. He was amenable. Close cooperation was absolutely necessary, however. No problem. It was almost too good to be true, but I was not complaining. We shook hands on the deal and went to work.

We told the public that DeSapio wanted Negroes like Adam Clayton Powell and myself to "stay in line," meaning that his word was command, in the Mississippi tradition. We wrote up little blurbs denying that Harlem was a plantation, although Carmine saw it that way and, unfortunately, there were always some Uncle Tom Negroes. Some observers thought the campaign was very racial, meaning racist on our part, but we never saw it that way. To us it was a campaign for independence, and the plantation symbolism was appropriate. So effective was our approach that on one occasion when Hulan Jack mustered up courage to address a Harlem crowd, he was given the "Bronx Cheer" by a number of his listeners. At another time when Adam said of Jack, "Send that Uncle Tom back downtown," the crowd became wild with laughter. Powell took care of the rhetoric because speechifying was his thing.

Since I was known throughout the New York area as the "petitions man," because of my long experience at the Board of Elections and my participation in the O'Dwyer campaign, everything in that area was entrusted to me. The key element was not whether Adam could be reelected or not, because once he was on the ballot he would be, but that we had to get him on the ballot. The petitions had to be absolutely in order, not tampered with in any way.

Much more recently, the *New York Times* has reported that: "Albert Vann, a six-term Brooklyn Assemblyman and one of the city's most prominent Black politicians, was removed from the September 9 Democratic primary ballots yesterday by a State Supreme Court Justice because of errors in his nominating petition." In this same article the *Times* explained, "In Albany, a State Supreme Court Justice yesterday upheld a ruling by a commission of the State Board of Elections that eliminated three candidates running for office on the ticket of Lyndon H. LaRouche Jr., the political extremist, on the same technical grounds, that the petitions lacked information required by law. [8]

What is seen here is that petitions law is very complex, and as I have noted previously, the uninitiated can be ruled off the ballot very easily if the reigning party so desires. Vann ran against Howard Golden in 1985 for the Borough Presidency of Kings county, that is, Brooklyn, and lost. Golden, a power in the organization, arranged in reprisal through the petitions process to prevent Albert Vann from running as a Democrat in 1986. Vann, by the way, had been thrown off the ballot before, in 1980, on similar technical grounds, but the Liberal Party picked him up and he won his seat. That was again probably the only route left to him.

Although we had a plethora of people asking to work for Adam as petition gatherers, I was very wary and made sure that only the people I knew and trusted would be used to gather petitions. It is important to remember that Adam was running for Congress of the United States, and that his Congressional district overlapped contiguous areas not generally considered part of the Harlem district. Because of the district's size, we needed petition gatherers in those Assembly Districts with leaders opposing Adam's candidacy, and supposedly supporting Earl Brown. When members of clubs in such neighborhoods came to offer their help, I would not allow them to do petition work for me unless I felt certain they could absolutely be trusted. In fact, I hung a plaque with "Beware of Greeks bearing gifts" above my desk at the Carver Club to let the many volunteers know that we were wise to charlatans. We simply could not risk Adam's removal from the ballot because of invalidated petitions.

As the campaign moved to its climax, quite a number of people in districts led by hostile leaders sought to make an alliance with us, so that in the next year's District Leader elections they could call on us for support. This was, indeed, tempting but I advised Adam not to make any arrangements with anyone in the Assembly Districts. If they wanted to make alliances, they could come and see me. Quite a few came in, but I advised everyone that we were now simply working to get Adam elected. Once the election was over, we could discuss other matters.

Adam's 1958 campaign was an exhilarating learning experience for me. As I have mentioned before, I viewed Adam in the 1940s as more of a social agitator than a politician. As such, he was able to bring into his orbit political support from usually apolitical constituencies. I studied this campaign to determine to what extent political and nonpolitical forces can be brought into political action when the issues seem to be more than the ordinary political ones; and I learned a very powerful lesson regarding the role of extra-partisan organizations.

In the very beginning of the campaign, we had Adam concentrate his speeches on the social and economic system of Harlem, benighted because of the bigotry and indifference shown to the area by the New York City government and the New York population generally. We insisted that we were fighting not only for Adam's Congressional seat, but also for the revitalizing of Harlem and for a better society. We argued that we could not accomplish this while taking orders from people like Carmine and his bunch, who were unconcerned about the problems of Harlem. This pitch had several consequences, all of which I regarded with delight.

Our plea attracted many organizations and I recall one Maude Gadsden, a powerful woman in the labor movement, who came to our aid. All the Black churches, and even some of the white ones, offered assistance. Social workers of all kinds who worked in the neighborhood assisted, and believe it or not, although Thomas Curran, at that time the Republican County Chairman, opposed Powell, practically all of the Republicans leaders in Harlem assisted.

In retrospect, the Republican County Chairman's behavior in 1958 now seems to me to be reminiscent of the behavior of Carmine DeSapio and that segment of the New York white community who were unaware of the changes taking place around them. That both parties, County Chairmen shared this view suggests that they were so embroiled in traditional politics and in the traditional perspectives of race relations that they were unaware of the changes taking place around them. Black people and progressive whites knew that the times and the manners had changed. A significant proportion of the white population in New York City had come to this realization and wanted to be part of this new morality and new politics.

But what had caused this and what was taking place? Certainly all this was not clear to me in 1958, but I knew that when Rosa Parks refused to give up her seat to a white person in a bus in Montgomery, Alabama, in December of 1955, and when, in the very next year, as a consequence of that small beginning, Montgomery's Black population organized a boycott which eventually desegregated the buses in that city, we in Harlem rejoiced. We knew that parents of Black children had faced fire hoses, stones, bottles, and even bullets and would not back down, in order to have their children attend integrated schools. Harlem knew that it was not a mere matter of integrating schools, not a mere matter of seeing to it that the Supreme Court decision of 1954 be adhered to; rather, we knew that Black people throughout the United States were serving notice that they would be treated equally *in all things* and that no longer would they be intimidated by police, dogs, and bullets, be denied their rightful place in American society.

The Little Rock confrontation seemed to have proven Adam Clayton Powell correct in supporting Eisenhower. He had been accused of making a deal in 1956 to ease his legal problems by supporting Eisenhower; however, Powell had always contended that he supported Ike because Ike was pro-civil rights. Although Eisenhower waivered at the beginnings of the Little Rock school uprising, he finally sent out the National Guard on behalf of the Black population of Little Rock, Arkansas. What is usually not remembered, which may have proven Powell's instincts correct, was that in the same year, 1957, Eisenhower himself presented a Civil Rights Bill to the Congress of the United States which, among other things, gave the Attorney General the power to seek injunctions in the federal courts to protect persons whose constitutional rights had been violated. [9]

According to the distinguished historian, John Hope Franklin, the 1957 Civil Rights Act:

authorized the federal government to bring civil suits in its own name to obtain injunctive relief, in federal courts, where any person was denied or threatened in his right to vote. It elevated the civil rights section of the Department of Justice to the status of a division, with an Assistant Attorney General over it. It also created the United States Commission on Civil Rights, with authority to investigate allegations of denials of the right to vote, to study and collect information concerning legal developments constituting a denial of equal protection of the laws, and to appraise the laws and policies of the federal government with respect to equal protection. One senator had called the new law a "sham", while another called it "a limited and modest step." The real significance of this legislation lay not so much in its provisions as in its recognition of federal responsibility and its reflection of remarkable and historic reversal of the federal policy of hands-off in matters involving civil rights. [10]

Professor Franklin's assessment of a "remarkable and historic reversal of federal policy" is absolutely correct because, except for obdurate, recalcitrant, and obtuse senators and representatives from the South, most members of the United States Congress knew that the time had come for a change in the relationship between Blacks and whites in this country. And as Professor Franklin has pointed out in another section of his book, clearly changes taking place in other parts of the world affected the relationship between Blacks and whites in the United States. For instance, at this time a number of African states were gaining their independence, with whom the Black American population had made connections and who reciprocally took an interest in the racial relationships in this country. In the Caribbean as well, countries had begun to march toward independence, and the knowledge of their changing status had an effect on the psyche, perception, and cosmology of Black people in the United States. In addition, certain local situations made for change. The United Nations had been established in New York City. In the avenues and streets of the city, people of African ancestry who were not United States citizens were being allowed into hotels and cafes and restaurants where Blacks had hitherto not gone. While this might seem to be a minor matter, these people set an example for many Black people who had not ventured in these areas before and who now walked in with confidence and impunity. Hotel and restaurant owners knew also that no longer could they keep out the indigenous population if they were letting in people of similar ancestry from other parts of the world.

What is very important here also, and so easily forgotten, is that through the so-called Black organization—the National Association for the Advancement of Colored People, the National Urban League, the Congress of Racial Equality—increasing numbers of whites lent their support to the drive for establishing a new moral order in the United States. There was something in the air, something uplifting, something spiritual, something moving, something that clearly Thomas Curran and Carmine DeSapio were incapable of feeling.

In the same year that Eisenhower presented his bill to Congress there had also been a March on Washington, reminiscent of the projected March on Washington of 1941 that did not come off, but the threat of which had forced President Roosevelt to sign Executive Order 8802 outlawing discrimination in those corporations that did work for the federal government. This March on Washington in 1957 is hardly ever referred to in the history books. But it did take place and may have affected Eisenhower's decision to send his Civil Rights Bill to Congress in that year.

Then, too, there was the question of Communism. Most white historians have treated the whole McCarthy era as a problem for the white population only, without any reference at all to what effect it had upon the Black population and the relationship between Blacks and whites. What is generally not noticed is that at the height of the McCarthy anti-Communist campaign, the Communists made much political capital out of presenting to the rest of the world the fact that in these United States Negroes were just as oppressed as they (had been) during the time of slavery. Learned, intelligent, and progressive whites knew that this would not do, because since the beginning of the Cold War the United States had been waging a campaign throughout the world to influence the hearts and minds of people positively towards the United States. It was the time of the ugly American, and Americans became uglier to people abroad the more they acted in an immoral and un-Christian manner in contradiction to that Constitution of which they were so proud.

Because of this, even Eisenhower, who certainly was not progressive, as President, with his advisors, realized that certain perceptions abroad about the country could not be allowed to go unchecked around the world, and was forced to do something. Thus Negroes throughout the country felt not as alone as we had previously but more and more a part of the world community. The isolated feeling in which we had spent all these years as a group entrapped in these United States without the power to fend for ourselves in the way we wished, had now fallen away. We believed, as did the young Martin Luther King, that the eyes of the world and God were upon us and that in some near future we would overcome. These feelings certainly were not felt by Carmine DeSapio or Thomas Curran, and so they continued in their traditional ways, oblivious to the changing times and manners, and to the deluge that would soon engulf them.

What I have just said I was not entirely aware of in 1958, but I knew something of it and I could sense, without knowing exactly why, that the Adam Clayton Powell campaign was not just a campaign against Carmine DeSapio and Tammany Hall, but a campaign to set a new tone in the politics of New York City. We knew from the large number of whites and Republicans who came to our aid that vast changes were in the wind. Yet, despite the new feeling of confidence that elevated us to a sense of near-euphoria, we knew all too well of traditional politics and we knew of the skullduggery that was possible. We were aware that our opponents might also sense the change and therefore resort to drastic measures. We were very careful in selecting those who spoke for us, and in the choice of those to gather petitions in our name. To placate people we distrusted and yet encourage them to feel they were a part of our organization, we gave each a list of signatures to obtain. When they returned we asked each to sign their petitions, witnessed by our petition lawyers, and when they left, we put their petitions in a dead file. This we had to do to prevent a critical number of petitions from being found defective to enable the Board of Elections to rule us guilty of "permeation of fraud." We also made sure that, once gathered, the petitions were to be filed on time and in accordance with every nuance of the petitions law. In this way we prevented these little-known subterfuges that can prevent a candidate's name from appearing on the ballot.

In 1958 we felt far more secure than we had been in the 1930s, but because of one's experience, one could not ever be too certain. I recall, for example, when I was working at the Board of Elections in the late 1930s, there was an election that pitted one established Irishman against an insurgent. In those days the insurgents always tried to file their petitions at the very last moment to avoid their being examined in time to be designated as "permeation of fraud." At that time the Board of Elections was in a building with elevators that usually closed around 5:00 p.m. The insurgents' messengers used to come piling in around 4:30 or a quarter to 5, barely beating the deadline and not allowing sufficient time for the petitions to be properly checked. In this instance, though, the ruling party was ready. Since they controlled the Board of Elections they cut off the elevators approximately an hour before the usual time. So the last petition messengers found no elevator service and others found themselves trapped between floors. They could not go up and they could not go down, and when they were finally released from their prison it was too late to file the petitions. We expected nothing as crude as this in 1958, but one could not be too sure of the creativity of Carmine and his group, who know everything that could be done in the bending of the laws.

As it turned out, we had done our job quite well because we had no problems with petitions. Possibly the boys in Tammany Hall knew that I was in charge and were afraid to do anything out of order, probably assuming that I knew more than I actually did. But getting on the ballot was only the first step. We had to carry the battle all the way to primary day, August 12th. To circumvent any last-minute surprises, we organized twelve poll-watching squads. We maintained telephone contact with them so that should word come in about a problem from one of our poll-watchers in any particular polling place, we could dispatch our squads to take care of the problem. We advised them of little tricks to watch for, for example, the use of sharp objects like rings, pen knives, and the like often used by opposing parties to render the ballots defective. Our precautions seemed to be unnecessary, however, because on primary day things proceeded in an orderly manner. Our fears were unfounded.

The campaign itself to defeat Tammany Hall was far more successful than could ever have been imagined. Earl Brown, who at the time we called "Look Down Brown" because of his penchant for not looking anyone directly in the eye, as Hulan Jack has pointed out, was indeed, a tired and sorry candidate. He was the worst person Tammany Hall could have picked to oppose Adam Clayton Powell. Brown seemed to be the epitome of a bossed person, unable to speak to a crowd, and, in consequence, his whole campaign was a sad scene.

But Powell rose to rhetorical and charismatic heights that Harlem had never seen before and probably will never see again. During the campaign Adam articulated in his person and his actions the long pent up frustrations and the unarticulated aspirations that had bubbled and seethed in the Black community for so long, and which this community now felt it would express one way or the other, even in the face of death. This was not a feeling that is characteristic of all Black people in Harlem. It had been expressed already in Montgomery, Alabama, and in Jacksonville, Florida, in Little Rock, Arkansas, and was to express itself even more fiercely before the end of the decade and into the next. Adam incarnated this burning desire for a sense of equality, these long pent up passions and frustrations, a willingness to let the world know by whatever means that as a people we would no longer be denied. Powell's incarnation of that desire held sway not just in Harlem but throughout the country. In Harlem Earl Brown became a symbol of the uncomplaining Black servant of the past whom no self-respecting Black could support. It was the end of an era.

The general election was anti-climactic, for there was no contest. The leaders of Tammany Hall realized what had taken place in the primaries and immediately announced their support of Adam in the general elections. Even Governor Averell Harriman and the rest of the state Party machinery came to Adam for support against Rockefeller and the Republican ticket. Despite Adam's support, Harriman lost, due to his own inability to campaign any better than Brown.

For myself, I had returned to politics at a most opportune time. I had retired from politics in 1953, one year before Brown v. the Board of Education decision. As I have said I did very little in the Presidential campaign of 1952, and nothing at all in the 1956 presidential election when Adam carried the ball in Harlem for Eisenhower. Thoroughly dissatisfied with the state of affairs of the Democratic party and politics in general in

New York City, I had let pass the 1957 mayoral elections. But I had not been unaware of what was taking place in Montgomery and what took place in Florida that same year, and I had viewed with increasing interest the treatment of Negroes in Arkansas and the behavior of President Eisenhower. My return to politics ostensibly was to help Adam Clayton Powell, but even now as I think about it, there must have been some awareness on my part that the times would change in such a way in the United States that the old politics would die, that what I had hoped for and had felt would not be possible for some time was now possible. The old politics were dying out and no longer could bosses, scoundrels and near criminals run the New York Democratic Party and the Black people in the city.

It is probable that the impulse to assist Powell was not as simple as it seemed to me then, but that there was something far more deep in my subconscious about which I was not really clear. As I think of it now, there must have been an intuitive feeling that these were the times for me as an individual and as a member of the Black Harlem community to return to work. If it had been otherwise, I would have returned once more to private life after the election of Congressman Powell, but instead I rejoined the Carver Club and without any pressure decided to run for the District Leadership the following year.

In this, Adam gave me all the help that could have been expected, and it came as a great satisfaction to me that all of those Harlem leaders who had sided with DeSapio against Powell and me in 1958 were defeated, with the exception of Hulan Jack. Adam's year might be 1958, but 1959 was mine and I knew that, with the Presidential election coming up the next year, sooner or later somebody would be in touch with me. Negroes were on the move throughout the United States. They were registering in increasing numbers, and a large part of the white population had now come to its senses and were supporting us. The election for the presidency could not be won by any white person without the Negro vote. As Theodore White was to point out later in his book, *The Making of the President, 1960*, "To ignore the Negro vote and Negro insistence on civil rights must either be an act of absolute folly or one of absolute miscalculation." White was right, as the Kennedy election showed, after which things could never be the same in these United States.

Chapter 6

From Harlem Leader to
Leader of Tammany Hall,
(1960–1964)

The presidential campaign of 1960

IN 1960, I was again in the turbulent
stream of Democratic politics. There were no quiet runs; everywhere there
were problems. After insuring a healthy victory for Adam Clayton Powell in
1958, my impulsive and compulsive colleague was already sniping at his
"good friend Ray." Of this, more later. In state politics we had lost the
governorship two years earlier, when Governor W. Averell Harriman, one of
nature's noble men, but a poor campaigner, had allowed himself to be
defeated by Nelson Rockefeller. In New York City, it was an open secret
that Robert Wagner, first elected Mayor in 1953, would run for a third time,
and it was just as well known that Carmine DeSapio and the other four
county leaders were thinking of adroitly dumping "His Honor." I was
cognizant of all these things and I had to think very carefully about my role
in Wagner's and the Party's future since I was now the Leader of Assembly
District 13 East, and a member of Tammany's Executive Committee.

It was known that I had been a long-time supporter of Wagner and in
1947 had become his Deputy Commissioner of Housing, a high post then
for a Black man in New York City. I would not forget either that when
Robert Wagner was Borough President of Manhattan in the early fifties, he
had called on me to find a Black person to be Commissioner of the Department of Water Supply. I knew of no one immediately, but I could not
let such an opportunity pass. To the uninformed, this post may seem

inconsequential, but it was indeed one of the most important in the City administration. It paid extremely well, controlled enormous power, and the perquisites, such as limousines and chauffeurs, were things coveted by the whites at the Engineering Club. To resolve the matter, I called an engineer I knew who was a well-known social worker with Catholic Charities. He promptly recommended Arthur Ford, a very bright young man who, because of his color, was employed in a minor position with the city. When I presented his credentials to the Borough President he exclaimed, "You've got a top man!" Indeed, I had; and so Ford became New York's first Black Commissioner of Water Supply. For such courageous acts, I respected and supported Robert Wagner.

In the early part of 1960, I focussed primarily on the Presidential elections but also kept an eye on matters that would affect my candidate for Mayor in 1961. As it happened, Congressman Adam Clayton Powell and I were delegates to the Democratic National Convention to be held in Chicago. Anyone trying to capture the Democratic nomination would have been foolhardy to ignore us in 1960. Adam, of course, was more important than I on the national scene, and his statements made national news regularly. There was no doubt about it: Adam Clayton Powell by 1960 was a folk hero to Blacks across the country, and the Democratic contenders knew it. To get Adam committed to a Presidential candidate, therefore, would be of great value, and they all wooed him intensely. Powell's early candidate, Senator Stuart Symington of Missouri, apparently had promised him something very important.[1] But Powell was shrewd enough to realize that if Symington had a chance, he was probably a third or fourth choice.

Since everyone was now wooing Adam, he needed an alibi, a good reason to keep in the good graces of the leading candidates, while not shifting his support from Symington. This alibi he found, without my knowledge, in me. The manner in which he did it was classic Powell. While apparently supporting Symington, Powell kept in contact with Sam Rayburn (Dem. Texas), the Speaker of the House, and when he was asked to support Lyndon Johnson, his answer went roughly as follows:

I would like to go with you, but you know I have just been through a campaign. My leader is J. Raymond Jones. I cannot go around him. I cannot afford to split my district in two. He and I worked together, and he and I have to go together. I have talked to him about the candidate. He has not made any commitment. He is still thinking about it, but I am working on him.

It was a classic stall, but I soon found out that not only was Powell using this ploy on the Johnson people, but also that Carmine DeSapio was using a variation on the same theme with the Kennedy group. Although DeSapio had suffered a number of setbacks beginning with his losing fight against Powell and me in 1958, he was still, in 1960, the New York County Leader, and his leverage was increased since it was widely held that he had the Democratic state chairman in his pocket. In addition, Carmine was, by virtue of his position, a Democratic National Committeeman. As the pressure increased, he avoided an early endorsement by telling the Kennedys that he wanted to move with a united, state organization, but that at the moment the Blacks were not in line. They were too significant a part of the party to be left out, he argued.

But although the ploy was working for Adam, it began to lose potency for DeSapio, for while the Kennedys courted him, they brought heavy pressure to bear in the counties around New York City and upstate. In a very short, time, they had outflanked the Old Guard of Eleanor Roosevelt and Herbert Lehman who were for Adlai Stevenson, and had gathered into their camp Charles Buckley and Stanley Steingut, the Bronx and Brooklyn County Leaders, and other powerful County Leaders around the state. Kennedy had worked around DeSapio, but could not do so with Congressman Adam Powell. He influenced too many votes outside New York City. They knew it and he knew it.

Adam's plea that "I can't go around my good friend Ray" soon brought about the logical result. Powell called me with the message that Rayburn, the Speaker of the House, wanted to see me, and of course, I went to see him, accompanied by my Congressman. At our meeting, the Speaker of the House was gracious and gentlemanly, but I had no illusions about him. I knew he was a Texan and that he had not distinguished himself in the cause of Blacks in Texas. But times were changing, and I was in Washington to make the most beneficial deal I could. I therefore adopted a pleasant and neutral posture and waited for the pitch. Adam departed immediately after the pleasantries, and "Mr. Sam," as he was called, said something like this: "Mr. Leader, I want to congratulate you on that splendid victory that you had. You know you've got a good boy, and I have a good boy. Lyndon is a good boy and Adam Powell is a good boy. What I want from you is a commitment as delegate to the convention to back my boy— you and Adam; and I will guarantee you right here and now that Adam Powell will be the chairman of the Labor and Education Committee when the Congress meets." I said, "Mr. Sam, you've got a deal." He stuck his hand out, we shook, and that was that.

To anyone observing the event, it would have seemed as if I had rashly and without meditation struck a dubious deal. Since at this time there was already a big groundswell for the Kennedys, why not join them? The smart money was already on Kennedy; the candidate had large sums of his own which his organization was spending with abandon. Besides being a very good-looking fellow, no doubt he would get a lot of the "charm vote." Yes, on the face of it I had made a weak deal. But at this stage I was not bargaining to be on a bandwagon. Adam and I could easily have done that. I had long reasoned that if we jumped on Kennedy's train early, what would we then be? Just two influential Negroes who might be rewarded with a few favors now and then. In this neither Powell nor I was interested. We acted on this assumption of Kennedy's winning, but no one could be certain of that. I had always figured Richard Nixon to be a mean and sneaky political infighter, and at the time I saw Sam Rayburn, I had already concluded that if Kennedy got the nomination, it would be a fifty-fifty election. As it turned out, I was on target. Kennedy's margin was infinitesimal, and although I am wary of the cliché that argues that Kennedy won because of the Black vote, it is difficult not to see it that way.

Win or lose then, the Kennedy option was never the most attractive. I thought that Lyndon Johnson had a long shot at the Democratic nomination, but in fact Johnson's possible candidacy was not overly important either. What was supremely important was that he was Rayburn's boy; therefore, in any eventuality Rayburn, being the Speaker of the House and a very formidable personality, could guarantee Powell's chairmanship of the Education and Labor Committee. It was only necessary to support Lyndon Johnson at the convention on the first ballot. If he won, we won. If he lost, we won. It was the kind of politics I preferred.

Immediately after our handshake, the Speaker pressed a button and a fellow came in. "Please take the Leader to Senator Johnson's office," Rayburn directed. When the young man took me in, Lyndon was walking to meet me at the entrance. He met me halfway, shook my hand and said, "Oh, you aren't short." I was not surprised by this because I knew he liked to give short people the business, and I had heard that he had poked fun at the New York leadership, which at that time had quite a number of short people. I was almost as tall as he and bigger in the shoulders, so I said, "You wanted short? You wanted pygmies?" at which he laughed loudly.

Soon, however, he was into his sales pitch. "Sit down," he said. "Make yourself comfortable. You smoke? Cigar? I am smoking," all this in one breath.

"A man of immense energy," I thought. I accepted a cigar and relaxed, and Lyndon began his speech. I took no notes, and it is, of course, impossible to recall that speech verbatim, but it went something like this:

"I know I am not the most popular man with your people despite the fact that I have done things that nobody else before me has done." Then he started reciting what he had done in the field of civil rights. "I can't convince your people that I am not a Southerner," he said. "I consider myself a Southwesterner, more Western than Southern." He went on along this line and then said: "I want your support. I need your support. Will you support me in the convention?"

I replied, "I have just pledged myself to Mr. Sam to support you."

"Thank you," he said, "I appreciate it. You will be hearing from me."

We shook hands again, and he walked with me to the door, where one of his aides took over and escorted me to Powell's office.

I enjoyed these visits to Rayburn's and Johnson's offices. These men, despite their past reputation, were becoming realists, and history has shown that my assessment of Lyndon Johnson was correct. There was no feeling on my part that these two men were carried away by their positions. They were not arrogant, at least not to me. I felt that a handshake would always seal a deal. It was also a joy to watch Lyndon go through his spiel, for I knew that by the time I had reached his office, Sam Rayburn had called him to give him the good news. If he hadn't, then something had gone mightily wrong, but when Johnson asked for my support, he was as earnest as a Texas Baptist preacher. It was a joy to watch him work.

I returned to New York that night and the very next day I received a telephone call from Ed Weizl, Johnson's New York lawyer, whom he later made a Democratic National Committeeman. Weizl informed me that Lyndon's top strategist, John B. Connally, the man who had masterminded Johnson's senatorial campaign in 1948, would like to see me the next day. This was fine with me, for I had made a deal and was ready to go to work.

I met with John Connally (later Secretary of the Navy and two- time governor of Texas) the following day at Weizl's apartment on Central Park South. He said that he knew we could help his man in New York, but asked what help we could give nationally. I advised him that we had connections with other Black people throughout the country, and since Adam was now the "political voice" of Black people there wasn't any doubt we could help LBJ. This was what he wanted to hear, for the possible image of Johnson as an anti-Negro Southerner was clearly on his mind. In the end we decided on a public relations campaign to sell Johnson as a Southwesterner and a supporter of civil rights. This could be done because Johnson's record was liberal when compared to that of his colleagues from the South. Connally liked the idea, and we agreed on a budget to put the plan into operation.

Immediately after the meeting, I telephoned my former executive secretary, Dr. J. Dayton Brooks, who at this time was working with Richard Daley, Mayor of Chicago. "Jay," I said, "I need you. We have a contract here." There was no hesitation on his part. He came the next week and we set up an agency we called the Holloway-Rand Agency, named after my wife and sister-in-law. The initial account was $25,000, which bought a lot more then than it does now, and with it we went to work. The operation was not complex. We did no polls or anything of that sort. Brooks simply researched Johnson's civil rights record and provided timely releases to the media in New York and around the country. This was not a very difficult assignment, for Johnson seemed positively liberal in 1960, since he had removed himself from the Southern Manifesto in 1956, had supported the Civil Rights Acts of 1957 and 1960, and had successfully distanced himself from the Southern segregationist bloc. As a result, we had no trouble promoting LBJ, and we reaped the rewards in many ways later.

An attempted bribe

Since I commanded some influence in 1960 and was closely associated with Robert Wagner and Adam Clayton Powell, it was inevitable that I would get a call from the Kennedy people. This summons came through the Mayor, who said Senator Kennedy would soon be in New York and would like to see me. Of course I agreed to see him and the meeting took place at a party at the Kennedy family's apartment on Park Avenue.

When I got to the apartment, it was filled with Kennedy supporters and, I suppose, potential supporters. I thought that they had me classified with the latter group, and very shortly my impressions were confirmed, for the candidate soon sought me out for a private chat. He told me that Adam Clayton Powell had told him that I was uncommitted, and before I could protest, the Senator informed me that he would make a good president for Black people, and went on with more of the usual. When he was through— and through it all, I kept thinking of the difference between his spiel and that of LBJ—I explained to John Kennedy that I was committed to Lyndon Johnson on the basis of his civil rights record. I told Kennedy that Adam was pledged also to Johnson, and explained to him that our commitments were for the first two ballots. At that John Kennedy gave me his famous smile, thanked me graciously, and moved on.

I should say at this point that I had been in politics long enough to know what that smile meant. It meant that the man felt certain of victory on the first ballot. I felt, too, that his chances were very good, for I knew of the awesome amount of money that was being spent in the primary campaign and the nearly overpowering effectiveness of his staff. And if there is such a thing as charisma, then there was no question that John Kennedy had it.

I went back to work for Lyndon Johnson, the Southwestern underdog, having decided to put the Kennedys aside until the convention, but Adam Powell and others would not have it so. About two weeks after the Kennedy party, Powell telephoned and asked me to meet a man named Sammie

Kaplan. I inquired about the subject of the meeting. "I don't know," said Powell, "but it is very, very important, Ray, very important that you meet him."

"All right," I told Powell, "I'll see the follow." This meeting was set for something like a week or so ahead.

A couple of days later I received a call asking me to meet with Robert Kennedy in the same apartment in the same building on Park Avenue where I had met his brother. My reaction was, "What is this? What does he want? I've told his brother where I stand." Although I was a bit surprised by this new invitation, I decided that it was better to find out what the younger brother had in mind.

At this point I had not made any connection between the two phone calls and the two projected meetings. It did not even dawn on me that they were to be two hours apart on the same day. I didn't connect them. On the appointed day, I went to see Samuel Kaplan, and it was the most horrible meeting I ever had with anyone. My mother had worked in a hospital in St. Thomas, and if there is anything that I find nauseating, it is hospital odor. As I walked into the room, the odor almost knocked me backward. The fellow was lying on his back in a bed, the dresser strewn with bottles of medication.

I hesitated, then began, "Is this . . . ?" He interrupted, "Yes, I am Kaplan." I said, "I am in the wrong room." To this he replied, "I will make this very short. I hear rumors that you are heading up a New York delegation to make a commitment to Senator Kennedy. Adam Powell says he will go along if you do, but can't afford to unless you do! You and Powell represent the Black vote. Since you defeated DeSapio, you are important. Some people recognize your importance, and here is a little something to show our appreciation." With that declaration, he handed me a blank check made out to me. "You can fill that in with six figures beginning with one," he said. These were his exact words. I was totally unprepared for this, so I said, "You haven't told me what I have to do for this." He said, "All you have to do is to announce that you and Powell will support John Kennedy at the convention." I said, "Thank you, but no thank you." With that I tore up the check, laid the pieces on his dresser and left him to his pills.

I was very angry with Kaplan, Kennedy, and Powell. If Kaplan had said, "Here is a package of $100 bills," the result would have been the same, but my reaction might have been different, because, with a check, it is an insult. If I were going to allow myself to be corrupted, I certainly would not be leaving the evidence lying around in the form of a cancelled check. I thought, as I walked away from Kaplan's hotel, that Kennedy's aides were the most arrogant and condescending lot I had seen in years. Obviously, they thought I was a fool who would allow myself to be bribed, and in such a stupid manner. So enraged I was by the whole sordid attempt, that when I reached Fifth Avenue in a righteous rage, oblivious to everything I stepped off the sidewalk and almost got run over.

Such a close brush with death sobered me. I had a little time before I was to see Robert Kennedy, so I found a cafe where I could sit and think things over. As I drank tea, I suddenly realized why Bobby wanted to see me within the hour. The realization shook me to my shoes. I was now angry at myself for not seeing the connection earlier, and thoroughly upset that I had allowed Powell to lead me into the situation in the first place. I decided that the day had not gone well, but I would end it on a clear note. With this resolution firmly in mind, I walked up to the Kennedy apartment.

The Robert Kennedy I met that day did not impress me favorably, as his brother had. My first impression of him during the brief pleasantries was of a steely, hard-nosed, and merciless character. Ambitious in the extreme, I thought, and ruthless too. That was my impression then, even before many people began to discuss it. As Bobby talked, my initial impressions deepened. His brother, he said confidently, would win the nomination on the first ballot. They had the votes. He only wanted to see me because Adam and I were holding up DeSapio's decision. This was an important matter which needed to be settled. Almost as an afterthought he added that of course to have the support of Powell and me would assist with the Negro vote.

As revolted as I was with the whole attempt to bribe me, I thought as I listened to Robert Kennedy, how different he and Kaplan were compared to Sam Rayburn and Lyndon Johnson. I thought how real and human were Ed Weizl and John Connally and how machine-like this little fellow before me was.

I was tired by now, so I said: "Bobby, evidently you were not told that I had met with your brother, that I like the Senator tremendously, but I have a previous commitment to Lyndon Johnson whom we will go with for the first and second ballot. After that we will be happy to support your brother." He replied, "So nothing has happened in the interim to change your mind?" I smiled and said, "No, Bobby, nothing has," and I emphasized "nothing has." With that I walked out of his presence. I could see his eyes as I turned, and I knew then that I had made myself an enemy, a mortal enemy.

Subsequent events proved my impression to be correct, for as soon as Robert F. Kennedy became the junior Senator from New York, he seized the first opportunity he could to try and discredit me. This occurred over the selection of candidates for the Surrogate Courts, of which more later, but here it might be said that Robert Kennedy, in my opinion, craved power more strongly than his brother, the President. Anyone who stood in his way, he regarded as an enemy. The desire to impose his will, to reshape the political landscape to his conception, was not to be interfered with by anyone, and while he presented a pious and almost ascetically saintly front to the public, those of use who knew him better realized that here was a Kennedy more in the mold of a conquistador than Jack Kennedy could ever have been. Recent books on the Kennedys seem to be proving me right.

On returning home, I was greeted by the insistent ringing of the telephone. Wearily picking it up, I heard the voice of Congressman Powell, full of bonhommie and good cheer. "Well, Ray, what happened? How did it go?" At first, I wanted to say something unspeakable, but I knew without thinking that such a response would have no effect on Adam, and furthermore, I was by then so exhausted that I merely said, "Nothing happened, Adam, nothing." "Nothing?" he asked incredulously. "Nothing?" "Nothing," I replied. He soon got the message that something unpleasant must have taken place and that I did not want to talk about it. I didn't, for there was nothing to be gained by spreading this story around without proof, when the Kennedys were riding so high. I would have been called a liar and an opportunist, and more important, such a revelation coming from me would surely negatively affect my constituents and friends in New York in some way. It was, therefore, impolitic to say anything. So, I didn't. One thing I knew; Bobby Kennedy would not soon forget me; nor I, him.

Between these events and the convention, I, J. Dayton Brooks, and our group did the best we could for Lyndon Baines Johnson. We knew by convention time that he was a long shot, and when we arrived at the convention it was clear that Kennedy would be nominated on the first ballot, which he was. The question now was, "Who shall have the vice-presidency?" I had thought that it logically belonged to LBJ, for the obvious reason, a balanced ticket. But not everyone saw it that way. As soon as the word was out that Johnson was being considered, a peculiar thing happened: I found myself surrounded by a large number of Negro delegates from the Midwest. They argued that Lyndon Johnson was no good, that I was no longer bound to him, since the balloting for the Presidential nomination was over. "But," I protested, "the Democratic Party seems ready to go for him." "Who cares?" said one. "We represent labor, and Walter Reuther doesn't like him." I was surprised by this reasoning; but as I looked around at the number of Black faces, it was clear to me that "labor" had more Black delegates at this convention than any other entity did. This realization came as such a surprise that while the delegates milled around me arguing, I stood still on the floor and pondered it all.

As a New York Democrat, District Leader, and member of Tammany's Executive Committee, I already knew that in New York, "labor" played a heavy role in politics. But that was always balanced by ethnic concerns for Jews, Blacks, Italians, and the Irish. In addition, there were always other interest groups that I called the "ideologues," that is, "reform Democrats," "conservative Democrats," and my group, the "regular Democrats." Because of all these groups contending (the women's bloc had not yet entered the ring), I had come to think in terms of them only. I had not given too much thought to the national scene except in improving the relationship between Blacks and others, thereby improving also Black political status. I was unaware of the swift rise to power of the "labor movement" within the Democratic Party nationally, and I resolved there and then to take a closer look into this matter when I returned to New York. Surely, something positive could be made of this.

As it turned out, the large gathering of Black labor delegates around me had the opposite effect from what they intended. Quite a few of the reporters there knew who I was and that I was a Johnson man. They and the Johnson floor managers also knew that my colleague, J. Dayton Brooks, had coined the phrase "All the way, with LBJ." The reporters, seeing this cluster of Blacks arguing, thought a story was in the making and rushed over. The Johnson people, seeing this move and spying me in the middle, reacted beautifully. They too rushed over, herded the TV boys towards me and prompted me to say that I was "All the way with LBJ." The other fellows were not asked anything, because it appeared as if I were speaking for the group. When the picture appeared, it looked as if a large number of Black people were for LBJ. Very sneaky it is true, but legitimate and good fun.

In retrospect, I have been pleased with my support of Lyndon Johnson. It is generally accepted today that Johnson lacked the social graces of John Kennedy, that he was a country bumpkin and, at times, very crude. But his lack of polish was not my concern. I had sensed in my conversation in his Senate office that Lyndon Johnson had, by the spring of 1960, undergone a spiritual conversion. It was my impression that he wanted to be President so that he could make himself one of a kind, an even larger figure than FDR, his hero, and I perceived a genuine desire to break out of the straitjacket of being a Southerner. To do this, he would have to deal positively with the problem of race relations. I thought then that if anyone could alleviate that problem, it would have to be a Southerner and one of more than ordinary stature. Who else but Johnson? Though I was less than elated that he received only the Vice-Presidential nomination, I convinced myself that he would have some influence on John Kennedy. It appears as if I was not too correct in this, but I would like to think that he tried. No one can say that when his time came, however tragic the circumstances, Lyndon Johnson did not do all he could to assist Black people and to improve racial relations in America. No President before (or since) tried as hard and made such substantial and lasting contributions in the field of civil rights for all people, including women, Blacks, and whites. For these achievements alone, I am certain he greatly surprised the skeptical labor delegates, for in the 1964 convention, I did not hear a single Black labor voice raised against my man. I consider LBJ one of our greatest presidents.

During the campaign, I was asked to do advance work for the ticket, mostly in the northern states. This job, although routine, was not lacking in stress and tension, for when my co-worker, Adam Powell, was in the neighborhood, tension was raised to theatre, if not high drama. At one point, I was in Los Angeles to coordinate the effort to sway a large Black ministerial convention taking place there. The chief presenter of the ticket would be Adam Clayton Powell. Fortunately for the Democratic ticket, Dr. Martin Luther King, Jr., chose this time to get arrested again. Although because of the new party platform Kennedy and the Democrats were now perceived by an increasing number of Blacks as considerate of the Negro vote, a significant segment of Black America was still supporting Nixon. It was decided by the Kennedys that Robert Kennedy, the campaign manager, would try to get King out of jail and, if successful, Congressman Adam Clayton Powell would break the news at the Black Baptist ministers' convention in Los Angeles before this news was broadcast nationally.

All of this required delicate timing, for Adam was to appear before the ministers at a certain time and there was no guarantee that King's release would be effected before the Reverend Powell was scheduled to speak. The decision to try this ploy had been made the previous day, and as the hour approached and no "go" signal came from Kennedy headquarters, Powell became so nervous he left his connecting suite without telling me where he was going. A few minutes before the appointed time, the call came to me from the Kennedys. King was not yet out of jail but would be within the hour. The question now was, What's best to do? I rushed into the adjoining suite to persuade Powell to begin his speech to the ministers' convention, hoping that before it ended, we could slip him the good news. But, of course, he was not there.

What happened next was very comical. While we searched for Powell, we had to find someone of stature to substitute for him and there was no one in the hotel of great stature other than the distinguished but very stiff former governor of New York, Averell Harriman. The governor, the good soldier to the core, agreed to give a prefatory speech until Adam could be found. I could not accompany him as I was directing the search for the missing Reverend and waiting for the call. I heard later that Governor Harriman did his nervous best, under the dubious stares of the Black ministers. Someone said that toward the end, Harriman did indeed, break out into a sweat and that when Adam finally showed up, the Governor looked like a man rescued from drowning. Fortunately, for all of us, the word came from Robert Kennedy at about the same time Powell was brought back to the suite, and off we rushed to deliver the news and rescue the beleaguered Governor. When we entered the conference room, there was instant excitement, and Harriman gave us such a look of relief that it stays in my memory even now.

Quite the opposite were the emotions of the Reverend Congressman Adam Clayton Powell, Jr.: he was in his element. Not only was he going to drop a bombshell, but these were his people. He was, with no exaggeration, levitated. I knew this the moment he struck a portentous pose and said, "Gentlemen." There was a pause and a hush, and then he said in Biblical and prophetlike tones:

I bring you tidings of great joy. I have just talked to Robert Kennedy and he has informed me that Martin Luther King is free. I tried to arrange for him to talk to you on the telephone, but I am sorry to say that we were unable to arrange it.

Although Adam was greatly stretching the truth of his role, it didn't matter much, for with such introduction, he could not miss. He outdid himself that day, and we could see, as Adam soared, quite a number of these dignified men of the cloth surreptitiously removing Nixon buttons from their lapels and putting them out of sight.

With Mayor Wagner against the bosses

Although Kennedy and Johnson won by a thin margin in 1960, the inauguration was anything but thin, and I attended in high spirits. However, my euphoria was soon severely undermined. In one of my strolls around the ballroom, I noticed early in the evening four of my New York colleagues sitting at a table with their heads close together. Immediately, my political radar sent me a warning, for the four were Tammany Leader Carmine DeSapio, Stanley Steingut, the Kings County Leader, Charles Buckley, the Bronx County Leader, and Arthur Levitt, Comptroller of the State of New York and one of the foremost vote-getters of the Democratic party. This get-together confirmed in my mind the rumors I had heard that there was a movement among certain leaders to reject Bob Wagner for mayor in 1961. I had known, since the summer of 1960, that the majority of the county leaders in New York were not happy with Mayor Robert Wagner. To them he was too independent and much too liberal. He had committed the sin of being too much a man of the people and was perceived as above party discipline. To Carmine and his group, this was heresy. Seeing the very popular Levitt with them, I reasoned that no other conclusion could be drawn but that he would be a candidate.

On returning to New York, I called the Mayor. "Bob," I said, "the boys are going to dump you, and the candidate I think will be Arthur Levitt." "How do you know this?" the mayor replied. "I saw them together at the inauguration of the President and they were not having a casual conversation. Their heads were together; they were very serious and their voices were muted."

After a moment of silence the Mayor said, "Are you going to be with me?" and I said, "Yes, I am." I don't know what the Mayor thought of my response then, and I never asked him, but after the campaign I was made to feel by gestures here and there, great and small, that my stand at this treacherous time meant a great deal to him.

The announcement of Carmine DeSapio about two weeks after the inauguration came as no surprise to us. In fact, despite the problems it would cause the Mayor and his supporters, I regarded the way in which Carmine did it as good theatre. He convened a meeting in a New York hotel of all the County Leaders, tipped off the press, and then, after a suitable suspenseful wait, he emerged with all the other leaders, to stand together like a phalanx and announce their candidate for mayor, Arthur Levitt. I am sure that this display of solidarity was intended to convince New York voters that the odds were overwhelmingly against the Mayor, and no doubt, they themselves were convinced of their own invincibility. Nonetheless, I saw the gesture as a serious political mistake, for it gave the impression, which we later exploited, of a bunch of Politburo "bosses" announcing who would be the next Secretary General. In any event, I was now relieved that the word was out and the battle lines were drawn.

Soon after this, when the mayor decided to set up his primary campaign organization, he called and invited me to a strategy meeting. He didn't say during his call what role he wanted me to play. But to be prepared, I asked Daniel Flynn to accompany me.

I have stated earlier that in a primary campaign, petitions are the most important element. Therefore, a skilled petitions person is, or was in the sixties, a very key individual. I thought I had some expertise in that area and so did my petitions' lawyer of many years, Daniel Flynn.

When I arrived, the group was already discussing petitions, because it was the first item on the agenda. Paul Screvane, the candidate for President of the City Council, had someone he thought was competent and was pushing his man. When my turn came to speak, I said I would have to think hard about working in a campaign in which I was not certain of the individual who would handle this critical job. I asked permission then to present my associate, Daniel Flynn, with whom I would be willing to work on petitions.

At this point I was not angling for the petitions job in the campaign, and I certainly was not looking for a position of power. I was thinking, however, that this was going to be a mean-spirited and no-holds-barred primary since we were fighting the united might of the leaders of Tammany and the other county organizations; therefore, everything had to be done perfectly. The Mayor, I think, knew that Daniel Flynn and I were the best petitions team, but adroit as ever, he decided not to make the decision himself. The manner in which he solved the problem speaks volumes of Robert Wagner's political touch.

There was a judge before whom Flynn and I had had a few appearances on petitions business. He was a Democrat, a friend of Wagner's, and an expert on political issues. I don't know how the Mayor arranged it, but while I was talking, this judge walked in and Wagner said to him, "We are talking about petitions and petitions men." The answer was prompt. "You have the best one sitting right there," he said, pointing to me. After this there was no more discussion on that issue, for political authority and legal expertise had spoken. The job was ours.

Within days, the Wagner people and I had the outlines of how the campaign should be handled. They agreed with me to emphasize the Wagner name and its identification with labor. We invoked the Mayor's father and the memory of the Wagner Labor Relations Act. We emphasized the personality of Robert Wagner, a simple, pleasant fellow, a man of the people and a hard worker. Levitt, of course, had nothing like this going for him although he was indeed a formidable vote-getter. In fact, the labor unions loved the slant of the campaign. Even Mike Quill, head of the powerful Transport Workers Union, a fellow as suspicious and wary of politicians as one can get, and later Mayor Lindsay's nemesis, gave us great support. The Hatters Union contributed workers. All segments of labor assisted, as well as a number of District Captains who did not follow their District Leaders in support of Levitt.

From all these districts, individuals volunteered for collecting petitions. A number of people were also lent by the Liberal Party, but I trusted no one at first sight. I checked every worker in every way possible. I was determined that we would collect far beyond the number of petitions required and, at the right time, demoralize the opposition with the size of the results. I was even more determined not to have my candidate bothered by any hint of petition irregularities. This was J. Raymond Jones and Danny Flynn at work, and no foolishness would be tolerated.

To ensure that everything possible was done to escape Murphy's Law, we set up headquarters in an Astor Hotel suite. In one room, a map of the five counties of New York City was hung on the walls. I had a code of yellow, red, blue, and pink pins on this map indicating what level of success we were having in every district. This room was always locked, whether I was in or out. In it I checked petitions and changed my pins as needed. But no pin was actually moved until petitions were double-checked by the indefatigable Daniel Flynn, who was also locked up, in an adjoining room. When we were satisfied, we tallied the petitions, moved pins, and put the petitions in the hotel safe. It was very hard work, and a number of nights Flynn slept in that room with the petitions, because we were determined to give our opponents the surprise of their political lives.

At the top of this team were Ed Kavanaugh, the nominal campaign manager, Julius C. C. Edelstein, the Mayor's Deputy for public relations, and me. It was a great team, for none of us was a prima donna and each was also aware that we were in a fight for our political lives. This awareness became more evident each day, not because of our opponents' actions, but rather because of a group that was supposed to be on our side, the Reform Democrats.

The philosophical leaders of the Reformers were Herbert Lehman and Eleanor Roosevelt, strong supporters of Wagner. However, early on, we noticed that although the Reformers were supposed to be gathering petitions, we, at the Astor, had not seen any of theirs the first or the second week. During those two weeks, leaders of this reform group were continually calling Wagner, seeking commitments for patronage in exchange for their support. Although they were professors of a new morality, they were playing the old political game. It soon became clear to us that certain members of the Reform group were not working in the spirit of their two eminent leaders.

In order to protect ourselves from the possible disaffection of the Reform group, we simply avoided asking them for their petitions, while the Mayor goodnaturedly refused to make any commitments. In the meantime, Reform leaders sought to persuade Lehman and Mrs. Roosevelt that our group, the "Astor Team," was not competent. The idea was to put pressure on the Mayor to turn the campaign over to them. We could hardly fault their conclusions because Flynn and I always at day's end reported the number of petitions we had gathered at approximately fifty percent less. We gave out this false information not primarily to discombobulate the Reformers, although we did not trust them, but more to lull Levitt, De-Sapio and the rest of that gang into a false sense of security. In the end, though, we wanted to show the Reform group that the "Astor Team" could put the Mayor on the ballot and have him win the primary and the election without them. They had too long been a political thorn in the side of the Democratic Party and they had to be pulled down from their high horses.

The day we comfortably exceeded the required number of petitions, we notified the "Reform" group, but we warned them that unless we had their petitions in ample time for review, we would not use them. This was very important, because to present dual petitions for a candidate automatically nullifies both petitions. This had already been decided by the courts. I did not want to be burned again with the problems of Section 135 of the election laws, which required the consecutive numbering of petitions. If the Reform group's petitions were to be used, then we had to do a careful job of collation. The certain knowledge that they were no longer vital to the campaign caused an instant change in their behavior. Immediately their petitions poured in, and it took Daniel Flynn and two other attorneys several long hours to put the entire package together.

Although petitions were my primary responsibility, I was also responsible for Harlem, for in that quarter Congressman Adam Clayton Powell had switched sides again, and was back once more on the plantation of Tammany Chief, Carmine DeSapio. Adam's defection at this critical juncture was mystifying. After all, I, if not Wagner, had assisted him greatly in 1958. In 1959 we had both been elected District Leaders without Tammany help, and in 1960 Adam, Wagner, and I worked closely together to elect John F. Kennedy. Furthermore, he and I had had no major misunderstandings. So what was the problem? I could not formulate any reasonable scenario, so I decided early in August not to worry about it.

By mid-August Congressman Powell not only restated his support for Arthur Levitt's entire ticket, which included State Senator Thomas J. Mackell, candidate for President of the City Council, and Joseph F. DiFede, candidate for City Controller, but announced his own slate in Harlem. This included the Reverend Oberia Dempsey, the associate minister at Powell's own Abyssinian Baptist Church. This Dempsey ran against Herbert B. Evans, my candidate in the 21st District. All this was unfortunate for Adam, but, worse, he supported John J. Merli, a friend of Carmine DeSapio, against another candidate of mine, Robert A. Low, in the 2nd District, part of which covered Central and East Harlem.

This move was very unwise, as the demographics of East Harlem and the Yorkville area had changed drastically since the 1950s. The area had become far more Black and Puerto Rican than Italian, and to support an Italian for City Council in this area seemed to me political suicide. In addition, Powell supported this same John J. Merli and his Co-Leader, Mrs. Ida Valesi, against Carlos Rios, a Puerto Rican, and his Co-Leader, Mrs. Henrietta Brown, a Black, for District Leader in the 10th Assembly District North. I did not know what prevailed upon Adam Powell to support this ticket, but in looking it over I thought he had clearly retreated from reality, because even if the Wagner ticket were to lose, such a ticket in Harlem could not possibly win.

This concern for ethnicity was apparent in the fine manner both tickets were nicely balanced. Wagner, who many people thought was of German origin, but who actually was of Austrian-Irish ancestry, was joined on his ticket by Paul Screvane for President of the City Council, Abraham Beame for Controller, and in Manhattan Edward Dudley for Borough President. Although Paul Screvane's name might suggest something French or maybe even Anglo-Saxon, his real name originally was Scrivani, and everybody in New York City knew it. Apart from his other credentials, he appealed to the Italian block. Abraham Beame was a Jew, and everybody knew that too, and as for the Borough President candidate, Edward Dudley, a Black, would bring in the Black vote.

Wagner's nominal campaign chairman, Ed Cavanaugh, Jr., reinforced the Irish vote just in case Wagner's mixed ancestry could not do it. On the Levitt side there was State Senator Thomas J. Mackell, the candidate for City Council President, an Irishman; balancing that for the Italians was Joseph F. DiFede. Arthur Levitt, a Jew, would bring in the Jewish votes.

Since ethnicity played such a great role in New York City politics, inevitably sooner or later charges of bigotry, racism, and ethnic discrimination would fly. And on September 1, six days before the primary, Arthur Levitt accused our campaign of being anti-Semantic. According the *New York Times*, "Mr. Levitt said that reports had been confirmed that six hundred sanitation department employees, campaigning in Queens, were using the argument that 'a victory for Levitt will leave a Jew to run against a Jew'."

The *Times* continued that, "Mr. Levitt called upon former Senator Herbert H. Lehman, leader of the anti-Tammany faction and a strong supporter of Mayor Wagner, to denounce and repudiate 'these racist tactics.' One of Mr. Lehman's associates reported that Mr. Lehman was so outraged by the Levitt charges that he did not trust himself to make immediate comment."[2]

This charge by Arthur Levitt was, it seemed to me, too calculated and most explosive because, although Abraham Beame, a Jew, was on our ticket, he was not in the top slot. Levitt, however, filled the top spot on his ticket. Furthermore, Levitt released photographic copies of the anti-Semantic pamphlets supposedly distributed in Queens, but these were unattributable, and I knew from my own position within the campaign that we had not put out any such literature, and that we had directed nothing of the kind to be distributed. To do such a thing would have been insane and suicidal.

In view of the gravity of the charges, Wagner's response was relatively low-key. He merely commented that he would match his record on civil liberties and civil rights with anyone else and characterized Levitt's charge as one of desperation.[3] But Edward F. Cavanagh, Jr., our campaign manager, was fit to be tied. Such allegations were like raising a red flag in front of an enraged bull. To him, Mr. Levitt had "evilly resorted to poison gas and hydrogen bomb warfare against our citizen's souls and their faiths."

"Never again," the *New York Times* reported him as saying, "will this stupid, frantic and frustrated man have an opportunity to stand up in the great theatre of this city and cry 'Fire!' " Rising to a crescendo, Cavanagh finished,

Decent people will judge him and his conspirators as the demons and depraved maniacs that they are, . . . and they shall reap the just reward of the damned. They have gone beyond the point of no return.[4]

Things were heating up to normal, because Ed's furious enfilade predictably brought out the Irish in Levitt's campaign manager, Daniel V. Sullivan. Returning very heavy fire, he said:

Instead of condemning and repudiating religious bigotry, Cavanagh turns his vitriol on those who expose it. Cavanagh does not choose to remember that we, Irish Catholics, have been victimized by these 'hate techniques' time and time again—in fact, as recently as the last Presidential elections.[5]

Mr. Sullivan was referring to the problem John F. Kennedy faced in 1960, when many Protestants had voiced concern about his Catholicism. Many thought that if Kennedy were elected President, then the Pope would have too much influence in this country. Kennedy, of course, had met the problem head-on by meeting with various Protestant ministers, particularly the Baptist leadership, forcing them to back down. The moment I heard all these charges from the Levitt camp, I knew things would be easier for us, even though during the last week of the campaign, the betting odds were steeply against us. Charges like these, against a man like Wagner, were simply stupid, for one could literally look at the man and sense his extraordinary decency. Such outrageous tactics would not yield any profits for our opponents.

As the campaign heated up towards the last few days of the primary, so did the temperature. The *New York Times* reported that the temperature on Saturday had been 95 degrees, Sunday 88 degrees, and that for Monday, September 4, it was expected to be 90 degrees. On that day, knowing that his charges of anti-Semitism were stymied, Levitt shifted his attack, accusing the Mayor of "weakness, incompetence, and indecision."[6]

These charges were weak, too late, and too shop-worn, and so we ignored them. More interestingly, on the same day Levitt accused the mayor of weakness, incompetence, and indecision, he made the mistake of saying that if he won the election in November, he would be "the only boss in New York City."[7] This silly statement caused cheer and gloating in the Wagner camp, because we knew that we would not have to make any response; others would do it for us. Indeed, the very next day, as expected, the *New York Times*, in its traditional preprimary editorial, had the following to say:

This newspaper finds no reason to alter the opinion it expressed on August 21 that Mayor Wagner should be supported for renomination next Thursday in the Democratic primary. This is not because Mayor Wagner's administration had been free from defects and scandals. In spite of some sound accomplishments, especially in his first term, the Mayor has not exercised a sufficiently vigilant control over some of his subordinates. One thing, however, he has done. He has declared his independence of Tammany Hall and such party bosses as DeSapio, Buckley and Sharkey. He might have taken this step sooner than he did. A political accident, rather than an excess of virtue pushed him into it. But because of this accident, he did take the step, and he is now clearly free of the old club house control.[8]

All this was to the good, and although I was always wary of the *New York Times*, yet what it had to say next thoroughly delighted me.

Mr. Levitt can make no such claim. He is an admittedly honest and able man who declared as recently as last Sunday: "If I am elected, there will be a boss in the City of New York and the boss will be its Mayor.' But we believed that Messrs. DeSapio, Buckley and Sharkey will have altogether too much to say in the operations of the city administration, if Mr. Levitt is elected.[9]

Levitt's accusations against Wagner, and his protestation that, if he were elected, he would be the only boss of New York City, showed that his campaign to be hopelessly hysterical. Despite the polls and despite the smart money, I now knew that we would win.

As expected, we got good news on Friday, September 8. Our candidates for the top spots of Mayor, Controller, and President of City Council outscored the opposition in all the five boroughs. In no borough did the Tammany leadership show winning strength. Nowhere was the race even close. In Manhattan, Wagner outpolled Levitt approximately 122,000 to 47,000, and citywide it was Wagner, 451,458 to Levitt, 291,672. Both Beam and Screvane had large pluralities and in Greenwich Village, Carmine DeSapio must have sensed that very soon his heyday would be over. Indeed, in November, he lost his District Leadership to James Lannigan and it was "Goodbye Carmine."

In my own bailiwick, Harlem, things were most interesting. In the 21st District where Herbert Evans, one of my people, ran against the choice of Tammany and Powell, the Reverend Oberia D. Dempsey, Evans won easily by a two-to-one margin. Robert A. Low, another Wagner candidate running in the 22nd District, defeated John J. Merli, in what was seen by some as an upset victory. Interestingly, in the 10th Assembly District, this same Merli also ran for the district leadership and both he and his co-leader, Mrs. Ida Valesi, lost disastrously to Carlos Rios and Mrs. Henrietta Brown. As the *New York Times* put it:

Mr. Merli's double defeat, plus the closeness of the leadership fight in East Harlem, involving representative Alfred E. Santangelo, appeared to signal the beginning of the end of the long political dominance by Italians in East Harlem politics. Puerto Ricans and Negroes now make up a majority of the population in the District. [10]

In this race Herman Badillo made his first big splash in East Harlem politics, running against Santangelo. Badillo's co-leader, Jacquelien Foster, outran Marie Lanzetta, Santangelo's co-leader. From this beginning Herman Badillo eventually emerged to become a congressman and later Koch's Deputy Mayor.

For myself, the *New York Times* had this to say:

In another bitter race, Mr. Jones and Mrs. Edrie Archibald, running on the Wagner line, triumphed easily over Tammany choices in the contest for the district leadership in the Thirteenth Assembly District East, in West Harlem. They beat Antonio Rasmus, clerk in the office of the Board of Elections, and Mrs. Elizabeth Barry by better than 4 to 1. Mr. Jones has been leader for the District for two years. [11]

The *Times* was properly perceptive in noting the importance of the close leadership race between Italians and Puerto Ricans in the 16th Assembly District South, as well as the defeat of John J. Merli and Ida Valesi, because, although it would be most desirable to eliminate ethnic politics in New York in 1961, the situation in West Harlem still reflected the domination of one ethnic group over another. When the ruling ethnic group refuses to show the proper concern for its constituents, then a most unhappy environment is created. This had been the case of Italian leadership in West Harlem for some time. The 1961 primary will ultimately be remembered as one in which profound changes were made, because Harlem finally moved closer to self-determination, for better or for worse, and certain elements of the white population could no longer take Black votes for granted.

September 8, 1961, therefore, was a banner day in my career, because practically all my expectations had been met. We had been in a bitter campaign and had triumphed against very long odds. We could now begin an administration, unencumbered by a reactionary group of people. We could do without people who no longer seemed to understand the changing political environment in New York City, and who, indeed, were beginning to give Tammany Hall the reputation for which it had been notorious in the 1920s.

The Mayor was jubilant after the primary; however, his unhappiness with the campaign charges of anti-Semitism tempered his joy. The charges were as unforgivable as the perfidy of the County Leaders. Barbara Carter, in describing Wagner's character in her book, *The Road to City Hall,* used the Mayor's performance during and after the primary as an example:

Take the 1961 election. The Democratic leaders were not too keen on Wagner. He already had broken with Tammany's famous Carmine DeSapio, and there were rumors of discontent in the ranks, rumors even of an effort to dump Wagner. Could he afford to alienate the other county leaders as well as DeSapio? Wagner's oft-quoted motto, handed down from his father, was "When in doubt, don't!" What was overlooked, however, was that the maxim had another side: "When not in doubt, do." And Wagner, no matter how shaky his position might seem, once his doubts were resolved, was like nothing so much as Macbeth's witch on the way to Aleppo: "And in a sieve I'll thither sail, and like a rat without a tail, I'll do, I'll do, I'll do."

Mayor Wagner was indeed "like a rat without a tail," because he did and did and did, and Carter's description is worth quoting:

He rode through to a smashing victory, and went on to win the election, without, it should be noted, incurring too much debt to the Reformers, whose local leaders, by election time, had fallen down on the delivery of the vote. But victory was not enough for Wagner. Indeed, before the primary month was out, moving men had unceremoniously put their dollies under DeSapio's desk at Tammany Hall and wheeled it away. For DeSapio had lost his minor post as District Leader in the primary to a reformer and on it rested, upside down, the pyramid of his power. Later judgements would decide that DeSapio had never really been as powerful or as shrewd as he had been pictured. In his hopeless attempts afterwards to regain his post, all that remained to him was his natural grace under pressure. Nothing became him so much as defeat. After DeSapio fell, the county leader of Staten Island was quickly dismissed, but Wagner was still not through. There was yet Brooklyn, Queens, and the Bronx, and the day after the election Wagner announced that Sharkey, Koehler, and Buckley would have to go—and Michael Prendergast, the state chairman, as well. And go they did, all but the late Charles A. Buckley, who not only had ties to President Kennedy but had learnt to master, better than DeSapio, the New York game of staying afloat with no visible means of support. It was, all in all, a pretty thorough affair.[12]

The campaign that followed the primary was for me, routine, lacking the drama of the primary fight. Although it was exciting to be part of a winning team, I had not lost sight of my priorities. If I had, Adam Powell would have been there to remind me in many ways, positive and negative. For me, the prominent part I had played in the Wagner victory was a victory for Black people and for the people of New York. I expected no great rewards for myself, but others thought otherwise, chief among them my friend, Dr. Kenneth Clark, distinguished Professor of Psychology at the City University of New York. He decided to lead a committee dedicated to engineering my election as Tammany Leader. To Kenneth Clark, I had impeccable credentials since I had had no scandals in my past and had been one of the first persons of some influence to break with the "Bosses" in early 1961.

Clark and his group thought that the Reform Democrats would support my candidacy because of my credentials. In this they were mistaken, for as reported to me later, Lehman told them that he did not know me very well, and furthermore, I was not counted among Reform Democrats. Such a response I would have expected, for support in politics seldom results from appeals to conscience. Lehman certainly knew of my work but he was correct in saying he did not know me. The point is that people are always more supportive of the individual they know intimately.

Appeals to conscience and fair play also motivated two groups of New York City ministers to exhort Mayor Wagner on my behalf. I was not privy to their deliberations, but the *Amsterdam News* quoted from the first group's telegram thus.

He has given 40 years of dedicated leadership both to the Democratic Party and to the community which he has nobly represented. . . . It will be a miscarriage of justice . . . to bypass Mr. Jones because he happens to be a Negro.[13]

This telegram was signed by the Reverend Dr. C. S. Stamps and the Reverend Melvin De W. Bullock, leaders of the Baptist Ministers Conference of Greater New York. The second group's letter was in a similar vein, but these ministers were from several denominations. On the one hand, I was pleased to see that after forty years of hard work, there was popular sentiment in Harlem and indeed among Black New Yorkers that I be considered. Such actions had been part of my dream in the 1920s because I was convinced that the times and the manners would eventually change in America. When this happened I was determined to be prepared for larger opportunities and responsibilities, and I wanted my community to be as prepared as I was. So I was gratified by the efforts of people like Dr. Clark and the ministers, but I knew that within practical politics, things are never as simple as they seem.

The combined might of the Reform elements was much too powerful in the fall of 1961 for petitions on my behalf to prevail, so Judge Samuel Rifkin, who had been the law clerk to the Mayor's father in 1927 but who was now a distinguished jurist, and partner in a very powerful law firm, was asked to serve temporarily while an acceptable candidate could be found. Rifkin served for a short period, and in the end a compromise was made to elect Edward Costikyan, a young lawyer in Rifkin's law firm. Costikyan was chosen simply because he was not a Regular Democrat, and neither was he a Reformer. Indeed, he was not so much a compromise choice as he was the product of a stalemate. Since the party had now fractured itself into what could be called Reform Democrats, Regular Democrats, and "Bossed" Democrats, it would have been very difficult for anyone who was vividly identified with any of the first two groups to be elected. As for the last group, they were now beyond the pale. So I, a Regular Democrat, quietly applauded the effort of my supporters; but I knew in December 1961 that as a practical matter, I too, more so literally than figuratively, was beyond the pale.

I run for public office for the first time

Not being chosen Tammany Chief in 1961 was not a catastrophe for me. I would have welcomed the job, but I knew that even if by some magic I had been elected, the schisms within the party would have intensified simply because I was Black. And why so? Because the last year of the Eisenhower presidency (1960–1961) and the first two years of John Kennedy's presidency were ambiguous ones for Blacks. The passage of the minimal Civil Rights Acts of 1957 and 1960 came about by pressure from organized Blacks supported by liberal whites. The spectacles of Little Rock, and Montgomery, and the student sit-ins in Greensboro, North Carolina, were in themselves weighty enough to exact from the political pipeline those two Federal Statutes. But, more important, these protests by 1961 assumed the shape of ominous harbingers. Things would get worse, it seemed, before they get better. Across the country, Black and white people sensed, with almost palpable urgency, that drastic and dangerous forces were massing in unknown quarters. For most whites, Black people were now regarded with caution, if not suspicion. They were not behaving according to expected norms. This subliminally threatening feeling was not just a Southern phenomenon. It also characterized the North.

In New York the feeling was also widespread; and within the Democratic Party a certain nervousness could be felt. On the one hand there existed the clear necessity to placate the Blacks before real trouble began. On the other, there was the deeper and more widespread feeling that a show of nervousness would be a sign of weakness. No one ever expressed these feelings to my face, but I sensed that the topic was discussed in the same way as ethnic ticket balancing, only with that special added ingredient of bigotry that only a few whites are able to resist when discussing Negroes.

I felt, rather than knew, in 1961 that the revolt of the Black population would be long-lasting, and that it would profoundly affect the Democratic Party and my role in it. The time was near when the Party, regardless of its various segments, would not be unable to disregard or deceive Black people. This expectation would not occur simply because of the civil rights movement. After all, this was New York City, not Mississippi. Nevertheless, there was work to be done to accelerate desired change and one area that desperately needed attention was the voting turnout of Blacks.

My Harlem colleagues and I reasoned that the time was drawing near where my dream of a Black mayor was possible, if we could increase the voting strength of the Black population. This would be no easy task in New York. We sometimes contended that it would perhaps be easier to do this in Georgia because the reasons for low Black voter turnout there was simply that Blacks were *not* allowed to vote! Since this was not the problem in New York, we needed to determine what were the actual voting levels and how they could be enhanced. As Mayor Wagner's "political secretary," I convinced him to persuade the Democratic National Committee to fund a study of Black and Hispanic voting patterns in New York. I wanted this study, not so much for what it would yield in simple quantitative terms, but more to get a better picture of why Blacks and Hispanics voted at lower levels than whites.

Our study revealed that Blacks and Hispanics generally voted at 45 percent of their eligibility, while others ranged between 60 and 70 percent. This we already knew, but we found in 1961 that Blacks and Hispanics were still skeptical of electoral politics. As they had in the 1920s, too many Black people felt that politics humbugged their lives more than it helped. The Hispanics also shared this view, and their disaffection was exacerbated by their difficulties with the English language. The decision we made then was to increase efforts at voter registration combined with a voter education program. This decision was timely, for the rising civil rights movement, combining moral persuasion and political involvement, greatly aided our small attempt. This confluence of efforts effectively changed a lot of attitudes that otherwise would probably have taken years to influence.

Although I had worked a long time to enlarge Black participation in politics and the electoral process in New York, I had not been interested in party positions for myself. It was ironic that I found myself in May 1963 being virtually drafted into electoral politics. My willingness to run for elected office was a departure from my long-standing rule to work only within the Democratic organization for fair and effective city government. But by 1963, I perceived changes in the wind, and it became apparent that perhaps I could do better for my immediate constituents and New York City by the adoption of a new rule.

The immediate occasion for my change of direction was the resignation of Councilman Herbert Evans, a Black from my group, who had been appointed to the Housing and Redevelopment Board. But there were other reasons. In the first place, I had come to view with alarm the habit of some of my colleagues in Harlem and elsewhere of putting forward ill-prepared candidates for elective offices and patronage posts. While formerly I could have depended on the Harlem Black leadership team to present a powerful, united front in Democratic councils, that assurance was no longer there after the 1961 mayoral elections. The main problem, of course, was Congressman Powell, who had lost a lot of local leverage by not supporting the reelection of Mayor Wagner. Second, although there was talk as early as 1962 of Wagner for a fourth term, I viewed this possibility with uncertainty. It wasn't that I did not believe Robert Wagner could continue to win, but that it was already obvious that what with Reform, Liberal, and Regular Democrats feuding, the possibility of Wagner winning again without a bitter struggle was remote. In fact, I was not really convinced that he would run in 1965 unless conditions were ideal. Conditions were definitely not ideal in 1963, at least not in our party.

Apart from the fractured factional condition of the Democratic Party in New York City, there was also the problem of the Liberal Party, and of Congressman John Lindsay and the Republicans. Rumors had it that Lindsay was thinking of the mayoralty in 1965. He was an attractive fellow, and although a Republican, he seemed to have that aura which transcended party. There was no question in my mind that he would be elected overwhelmingly to Congress in 1964, and this certainly would not hurt his chances. Besides, the Congressman had read correctly the political winds. While he was no Adam Clayton Powell, he had said all the right things on civil rights. This caused him no problem in his "blue stocking" district and endeared him to Black voters despite his Republican label. As I considered Lindsay in 1963, I thought of him more as a closet Democrat, which he later turned out to be.

Because of those conditions and their implications for the future, I was presented with a dilemma. If I remained as District Leader without a Democratic mayor or governor in 1965, I would have very little political power. If, however, I became a councilman in a Democratic City Council, I would automatically have a very strong power base. I would certainly have more leverage than any new councilman, because of my years of service as a District Leader and member of Tammany's Executive Committee. My powers would probably be second only to the President of the City Council within the Council and more so outside the Council. If Lindsay were ever elected and I were on the Council he would have to deal with me, and whatever Democratic coalition I would join or put together. The deciding factor which propelled me into the race was that, in the present instance, I did not have to run in a primary or face an election for several months. This was so because in filling a vacancy on the City Council caused by the resignation of a member, the replacement is made by the City Council itself—that is, the person is elected by the majority vote of the majority party in the Council. It was understood, of course, that the County Leader forwards the recommendation, and in my case, after some hesitation, Edward Costikyan made the recommendation.

I was elected in May 1963 for the 21st Council District, and while I viewed it as a step forward in my crusade to gain leverage for my immediate constituents in Harlem and for Blacks in all of New York City, this view was not shared by a number of my own colleagues on the Harlem leadership team. It was a complicated situation, and was a serious problem for me but it never caused any great personal animus on the part of my colleagues. In fact, the responses of most of these men were conditioned by their desire to enhance their own power and to pay off political debts they had incurred. The manner in which these complications arose was illustrated by the positions taken by my former friends as the September City Council primary elections approached.

Since I had been elected by the Council in May, I had to face an election in November, as well as a primary in September. I expected to be challenged. Apart from how I was viewed by some Harlem colleagues, I expected opposition for structural reasons as well, for the 21st City Council District not only encompassed my Assembly District, the 13th East, but also the 11th and the 7th. The leader of the 11th was Assemblyman Lloyd E. Dickens, who had a candidate of his own—Henry Williams—from his Assembly District. This desire to have his own man on the City Council I understood. It is normal politics, but the situation had become a little less normal since Hulan Jack, the former Borough President, was supporting Dickens' efforts against me. The situation became really interesting in early June when Congressman Adam Powell, who was again in one of his "eras of good feelings," had decided to aid my campaign. But Adam's support soon presented a problem, because I learned later that he was supporting John Young III for Councilman-at-Large, while Paul O'Dwyer, my friend, was running for the same post.

To the lay person, the situation in 1963 may have seemed dauntingly complicated but I was now used to these internecine battles and I viewed the coming fray with bemused benignity. To be honest, I expected to win and also to learn from the moves I had made to bolster my campaign. One such move was to promote Charles Rangel, an attractive newcomer, subsequently a Congressman, who was contesting the leadership of Lloyd Dickens' 11th Assembly District. Since by 1963 I still had some influence, I knew I could help Rangel, and I reasoned that my support would give Dickens some pause. Another move, calculated to frustrate any instability on the part of Adam Powell, was to get former Governor Herbert H. Lehman to serve as honorary chairman of my election committee. Thus, should I lose votes from the likely bad behavior of Powell, the Reform elements would follow Lehman and support me. At least, so I figured.

I have never been so sure of myself as to believe I could assuredly predict the result of a political campaign, or the behavior of politicians, but in this instance, things went the way I thought they would. Adam Powell stayed with me from July to September, but as I had feared, he turned against me on the Sunday before the primary, and endorsed my opponent Antonio Rasmus for the leadership of my Assembly District. Since I was also running for City Councilman, he also endorsed my opponent, Henry Williams. I would have worried if Adam had broken away earlier, but the abruptness and lateness of his moves worked in my favor, for on primary day I retained my district leadership by a five-to-one margin, and in the nomination for City Council, I prevailed over Henry Williams by 1,300 votes.

In the Council race, quite a number of white voters voted for me, a vote I ascribed to their awareness of my record of fair play in racial matters and my brief, though proven, record of being a representative of all my constituents, white and Black. Congressman Powell did not interpret the vote that way. According to the *New York Times*, Powell stated that, "Black voters in central Harlem" had rejected me for councilman and that it was the white voters who had insured my victory.[14] Such statements were typical of Adam, as was the ability to ignore unpleasant details such as the fact that I had beaten his candidate in central Harlem by a wide margin. His actions held meaning far beyond mere fickleness, for to this day, quite a number of people question my politics on the basis of Adam's pronouncements. I therefore resolved once again to deal even more carefully with this charming but mercurial man.

The elections in November were anticlimatic compared to the primaries, for the Republicans had no one of any stature to oppose me. The satisfaction of my reelection was marred only by the death of John F. Kennedy in the same month. I mourned his passing, for although I had little regard for Robert, I saw John F. Kennedy as an essentially decent person who had begun to learn while in office that he had to become the president of all the people regardless of race. Yet even though I mourned his passing, I was happy to see my old friend Lyndon Baines Johnson elevated to the presidency. I had worked for him in 1960 and I had always believed he would do the right thing for Black people. In this he never let me down. In fact, he was, all during his term in office, a source of pleasant surprise, and I have mourned his passing, too.

In politics one is seldom allowed enough time to mourn, to bask in the glow of victory, or to struggle with the agony of defeat. Defeated, the seasoned politician is, or should be, the next morning planning a campaign for victory. This is so because there is always someone ready to take your place, ready to demonstrate that he can do a better job than you. Such is the compulsion if not the confidence of the breed. As my friend, Senator Daniel P. Moynihan, has noted, "New York politicians don't stop, until they die and are carried away to the Holy Sepulchre."[15] Politics, then, is a never-ending game, and even in victory the wise person is either thinking of something to do to bolster his or her position, or to aid his or her other constituency, which some might perceive as being the same thing. So many times, however, one's feeling of well-being is abruptly terminated by unforeseen and unwanted developments.

The Constance Baker Motley–Noel Ellison case

The story began on the same day I was reelected to the City Council, for in that election James Watson, a member of my own club, was elected to a Civil Court judgeship. This meant that he had to resign the post of State Senator for the 21st Senate District, and a replacement had to be found. It was not a situation that I viewed as pressing because although "Skiz" Watson was from my club, there was no understanding that his replacement had to be from my district, the 13th Assembly District East. I was willing, in fact, to go along with any qualified candidate from the 7th, the 11th, or the 13th Assembly District West, which together with mine made up the Senate District. In early January I was more than a little startled to learn that leaders in the 7th A.D. had selected a Noel Ellison to fill the Senate seat which Watson had vacated the previous December. This Noel Ellison I had known for some time, and I knew also that he had been found guilty on three occasions of participation in the numbers game. Although he had never gone to jail and the fines he had paid were very small, he neverthe- less was, in my opinion, an unacceptable choice. I was furious also with the thinking I knew had produced this choice.

It was obvious to me that the white leaders in the 7th A.D., which was approximately seventy-five percent white, thought that since the Senate District was predominantly Black, we Blacks would be satisfied with even an unqualified person, as long as he was Black. This was particularly shocking since the leader of this West Side group was none other than the great liberal Reformer Congressman William Fitts Ryan himself. Ryan and that group's standard pitch was "the best candidate at all times"— yet here was Ellison. It was unbelievable! The more I thought about this, the more determined I became to prevent it. I consulted with my friend Judge James Watson, and he suggested as an alternate choice Mrs. Constance Baker Motley. Mrs. Motley, a lawyer, was well known for her role in the 1962 fight to enroll James Meredith of the University of Mississippi, and was now general counsel to the NAACP's Legal Defense Fund.

I was absolutely delighted with Watson's suggestion, because she was the kind of candidate my club, the Carver, was always looking for. Her credentials were impeccable, and we at Carver immediately realized that given her education and experience, she clearly had the potential for going much further than the State Senate. This was an important consideration not only for our club but for the Black community. When it was noted that she was very tall and stately, and a very assured speaker, she seemed ideal. Besides, she was already a registered Democrat. With all this behind her, we thought, as we considered her for State Senator, that in time and with luck we could make her the first woman Borough President (and a Black woman at that!) and then move her into the mayor's office. Eventually, we were very successful in the first two plans, and although we decided not to try for the mayoralty, Mrs. Motley certainly has achieved high office in the Federal Courts. I have always regarded her progress with a special personal interest.

It was agreed then that Judge Watson would sound her out. He reported that she was willing to run if she received the endorsement. I passed on her name to the Borough President, Edward Dudley, a member of my club, who was overseeing this operation for the Mayor and the County Leader.

At the same time Watson and I had come up with Mrs. Motley against Noel Ellison, Lloyd Dickens, as one of Adam Powell's surrogates, put forward the name of Andrew Tyler, then president of the Harlem Lawyers Association. Tyler was a good choice, but the way things had developed I could not support him. Edward N. Costikyan, in writing about the affair in 1966, contended that I would not support Tyler because he was Dickens' candidate and Dickens was my "old enemy."[16] This interpretation is very wrong, because Dickens at this time was of minor concern to me. I was, in fact, disturbed by Ellison's poor reputation, and by the bad publicity his choice had generated. To counteract this poor image, we had to promote a candidate of the utmost integrity, with a well-known record. Tyler, though an excellent choice, simply could not compete with a Motley. Furthermore, I didn't want the Republicans in the special election, set for February 4th, to find any chinks in our Democratic candidate's armor. About Motley, I could be as certain as anyone could be that there weren't any.

Ed Costikyan has written that in the early rounds of the selection process,

Motley had no one's avowed support. This fact led me to believe that J. Raymond Jones, a regular district leader of the Thirteenth East known as "the Fox," was her unavowed sponsor. . . . [17]

It wasn't that I was "unavowed," it was that I did not conceive of the County Committeeman of the Senate District picking an Ellison, or Tyler for that matter, over Motley.

The meeting to decide on the matter was held on Monday, January 13, with Ed Dudley, the Borough President, presiding. As it turned out, I got the biggest surprise of the new year. In a series of moves reminiscent of "Boss Tweed," the Reformers rigged the meeting in such a way that Ellison was nominated with a plurality of 3 votes: 179 for Ellison, followed by Motley with 104 and 72 for Tyler!

How did this happen? The answer became clear after several meetings and a lawsuit brought by the County Leader Ed Costikyan, aided by Justin Feldman, the Chairman of the New York County Democratic Law Committee. In the case we are discussing, a candidate is agreed on when a nominee has a plurality of votes over the other nominees. We had in this instance, as I have noted, three Assembly Districts involved, but the number of committeemen varied with districts. Furthermore, the 13th was split in two: the 13th A.D. West, of which Angelo Simonetti was the leader, and the 13th A.D. East, my district. As regards numbers, the 7th A.D., led by a triumvirate of Franz Leichter, Eugenie Flatow, and Congressman William Fitts Ryan, had by far the largest bloc of votes—176. The 11th A.D. led by Lloyd Dickens was next with 133 committee votes. My district, 13 A.D. East, had 97, all were committed to me in support of Mrs. Motley. This was not the situation in the 13th A.D. West, for although it had 51 County Committeemen, its two leaders, Angelo Simonetti and Margaret Cox, were feuding, and Cox controlled 34 of the 51 votes, votes she had pledged to Ellison.

On a cold night in January in New York City, not everyone is going to attend a Senate District Committee meeting. While all the other districts had a turnout of between 65 and 70 percent, the 7th had an 85 percent rate. They had more zeal, one might conclude, since we were dealing with Reformers; yet, the diametric opposite was the truth. As the case began in court, the leaders of the 7th A.D. admitted that they had been guilty of "irregularities." This admission stopped the case and spared the embarrassment of a public admission that they had, on the night of the County Committee meeting, filled nonexistent vacancies on their committee. This they did in order to have warm voting bodies to vote in place of people who were not at the meeting. And so it came to pass that Ellison was able to get a plurality of three! Once this holier-than-thou front collapsed, I knew it would take little effort to nominate and elect my candidate.

In such an emergency as this, the Committee on Vacancies, elected by the same committee that elected Ellison, had the right to nominate the replacement for Ellison, who now had to bow out. On the Vacancies Committee were Eugenie Flatow, Margaret Cox, Angelo Simonetti, Lloyd Dickens, and me. Finally, Flatow and Cox, probably depressed from being caught doing unthinkable acts—for Reformers anyway—abstained from voting. Simonetti and I had already agreed on Motley, so that left Dickens. In the end, he voted with us and Mrs. Motley was in.

Edward Costikyan recounts that he had to work on Dickens to vote with Simonetti and me. It is most likely true, although I was not privy to these discussions. I do know that it would have been useless for Dickens not to vote for Mrs. Motley, who even in the rigged election had placed second by a wide margin above Dickens' candidate, Andrew Tyler. Furthermore, if either Cox or Flatow were constrained to vote, they would, in their wounded condition, have to go for someone of unimpeachable credentials. It wasn't that Tyler was tainted, but it was that Motley was so clearly the best choice.

In this context, Costikyan was not entirely correct in declaring that at one point I wanted to drop Mrs. Motley. In reference to a meeting of the County Executive Committee, called to decide whether to press a lawsuit to have Noel Ellison removed, he writes:

But the big surprise came from J. Raymond Jones, Motley's original sponsor. He wanted no lawsuit. He no longer wanted Motley. He wanted Ellison, so he could use Ellison and his record to beat reform, Ryan, and the Seventh Assembly District over the head for the next nine months. Then, in November, he was sure *both* Ellison *and* Ryan, along with reform could be demolished.
So he made the best speech of the evening.[18]

I don't know if I made the best speech of the evening, although it is gratifying to read that compliment now. It is true that I argued against a lawsuit, and my reasons were clear. The Reformers had done something to damage the party, and this was not the last thing I expected them to do. In fact, because of such behavior I viewed the Reformers as acting not as Democrats but more like a new party. I did not see all this as boding well for the future of the Democratic Party. I did desire to use the occasion to reform the Reformers, not merely "to beat reform," for to beat them in November would not be enough. I wanted them to be bothered by the stigma of it for the next nine months so that a better group could take over. In this way, the party would have been strengthened by new leadership.

I objected to a lawsuit, also, because I thought it a dangerous precedent to set, whereby, for other less laudable reasons, the County Executive Committee could challenge and remove a duly elected candidate in other circumstances. I thought, too, that the damage had been done already and that a lawsuit would not significantly reduce the damage. I was aware, however, that a lawsuit would aid my candidate, which it eventually did, but I believed Mrs. Motley could and would wait a few months, by which time she would be unbeatable. So, to the County Leader it may have appeared as if I did not want Motley, but my posture was not one of abandonment, but one of principle and timing. These two elements, I believe, are the hallmarks of any truly successful politician.

Adam Clayton Powell and the Clayton apartments scandal

With the Ellison-Motley affair resolved in late January, I thought that I was due at least a brief period of respite. But that was not to be, for Adam Clayton Powell, lacking both principle and a proper sense of timing, immediately commenced one of his periodic guerrilla attacks on me. This attack took up an extraordinary amount of my time in 1964. In the end, these contretemps proved to be advantageous to me and my program, but they were exhausting and at times very discouraging. I often wondered why I had to be burdened by this very brilliant but oh so mercurial colleague.

I think it is important to recall my relations with Congressman Adam Clayton Powell at this juncture because he and his accomplices involved me in a lawsuit during all of 1964, a suit that, though it appeared personal, was politically motivated. I recall its history to illustrate the problems faced by anyone in politics who is opposed by another with principles that may be described as personally opportunistic.

For years Adam Powell and I had been struggling to secure middle-income housing for Harlem. After my return to politics in 1958 to manage Powell's successful campaign against Carmine DeSapio, Adam and I intensified our efforts to this end. Our strategy, given Adam's personality, would be that he would act as a prod and I would do the spadework, so to speak, with the city and state government. Although I held no city or state government office, I was a District Leader and as such I possessed some leverage.

Our efforts to provide better housing in Harlem were aided by the passage of the Mitchell-Lama Act by the state legislature, which authorized New York City to provide middle-income housing for its citizens. In order to involve local citizens in housing development, the law required that the project be "sponsored." Sponsorship required no depositing money but insured that the sponsors would be responsible for site selection, finding a developer and builder, as well as supervising the entire project to its completion. The sponsors were responsible to the city, for the city provided 90 percent of the mortgage at 4 percent interest, as well as a tax abatement on the project for fifty years. To have projects approved, the entire scheme had to be reviewed by the Housing and Redevelopment Board, and funds would not be forthcoming unless the entire proposal was approved by the City Controller's office prior to 1962 and by the Housing and Redevelopment Board after that.

Early in 1961 I participated with Congressman Powell in the sponsorship of the Clayton Apartments located at 135th Street and Seventh Avenue. I became involved by invitation, when Powell's surrogates, the firm of Brooks, Hampton, Levy and Walker, Inc., after taking a $6,000 fee from Balaban and Gordon, Builders, for the procurement of a site, were unable to deliver. Since this meant the apartments might not be built, I agreed to join in and save the day. I did this because I had worked too hard to bring lower- and middle-income housing to Harlem to allow this real possibility to be blown away by greed, combined with incompetent and unscrupulous behavior.

To save the project, I asked friends of mine to assist in finding a site, and through their efforts we came up with the abandoned Public School 89 at 135th and Lenox Avenue. My next step was to take Balaban, the prospective builder, down to the Controller's office and add him as a sponsor of the project. Despite their having failed to find a site, the firm of Brooks, Hampton et al. tried further to participate in the Clayton project. Its representatives, led by William Hampton, wanted to broker the demolition of the building. I went along with this because they had a Black firm involved. This emboldened them; next they wanted to broker the insurance, the electrical fixtures, and the plumbing! This seemed to me greedy and selfish and I decided that I could not approve it. When Balaban informed me further that Hampton's brokerage would increase the cost of the building by 20 percent, there simply could be no negotiation. I broke with them, and they received no contract.

While the Clayton Apartments were being built, I was able to secure, as part of a $201 million Housing and Redevelopment Program, a $40.4 million housing cooperative for Harlem. These apartments would take up two city blocks and were to be located on the site of the subway yards controlled by Mike Quill and the Transport Workers Union. This was riverfront property and many groups desired it for commercial development; but the Mayor and I convinced Quill, President of the T.W.U., that it would best be used for housing. When the news got out in October 1963 that the Esplanade Gardens Apartments, as they came to be called, would soon be a reality, the firm of Brooks, Hampton, et al. sued to recover money they claimed as owed to them for participating in the development of *both* projects. This suit created quite a stir in the newspapers and, I am sure, in private conversations. As late as March 1964, the *New York Times* devoted several columns to the story, under the heading "Powell and Jones Battling Over Harlem Cooperative," and noted:

In the background of the controversy is a cleavage between two groups polarizing around either Councilman Jones or Representative Powell as primary elections approach.[19]

I had to give the reporter, Edith Evans Asbury, good marks for perception, for nowhere in the suit had Congressman Powell's name appeared, and strangely, he had refrained from his usual pontifications. But I knew his deft hand was at work, for William J. Hampton had been Powell's secretary, and Leroy J. Walker, the president of Brooks, Hampton, Levy and Walker, Inc., was a Powell man. I felt certain also that my "on and off" colleague was pulling the strings from some dimly perceived background, for the charges made in the media were hallmarks of Adam's rhetoric. I was charged, for example, by Henry Williams, the man I defeated in the 1963 primary and one of Powell's lawyers, with employing a white lawyer for the Clayton Apartments and for giving the insurance business to whites. Such statements delivered in 1963 in Harlem were potential political dynamite, but I did not allow myself to be intimidated by them. In response, I noted that all contracts could not and should not go to Negroes, and further that I did not intend to get involved in any racism. It may have been that by 1964 my political standing insured me against the potential damage of this charge because, in the end, I experienced no injury from this attack.

The case of *Brooks, Hampton et al. v. Jones et al.* yielded nothing for the plaintiffs, including Congressman Powell. Their loss enhanced my stature with Harlem voters and all elements of my party, particularly those in New York county. The suit, in effect, cleared me of "suspicions of corruption" which are so easily generated in politics. This official bill of health now cleared the way for previously suspicious and/or cautious colleagues to regard me with favor. Even near-enemies felt the scales fall from their eyes as they began to perceive that I was now immune to my most powerful "friend" but also becoming more influential in the regular Democratic Party councils.

I become Chief of Tammany

One such near-enemy was Margaret Cox, co-leader with Angelo Simonetti of the 13th A.D. West. She had opposed me strenuously in the fight to nominate Constance Baker Motley for the State Senate, and had gone down to defeat with the Reformers of the 7th A.D. It was this same Margaret L. Cox who, realizing sooner than most that I still had a future in New York politics, called me in early November 1964, while I was in the Virgin Islands, and stated that she had put my name in for County Leader. She had done so without asking my permission and she called for approval. This was all right with me, and I informed her that I would run if Mayor Wagner thought I should do so.

After the telephone call, I found myself thinking of the odd turns of political life. It is not unusual for opposing political candidates on a particular issue to appear often as mortal enemies to the outsider, yet to be great friends on another issue. That is quite normal politics if both participants are of the same party. Margie Cox was of my party but with a difference, for, although in 1964 the schism between Regular and Reform Democrats in New York was real, Cox was a Black woman. As such she had very little in common with the Reformers, because as the Ellison case revealed, they had, with the exception William Fitts Ryan himself, very little real respect for Blacks. I had always thought she was miscast in the role of Reformer, but I concluded that perhaps she saw it as prestigious to be a Reform Leader, far removed from scoundrels like me in the Regular Democratic organization. I thought after her call that she must have begun to see through the pious facade of the Reformers in the Ellison case.

As I sat on my porch, overlooking the harbor lights of Charlotte Amalie, I thought back to 1949. In that year, when William O'Dwyer was reelected Mayor, Hugo Rogers was the County Leader. For reasons not clear to me at the time, O'Dwyer wanted to be rid of Rogers. The Mayor's angst coincided with some good work I had done for the party, particularly the role I had played in removing the stigma of Communism from the New York City Council. I did not think this work was the reason the mayor called me in, but I was summoned and he told me bluntly that he felt he could make me Tammany Chief if I desired the job.

I suppose that if I had been less informed I would have jumped at the chance to be leader in 1949, but having worked at a fairly high level in the Democratic party since 1947 as Deputy Commissioner of Housing, I learned rapidly of the prospects of our party and leader. I knew when the Mayor spoke to me that he was already in trouble and that if I accepted this post as his protege, my tenure would not only be turbulent, but also short. With a certain sadness, then, I told the mayor I was not ready. Soon after, Carmine DeSapio was elected leader and the acceleration of the party's fragmentation among Reformers and Regulars began. Within a year, Bill O'Dwyer was forced to resign "under a cloud," and President Harry Truman in his generosity made it possible for him to continue in political life as Ambassador to Mexico. President Truman's action pleased me because Mayor O'Dwyer had been always considerate of me, and, as I have noted before, he had directed Robert Wagner, Commissioner of Housing and Buildings, to appoint me as his deputy in 1947.

District Co-Leader Margaret Cox saw to it that her telephone call made the newspapers. All of them were noncommittal on my abilities, but Margie got the *Post* to print her view that I was "the party's most distinguished and able leader."[20] This accolade was useful, although one could never be sure how many people would accept it, particularly when I was already well known as "The Fox." For years people had called me that, and in truth I had never been too comfortable with it. Reporters especially seemed to delight in a name like that, much more so than I did. In the early stages I had tried to discourage its use, but after a while I gave up because the press blithely ignored my beseechings. I wondered now, though, if in the run for a position that was expected to bring so many disparate elements together, whether the designation "Fox" would not inordinately bother some groups.

I wasted no time on this, however, and returned to New York in time for my sixty-fifth birthday party on November 19, 1964, given by my Carver Democratic Club. It was an exceedingly happy occasion, for the testimonials from my club members and from others high in the city leadership, I knew, were genuine. There was excitement that night among the Carver group, particularly when Mayor Wagner said he hoped I would stick around because he needed me. Several people interpreted this to mean he would endorse me for the leadership, and I expected him to, but in a political development such as this one, where there was bound to be opposition, timing and even the phrasing of support is vital. So on that night, with the decision to be made on December 4, that was all the Mayor, cautious as ever, said.

The selection of the County Leader in New York County is actually quite straightforward. In effect, the 66 District Leaders and Co- Leaders who form the Executive Committee of the Democratic County Committee meet and select the candidate by a straight majority vote. Simple! Things get a bit complicated though, when it is understood that I do not mean at least 34 out of 66 votes. That would be too simple for New York City. In fact, I mean 16 votes, for no leader that I remember had a full vote. The votes were in fractions, depending upon the Assembly District. Simple arithmetic will show that some districts had less than a full vote, and since there must be two leaders from each district, one male and one female, the *individual's* vote is never more than ½. For these districts that were apportioned a ¼ vote, then the individual's vote would be ⅛. To be elected I would need a minimum of 8⅛ votes.

In a situation such as this, it is foolish to campaign, and I would not have tried even if it were possible. I felt the post of Tammany Leader should and would be determined on my record, and in this case, more important, on how the various factions in the party felt about me. About my record, I had no qualms. I had worked for the party a very long time, and I think I had shown independence and prudence in all my political dealings. This was my view and I was satisfied with it. I knew, though, that certain elements of the party perceived me in none too flattering ways and that I could never hope to get their votes. The West Side Reformers, for example, had not forgiven me for the election of Mrs. Motley, and the group allied with the Liberal Party viewed me dimly, I thought. My base, then, was with the Regular Democrats, but within that group there would be favorite sons and daughters. The only person who could lead this group was the Mayor, and so I relaxed and left that role to him.

The Mayor, showing his usual deft touch, said nothing to the press or anyone else about me until the last moment. In fact, that disconcertingly astute man waited until the very day of the election, when the majority of the Regulars, unable to develop a consensus, began to ask, "What does the Mayor want?" This was the critical moment he was waiting for: when he telephoned a few District Leaders and announced I was his choice, the Regulars rallied around me.

Although the vote for me was not unanimous, I was pleased with the outcome. As expected, Robert Wechsler, the Reformer candidate, received 5¼, and I, 10½, which, being a two-to-one ratio, was most gratifying. I was particularly pleased when Wechsler moved to make my election unanimous and carried all the Reformers to my side with the exception of Franz Leichter and Eugenia Flatow. Leichter and Flatow's opposition simply demonstrated that animus still remained from the Ellison-Motley campaign.

To a great extent politics, at least at the organizational level, is the art of getting along with or leading diverse personalities and movements. Since I was now the elected Tammany Chief, or as I preferred it, New York County Leader, I was not about to be troubled by the two abstaining votes of Leichter and Flatow. I considered Wechsler's gesture gracious and I said so in my acceptance remarks, but Wechsler's gesture and Flatow and Leichter's behavior were polar reminders of the job I had to do. It was obvious from the vote that we had a serious schism in our party, and I regarded the elimination of that schism as one of my top priorities. To do so effectively on a countywide basis, I first had to take care of schisms in my own bailiwick, and that meant I would have to show all New York that I could pacify, if not tame, that temperamental leopard in my backyard— Congressman Adam Clayton Powell.

I had given Adam Powell a great deal of thought in the week prior to my election as Tammany Leader. I knew that if I won, I would immediately be confronted with a number of pressing and troublesome problems. There would be the problem of filling the position of Borough President, now that Edward Dudley, a member of my club, was resigning to take a seat on the New York State Supreme Court. This was not going to be easy, for Mayor Wagner had so far for that job supported Deputy Borough President Earl Brown, to whom I was very much opposed. There was also the looming problem of organizing the State Legislature, in which Democrats had won control of both houses, something we had not done in the past thirty years. Since the Governor was a Republican, that situation required intervention from the Mayor, then the most powerful Democrat in the state. If the Mayor was involved, I would be too. Furthermore, there remained the continual problem of refinancing the New York County Democratic organization, which I knew to be in a most precarious financial state. And finally, the problem of the new junior senator from New York, Robert F. Kennedy, loomed large. I knew he remembered me and the Lyndon Johnson campaign in 1960. Knowing his personality first hand, I expected him to attempt a power play for the leadership of New York State, which he very soon tried. All these problems would soon require attention, but I was determined to begin my term on a positive note and to end the calendar year with some appearance of the beginnings of harmony.

The key to this first stage was Powell, who, by reason of his seniority in Congress, was in December 1964 no ordinary Democrat. Though excoriated in the New York press from time to time for his flamboyance and personal excesses, he was known across the country as the champion of Blacks and a thorn in the side of segregationists, states righters, and bigots, various and sundry. More important, he was the chairman of the powerful House Committee on Education and Labor. As such, Powell was courted by party leaders not only in New York but in many other states. Even Presidents Kennedy and Johnson found it necessary to be considerate of him because of his chairmanship and his charisma. Among Democrats of New York County, the regard for Adam was less lofty, for we knew him better, but all of us knew that despite his faults, Adam was a hard worker and an intelligent leader when properly motivated. In fact, he enjoyed the national reputation of being a strong and productive chairman. Since I was now County Leader, the first Black person ever to be so honored, I knew Adam might view my elevation as a further challenge to the stature he loved so much even though he had, indeed, supported me for the leadership. Such a development would not be useful for anyone, and some alternative would do Adam and me and the party a great deal of good. It was in this context, therefore, that I journeyed to Washington, D.C., on Friday, December 4, the day after my election, to see Adam.

Despite published speculation to the contrary, we made no secret deals at that meeting. My proposition was simple: I was now the County Leader and the possibilities were there for making the Democratic Party progressive and strong in New York. Since he was known as "Mr. Civil Rights," I pointed out that in New York he could be of assistance in furthering civil rights in a substantive way, without the inflammatory rhetoric. In sum, I tried to show the Congressman that in his present position, unable to visit his own constituency in fear of being arrested for failure to pay on a civil judgement, we could be of assistance to each other and the party. This he saw only too well, for he knew that I could have carried on without him, and I felt that in his emotional way, he was thoroughly pleased, if not touched, by my gesture.

There was one little personal matter I could not resist throwing in. When I suggested that he restrain his boys who were still trying to make trouble on the Esplanade Gardens affair, Adam was all innocence. "I have nothing to do with that, Ray," he said, waving his cigar airily, but with injured aplomb. "It was all their doing. I had nothing to do with it." Of course, I didn't believe a word, but since he was now for the moment cooperative, there was simply no point in pressing the issue.

In the corridor, after our meeting, we met the press. Television lights lit up the place—I think Adam had seen to that—and he was in his element. When asked about our battles in the past, he answered in that breezy, devil-may-care style so beloved by journalists, "We've never been opponents," he said. "We merely differed once on a candidate. Ray and I have been close together all our lives."[21] All our lives? This was a bit much, but he did not stop there. He told the reporters that I had been his choice for Tammany Leader and that he was for me 101 percent! It was interesting to watch this man at work. He charmed his audience. He was assured, unconcerned and debonair. When he was asked why I had come down to Washington instead of Adam going to New York, he replied with sly insouciance and a conspiratorial wink, "Conditions are not normal now."

Such a charmer he was that no one pressed the subject. But for the *New York Times* reporter, Warren Weaver, Jr., this was almost too much. Reporting on the scene he wrote:

To hear Mr. Powell this afternoon, however, one would not have guessed that any feud had ever divided him and the new county chairman.[22]

After Adam's cheery dismissal of our past problems, no one pressed that point either, and with Powell as cheerleader, everyone seemed to want to celebrate our reunion. For my part, I was very pleased with my visit, for the whole affair had turned out better than I had envisioned. Although I could not be sure how far in the future our rapprochement would last, I was very aware that the present drama played in New York, and that was what I had come for.

I had considered my trip to Washington a success, at least for the present, and I knew most Regular Democrats agreed. I had expected that some Reform elements would not be too enthusiastic, but this I could deal with after a brief rest over the Christmas season. No respite, however, was to be given me by the press. Being Black, the national magazines used that angle for their stories. *Newsweek*, for example, commented that my election did not mean "that the British are coming." "Tammany's new sachem, like 1,087,931 increasingly vocal New Yorkers," it noted, "is a Negro."[23] The local papers quickly reminded their readers that I was the first Black person to be so honored, but being local, they had other things on their minds. The *New York Herald Tribune* was very kind to me, but wondered whether a Negro would also be President of the City Council the next year and what role would I play. The *Herald Tribune* thought that my election would give the Negro "more recognition in the city" and obliquely hinted that I would be there with Wagner for his fourth term.[24] The *New York Post* was the kindest and most realistic. It, too, understandably noted the hue of my skin, but it remained clear-eyed about the very large problem I faced. "He inherits a divided organization," the *Post* editorialized, and went on,

there will be many snipers and hatchet men standing in the wings. It is our hope that the reform bloc, which could not genuinely unite in a fight for its own candidate, will give him a real chance to demonstrate his capacities for leadership and independence.[25]

Only the *New York Times* was unkind and at the same time foolish. For some time a hostage to the Reformers, it deplored, in its ignorance of practical politics, my attempt to reconcile problems with Congressman

Powell. And, as I had wondered weeks earlier, the *Times* found it possible and necessary to remark unfavorably on my sobriquet, "The Fox."

Mr. Jones's rise to wealth and power through four decades of politics has won for him the sobriquet of The Fox—a tribute perhaps to his subtlety and cunning, but hardly suggesting a high standard of political or moral leadership. He is acknowledged to be a master political craftsman. He played a major role in Mayor Wagner's victory over Carmine DeSapio, Charles A. Buckely and Joseph T. Sharkey in the primary before the mayoralty election of 1961. He has achieved his successes primarily as an organizer and distributor of patronage. Significantly, Mr. Jones's first action after his election was to go to Washington to make a public demonstration of friendship with Adam Clayton Powell, unquestionably the representative of the worst element in the Democratic party in New York City today. Such a bad start will hardly recommend Mr. Jones to citizens who would like to see the Democratic party here more devoted to furthering clean, honest, progressive government than the pursuit of jobs and contracts.[26]

Not content with this initial fusillade, the *Times* issued a stern rebuke to Wagner and me, for "stiff-arming reform," and called the mayor a "Boss."[27] These statements were as untrue as they were unrealistic and unkind, so I read them with a new-found equanimity, a posture I knew would be necessary in the New Year, if I expected to solve the formidable problems that lay ahead.

As Christmas approached, I reflected on my more than forty years in the Democratic party. Beginning in the 1920s, I had expected to raise myself to a respectable level of achievement, but I had not thought that at age 65, I would be taking on a new challenge as the Leader of my own county, the most powerful and talked- about county in the nation. I felt as if I had finished another phase in my life and was about to embark on another. Once again, the times and manners in America had changed. I did not feel as alone as I had in earlier years. In the United States we had newly elected a president from the South, a man I had supported in 1960 and one who had seen to it that a Civil Rights Act of far-reaching implications had been enacted. I was certain there was more to that man; I expected more, and he later delivered. There were, of course, confrontations between Blacks and whites, between Native Americans and whites, and between the Hispanics and whites. There was talk of racial wars, and of a separation of the races by extremists on both sides, possibilities against which I had worked all my life. But amidst all this were the giant and noble figures—James Farmer, Fannie Lou Hamer, Martin Luther King, Jr., President Lyndon Johnson, and others. I viewed all this ferment as positive. I could discern, beyond all the real fires and fiery rhetoric, a struggle for harmony and a common humanity, and I felt fortunate that in New York I was now in a position to play a more influential role in that struggle. At last my time had come and I was determined to do my very best for my party, for Harlem and for the country that in 1917 had, indeed, literally claimed me.

Chapter 7

The Fox of Tammany: Early Victories, *(1964–1965)*

HAVING BEEN ELECTED Tammany leader, developments originating in the 1961 mayoral election of Robert Wagner severely tested the grandiose ideas I had entertained during the Christmas holidays of 1964. In that election as Edward Costikyan has noted,

a far more basic and yet more complicated situation arose when the five county leaders opposed Mayor Wagner because they accurately appraised his intentions as being directed at the destruction of the power of the county leaders. Many district leaders followed suit because they were aware of great voter dissatisfaction with the mayor, but were unaware of the even greater latent animosity directed towards incumbent New York County leader, Carmine DeSapio.[1]

Costikyan is correct in his assessment of the great dissatisfaction with DeSapio's behavior and that of the rest of the County Leaders. But he is wrong on one point, and he did not develop another implied in his observations, that is the increased power of the Mayor under Wagner.

In the first place, the Mayor was not intent on the destruction of the County Leaders or on taking over the leadership of the counties. In the second place, what the mayor was interested in was reestablishing himself as a leader of the Democratic Party of New York City so that County Leaders would understand that they would have to deal with him for the next four years. Mr. Costikyan did not explain why the mayor viewed the election as so important.

What happened was that Robert Wagner had become a very popular mayor during his previous terms; he had also become a very independent mayor—so much so, that the County Leaders viewed him as less and less a creature of their own making. Furthermore they feared that if he continued in the office of mayor he would establish an authority similar to that established by FDR, simply on the basis of his popularity and his longevity in office. It was important, then, to get rid of Wagner as Mayor in 1961 before longevity made him even less tractable. Of course they lost, and before year's end Carmine DeSapio was no longer the New York County Leader. Shortly after this, all the others, with the exception of Charles Buckley of the Bronx, were also gone. It would have been impolitic for Mayor Wagner to keep them. They were untrustworthy, and, more important, the voters had repudiated them.

The popularity and reelection of Wagner, his independence, and the gradual political demise of DeSapio made for troubles in 1965, and made it impossible for me to proceed in my usual idealistic manner I envisioned while on Christmas vacation.

What I had intended

I had hoped that as County Leader I would find some means of bringing about a better relationship among County Leaders through the process of what one might call a demonstration of shared interests. Since Wagner had emerged as the pivotal figure of the Democratic Party in New York City, I wanted to use his tenure and popularity to bring about party unity—as much as was possible—so that should he choose not to run in 1965, the party would have sufficient focus to ensure a Democratic Mayor and City Council. Unfortunately, this turned out to be far more problematical than I had ever imagined.

I had other grandiose ideas, too. When I took over as County Leader, it became clear to me that the New York County Democratic Party was broke and fund raising quickly became foremost in my mind. I had planned nothing new, but it occurred to me that the normal processes could be done on a larger and higher scale—perhaps a few more dinner dances, testimonials, and such, where all invitees would contribute a bit more than in the past. After all, it was our party.

I thought also, since this was 1965, the height of the Civil Rights Revolution, and because the Democratic Party, particularly in New York County, had established good links with the Black and Puerto Rican population, that with me as the first Black County Leader, we had a unique opportunity to maximize the membership of the minority groups in the Party. I had not devised any precise method for doing so, because I thought I would have time to think this matter through, get advice, and devise a plan of action sometime during the spring. But by January, troubles muted in the fall came to full force and denied me the opportunity to test my ideas in any orderly fashion. My first problem in 1965 concerned the party reorganization of the New York State Legislature which initially had seemed a blessing. The Democratic Party had swept both houses the previous November, which had not occurred for the past three decades. Thus, the power of the Republican Governor was seriously attenuated. This situation should have been cause for rejoicing; however, for the Mayor and me it soon turned out to be a nightmare.

Another development that bore directly on this seemingly wonderful scene was the November 1964 election of Robert Kennedy as junior Senator from New York. He had won the Senate seat with ease, with only routine assistance from me, leaning heavily on the mystique of his brother and the Kennedy family. While ordinary Democrats rejoiced at his election, I recalled the confrontation we had had in 1960 when he managed his brother's campaign, and I knew instinctively that this man would become a source of trouble for me. I would not have been concerned had he kept his animosity at the personal level, which is what I thought he would do, but he soon proved me wrong, and turned out to be a source of serious bother not only for myself, but for the Mayor and the party as well. All of these things came together in the party's attempt to choose its leaders for the State Legislature.

The fight to reorganize the New York State Legislature: The treachery of Robert Kennedy

I am certain that in January 1965 Wagner had not yet made up his mind whether he would run for another term later that year. If he contemplated running at all, he would have to assert himself in the larger affairs of the state, particularly if he wished to continue a life in politics, moving from the mayorality to the U.S. Senate or to the state capitol. This is not to say that I knew of such ambitions, but it is a normal progression for most politicians in the position that the Mayor enjoyed. Because he was the foremost Democrat in the state, Wagner decided in January to make his influence felt in the reorganization of the State Legislature. He and I had not counted, however, upon either the imaginations of the other New York County Leaders or on the ambitions and tactics of Senator Robert Kennedy.

When the Democrats were the minority, Joseph Zaretski of New York County was the Senate Minority leader, and Anthony J. Travia of Brooklyn, the Assembly Minority Leader. As a reward for their work, the mayor wanted Joseph Zaretski to be Senate Majority Leader and Anthony Travia to be the Speaker of the Assembly. We thought that, given these men's long service in the Democratic Party in the State Legislature, there would be little objection from any source as to their qualifications and deservedness. The Mayor, though, had not counted on the continuing hostility of such County Leaders as Charles A. Buckley of the Bronx, John F. English of Nassau, and Stanley Steingut of Brooklyn. Neither had he anticipated the animus of Peter L. Crotty, Democratic Leader of Erie County, and of William H. McKeon, the Democratic State Chairman who in fact owed his high office to Mayor Wagner. Between November and December a number of Democratic Party county leaders across the state and all the county leaders of New York city, with the exception of Moses Weinstein of Queens, had come to the conclusion that Robert Wagner would run for Governor in 1966. If he ran and won he would become a most powerful figure. This would not do, because Robert F. Kennedy was now a rising power in New York and it soon became very clear they thought Kennedy could do more for them. Thus, led by Stanley Steingut and Charles Buckley, they fielded an opposing slate for the leadership. For Senate Majority Leader, they presented Senator Julian B. Erway of Albany, a protégé of the State Chairman, William McKeon, and for Speaker of the Assembly, Stanley Steingut, whose father had held that same position some thirty years earlier.

It was never announced that these were Senator Kennedy's candidates. Rather, they were presented to the press as the choice of the majority of the democratic legislative delegation. I knew better, for I had detected from the beginning that the fine hand of our freshman Senator was involved in this entire stew, and as the fight progressed throughout January, my conclusion was proven correct.

When it became clear to Mayor Wagner that his position as the titular head of the Democratic Party in New York State was under serious assault, he sent me to Albany as his personal representative. My job simply was to hold the line and prevent a take-over by Senator Kennedy and his henchmen. Luck came to our aid and in the form of the problems of Senator Erway, for the anti-Wagner forces had not done their homework on his record. Had they scrutinized his background, they would have found that a damaging case could be made against him for being anti-civil rights. As the *New York Times* pointed out on January 3, 1965, Mr. Erway, very conservative in his views, had voted against a bill to make discrimination illegal in private apartment hosing. As this information surfaced, his candidacy became less and less attractive, and Kennedy's group suffered its first embarrassment. By January 6th, the Erway candidacy had bitten the dust, and the Kennedy anti-Wagner forces were locked in a struggle over an alternative. Charles Buckley pushed Senator Ivan Warner, a Black man from his own constituency, the Bronx, but others supported Senator Jack E. Bronston of Queens.

While the division grew within the anti-Wagner forces, the mayor made it plain that there was no change in his position. On January 6 he stated, "I see no possibility of establishing a boss-rule consensus for legislative leadership other than by invoking the rule of legitimacy and choosing the men already designated in the past to bear the burdens of leadership, Tony Travia and Joe Zaretzki."[2] By Sunday, January 10, the press was convinced that Erway would be out, and that he would be replaced possibly by Senator Bronston of Queens. The thinking was that since the concentration was on the Senate leadership, Stanley Steingut would be elected as Assembly Speaker and that Bronston would prevail because he was from Queens where Moses Weinstein was Mayor Wagner's lieutenant. Somehow the Mayor would support Bronston, if Weinstein supported him. In this, the press was mistaken, because Mayor Wagner did not operate this way. He had given his word to Anthony Travia, and since keeping his word was a hallmark of the man's character, I did not expect him to deviate one iota from it! Anyhow, Weinstein did not pressure the mayor to support Bronston and it soon became obvious that Moses himself was not committed to Bronston.

By Monday, January 11, things were getting intractable. That night, State Chairman McKeon called a meeting in Albany to propose a solution to the problem. McKeon suggested that if all candidates withdrew, then Senator Bronston could be chosen Majority Leader. To make Joe Zaretzki happy, McKeon proposed Zaretzki be made the Chairman of the Senate Committee on Codes, where he would have, as chairman, a personal fund of five thousand dollars for entertainment. To sweeten the pot, McKeon suggested the budget be boosted to ten thousand dollars. This sounded like a bribe to me, but I kept quiet. Furthermore, if we withdrew the name of Anthony Travia, then he could be given an additional judgeship in the Court of Claims to appoint. This struck me as peculiar at the time because I was certain that the Court of Claims judges were appointed by the Governor. Nevertheless, I listened to the suggestions, made a few comments about the inadvisability of dictating to the Democratic leadership, and promised to make these suggestions known to the major.

I had brought the New York City Election Commissioner, Maurice J. O'Rourke, to this meeting with the State Chairman and the others. On the train back to the City, he followed me to the smoking car and asked, "What in the hell do these guys think they are doing? They're trying to bribe you!" I replied that it seemed that way, and I would have to report the matter to the Mayor.

When I got back to New York, the Mayor called a meeting with Julius Edelstein, still his personal aide, and me to discuss the whole matter. First on the agenda was how to handle this whole mess. The press was making a lot of angry noises and had begun to blame the Mayor for not bringing about some solution to the impasse; something had to be done quickly. I suggested the Major telephone Senator Kennedy and ask him to withdraw the candidates pledged to him. We would also withdraw our candidates and we would leave it up to the legislative caucus to choose the leadership. I suggested this because I wanted Senator Kennedy to realize that we knew he was behind this sorry mess. The Mayor liked the strategy and immediately placed the call. Yet when the Mayor suggested Kennedy withdraw his delegates, the Senator strongly protested that there were no delegates pledged to him.

This was ridiculous because we knew better. What we should have immediately done, but did not, was to go to the press and reveal the conversation. That way, the press would have pressed Kennedy for corroboration, and he would have had to do one of two things—either he would have to stand publicly with his supporters, or he would have to deny them, thereby creating severe problems for himself and them. Not going public on this issue was a mistake which further prolonged the deadlock until February, at which point the energy of Kennedy supporters began to lag.

Governor Rockefeller, fed up with the situation, decided to jump in on our side. In a round-about way, I knew beforehand that Rockefeller was ready to join us. For some time I had been on the Board of Overseers of the College of Virgin Islands and I was friendly with former Governor Ralph Paewonsky of the Virgin Islands. In a meeting concerning the College, Ralph leaned over to me and said, "I think you are going to win your fight in Albany." In surprise, I asked, "What do you know about it?" He replied, with an enigmatic smile, "Never mind. The Governor will see to it over this weekend." It struck me that if Republican Governor Rockefeller were going to step in, it meant that he would prefer to ally himself with Wagner who was more of his political views, though a Democrat, than with somebody so power-hungry as his opponent, the freshman Senator from New York.

As it turned out, Paewonsky was correct, for in mid-February when the Legislature met to elect its leaders, the Governor delivered the necessary Republican votes: Anthony Travia became the Speaker of the Assembly and Joseph Zaretzki, the Senate's Majority Leader. I considered this a defeat for Robert Kennedy and a victory for the Mayor. But as it turned out, this struggle was only the beginning skirmish of a long battle that lasted throughout my entire tenure as New York County Leader.

The business of "lulus"

One of the things that came out of the struggle to reorganize the New York State Legislature was the question of "lulus." As I stated before, at one of the meetings, Chairman McKeon had made the suggestion of a double lulu—that is, ten thousand dollars expense money a year, rather than the usual five thousand, for the Chairman of the Senate Codes Committee. I had dutifully reported this to the mayor, who then reported it to the press. The upshot was that Chairman McKeon denied that he had ever made a bribe offer, while the Mayor and I insisted that it sounded like a bribe to us. Soon the State Investigation Committee (S.I.C.) got involved and asked for hearings. I thought that Maurice J. O'Rourke, the Elections Commissioner, would corroborate what I had reported to the Mayor because he was the one who had followed me to the smoking car and asked me, "What in the hell do these guys think they are doing?" But when we were called before the State Investigation Commission, O'Rourke, who had by this time gone over to the Kennedy forces, claimed that he had not heard any such thing. In addition, Moses Weinstein, the Queens County Leader, also decided not to corroborate my story.

At this point, I was very upset with the way things were going before the S.I.C. I did not want the investigation to end on a note that suggested I had not been quite clear about what happened, but Julius Edelstein once again came up with a brilliant idea. He suggested I demand a lie detector test for all the participants, which I did. My challenge was picked up by the newspapers, and as reported by the *New York Post*, a spokesman for McKeon said that the State Chairman would not comment on my challenge because "the testimony before the S.I.C. speaks for itself."[3] Regrettably, the S.I.C. did not take me up on the challenge either, although polygraph results were admissible as evidence in those days.[4]

The outcome of this whole affair was that the State Investigation Commission sent the report to Rockefeller with no recommendations.[5] For myself, I felt that I had been vindicated because I was the only one in this affair who had offered to take a public lie detector test, or undergo whatever examinations that would prove the veracity of my statements.

My adventures with Edward Koch

Edward I. Koch became the Mayor of New York City in 1977, and by most assessments, he has been a successful mayor. But in the late spring of 1965, the Koch I knew was not the more mellow and accommodating fellow we know today.

In 1965, Koch considered himself part of the Reform movement in the Democratic Party. He had been successful in wrestling the leadership of the 1st Assembly District, comprised of the greater part of Greenwich Village, and formerly controlled by Carmine DeSapio. Koch was insecure in his victory, always expecting the possibility of DeSapio's making a comeback. In the 1965 redistricting of Manhattan, the Party drew lines in such a way that Koch thought would give DeSapio a chance to make that much-feared return. This he was determined not to let happen. In conversations with him, he asked that the lines be redrawn to prevent the return of the man in the dark glasses. He argued that he could not win with all the Italians in his district and accused me of setting up a district to assist in Carmine's return. I considered that statement most outrageous, and I informed Koch that if he heard of this statement later on, he should not be surprised. This was not the first time that Koch had accused me of trying to bring Carmine DeSapio back to power, and I decided to make public his remarks about the Italians, and I promptly did so.

In retrospect, I am not at all certain that I did the right thing, but I was indeed very angry at Koch's accusations; and furthermore, I was disturbed by statements that I considered prejudiced. As County Leader, I was trying to bring all ethnic groups together within the fold of the Democratic Party, carrying on a useful tradition which we'd had for many, many years.

When the news broke, Koch, as expected, vehemently denied every word of it, although my statement was corroborated by Richard Levy and Louis Grossman, members of the County Law Committee. I'll say one thing for Edward Koch, then as now, right or wrong, he had the courage of a kamikaze pilot. The very next day, I read that he had been a guest of the McDougal Street Area Neighborhood Association, an association made of mostly Italians. When questioned, he said my statement was "utterly false," and that I had made it because "he, Raymond Jones, cannot control our votes."[6]

I had not wanted to control Mr. Koch's vote nor the votes of his Club. As County Leader, I needed someone in a leadership position who would not be divisive, except on a matter of principle, and on whom I could count to consider the welfare of the Party. As it turned out, my initial problems with Edward Koch, and my suspicions of his undependability at the time turned out to be true when Republican John V. Lindsay ran for Mayor in 1965.

In that election, the Democratic candidate was Abraham Beame, who lost to Lindsay. On the day before the election, Koch, to everyone's surprise, came out in favor of John Lindsay. Here was Edward Koch, a District Leader, responsible for securing the polls and getting out the vote for the Democratic Party, supporting at the last moment the Republican candidate! His declaration certainly swayed Democratic votes for Lindsay, and left the polls unprotected. This was, to me, the most reprehensible thing a District Leader could do. Koch's action also vindicated, in my own mind, that sense of untrustworthiness I had felt about the man in the earlier confrontation, when he wanted the Italians gerrymandered out of his district.

This time I felt Ed Koch had gone too far, and I suggested the County Executive Committee meet so that questions of censure, expulsion, or whatever move was appropriate, be discussed. I scheduled the meeting for November 18. Some of my colleagues, however, did not share the sense of outrage that I felt at Koch's dereliction of duty. Frank O'Connor, the new City Council President-elect, made a public stand that he was opposed to the expulsion of Koch and his co-leader, Mrs. Carol Greitzer, because "the Democratic Party cannot afford to splinter itself in the pursuit of political heresies."[7] I had been a supporter of Frank O'Connor for some time, but what he meant by that statement was beyond me. Questioned on the matter by the reporters in the wake of O'Connor's statement, I said with respect to Koch's action, "In my opinion, sir, this is irresponsible, dishonorable, and reprehensible, and no excuses can justify it."[8] I meant it at that time, and I mean it even now. Such behavior by a leader on the eve of election, when he is bound to support the Party's nominees, is reprehensible. It wasn't that I was obsessed with expelling Edward Koch, but I felt some public action had to be taken, as a message given to any other person who contemplated similar behavior in the future.

Several Reform leaders sided with Edward Koch, and announced that they were against "purging, censuring, or chastising Koch and Greitzer." But, in the same breath, this particular group stated, "While we do not agree with their [Koch and Greitzer's] action, we believe it is not the responsibility of the Executive Committee to pass judgement on the political views of its members." They suggested that these judgements should be made by the Democrats who elected Koch and Greitzer.[9] Of course, this argument was nonsense, merely a verbal smokescreen designed to obfuscate the issue. As County Leader, it was my responsibility to make sure that the various segments of the Democratic Party in New York County support the candidate of our choice. I knew that my position was responsible, fair, and reasonable, and that the majority of Democrats agreed with me, so these statements made prior to our Executive Committee meeting did not cause me grave concern.

When the Executive Committee met on November 18, it accepted a resolution declaring the obligation of all District Leaders to support properly nominated candidates. The resolution stated, "We condemn the actions of any members of this body who have violated this obligation without resigning from this body, with sufficient notice to enable the party to replace them, and believe that they have betrayed their Party, their obligations as Democratic district leaders, and their constituencies."[10] The vote for censure was a solid two-thirds majority, but consistent with his view that he can never be wrong, Koch told reporters that this resolution had nothing to do with him and Mrs. Greitzer! The reasoning he gave at that time was characteristic of the man, then and later. Speaking to me, with reporters present, he asked if he was the person being censured, how was it that his name was not mentioned?

Four years later, when I was no longer County Leader and when I supported Lindsay, he wrote to remind me that now the shoe was on the other foot. His unprincipled thinking prevented him from seeing that I could support Lindsay because then I was neither the County Leader nor a District Leader. I had no responsibility for manning the polls and getting the vote out. Furthermore, I had not been committed to support anyone, either through organizational position or previous statements. Consequently, I was free, morally and politically, to do whatever I wished. He seemed to enjoy a psychological lift, as perverse and incorrect as it was, in contending that I was doing the same thing he had done in 1965.

Edward I. Koch has been a very popular mayor. But anyone who has done a close reading of his autobiography will soon realize that Koch is an individual who can do no wrong, even if he has to go through what may be called bizarre psychological contortions to reach unreasonable and irrational conclusion. He seems to have improved with age, and he may yet turn out to be a very good mayor. But as of now, my vote is still out.

The fight to make Mrs. Motley borough president

Another of my immediate concerns in early 1965 was that of making Constance Baker Motley Borough President. It had been a ticklish and delicate operation to secure her the State Senatorial nomination the previous year. At that time, as District Leader and leader of the Carver Democratic Club in Harlem, I wanted to promote Mrs. Motley's candidacy for State Senate because her yeoman work in the NAACP's legal department assured her credentials, and, more important, I wanted to see a woman representing the Harlem community. I strongly believed more women should have highly visible posts in the Democratic party. Mrs. Motley's candidacy would have great significance for Black women in New York City and State, and this added to the value of her candidacy. Of course, in all modesty, I thought that eventually it would reflect well on me to have sponsored her candidacy, and I have never had anything against good reflections!

Thinking of Constance Motley, it occurred to me that somewhere in the future it might be possible to engineer things so that she could become the first Black woman mayor of New York City. Such ideas I kept strictly to myself, and to my wife, a staunch feminist and civil rights supporter. Familiar with the system, I knew there would have to be an intermediate step before anything like what I envisioned could be accomplished.

The opportunity to move her one step further toward my secret ambition came with an opening occurred for the Borough Presidency of Manhattan, when Edward R. Dudley, a member of my club, left that post for the Supreme Court of the State of New York. During Dudley's administration, Earl Brown, a Black man, had been the Deputy Borough President. In the beginning it was clear that almost everyone favored Earl Brown except the mayor and me. And, believe it or not, Brown turned out to be the favorite of the Reform Democrats! They met some time in mid-February, and as reported by the press, gave Brown a 33–14 preference vote over one of their very own, Francis W. H. Adams. On the City Council, of which I was a member, I knew in early February that the majority of my colleagues were for Brown. They knew him, felt comfortable with him; their sense of familiarity did not breed contempt but rather contentment, even though they called him "Look Down Brown." But I was not happy with Brown, and I informed the Mayor that I would not support Brown under any circumstance. Judge Watson or Mrs. Motley would be acceptable to me, but not Earl.

Outside the Council, the press and interested observers saw the contest as between Judge Watson and Earl Brown. But the moment Mrs. Motley's name was placed in contention, the politics became labyrinthine. The Kennedy camp made the first move in this complicated game by leaking the story that Senator Kennedy had nominated Motley for a Federal judgeship. The press widely reported this story, which was never contradicted. I was not fooled by this, because Mrs. Motley had given me the word that she would accept the Borough Presidency if the City Council elected her, and I felt certain that she would not renege on her commitment despite the blandishments of Senator Kennedy. My concern was therefore fleeting, and I left the promotion of Mrs. Motley as the first woman Borough President of Manhattan in the deft hands of the Mayor.

I should have known, however, that, even with only six days to go before the election, there would be trouble. It came when Congressman Powell, along with Hulan Jack, Mark Southall, and even my old friend, Percy Sutton, insisted that Mrs. Motley would be "much more effective as a Senator than a Borough President."[11] In this, several Harlem groups joined Powell and Jack in support of Earl Brown, but these orchestrations got nowhere.

Some voices also argued that the position of Manhattan Borough President had become a "Negro preserve," because a Black person had held that position since 1954. The *New York Times*, in its usual high-flown flight from reality, commented:

The only candidates mentioned are Negroes, because the post has come to be regarded by many politicians as a vested preserve of the Negro segment of the city's population. Since 1953 the office has in fact been held only by Negroes. This is an unfortunate, undemocratic and unwholesome development.

It is intolerable that any public office should be regarded as a private property of any special group—racial, religious, economic or social—within the community. Merit, not color of the skin, nor place of worship, nor country of origin is what should count; but, unfortunately, as often as not in this city it doesn't. . . . [12]

I read this editorial with great amusement, because the editors of the *New York Times* knew better. They pretended, disingenuously, not to know that in New York City exactly this kind of political job distribution was what made the Democratic Party and the city work. At all times in my years in politics, the concerns of the Jewish constituency, the Irish constituency, the Catholic constituency, and all constituencies, had to be taken into account if the entire community were to feel that its problems, interests, and perspectives were always taken seriously and dealt with in some even-handed way. What seemed to bother the *New York Times* most was that because the Black electorate had now made its position clear and the power of its votes felt, Black people were somehow at fault.

As it turned out, Mrs. Motley was elected by a unanimous decision of the City Council, with the first round vote of 5 to 3 finally being resolved unanimously. Even the two Manhattan Republicans came to the realization that she was the best possible candidate, the most deserving of the job. They knew that if word got out that they had opposed a Black woman so obviously qualified, it might have a negative effect on their political fortunes, perhaps from the women's constituencies, and certainly from the Black constituency. These men were too smart to allow themselves to be distracted by blandishments from Powell and his group or even from the *New York Times*. With Mrs. Motley's election, I breathed easier, because I felt that the intermediate step had been taken towards my ultimate goal of one day seeing her as the first Black woman Mayor of New York City.

The election of Mrs. Motley to the Borough Presidency of Manhattan did not end this saga. She remained prominent in New York City Democratic politics into the fall of the next year. her election by the City Council meant that she would have to run in the November elections for a full term. I knew full well that come primary time, she would again run into opposition from Adam Powell and the rest, since the wound of their loss in their earlier opposition would not have healed by then. I believed they would make at least one more try to elect their own candidate. I reasoned, though, that she would use the time between February and the September primaries to mend fences and establish a high positive profile, preventing any late bushwhacking by the Powell forces; Mrs. Motley was too brilliant and astute a woman to do otherwise. I was convinced she could carry on on her own and make a name for herself, as she had done in her short term in the State Legislature. In this view I was not disappointed. Neither was I disappointed in my expectations of Congressman Powell's opposition.

In mid-June Powell threatened a primary fight. The argument was the same as in February: that Mrs. Motley had been chosen by Mayor Wagner with "absolutely no consultation with Negro leaders, including J. Raymond Jones." In fact, the Mayor had consulted with me, so the Congressman's remark was without basis, as were all his remarks about Mrs. Motley, except for his qualification that Mrs. Motley was "a very fine person and I have the utmost respect for her."[13] The real objection to Mrs. Motley was not that she was not qualified, and not that she would not represent the interests of Black people as well as the entire Manhattan community, but because there were several people within the Powell organization desirous of the job and Adam had to say something to placate them. Adam's wild inventions did not worry me, because having sounded out the members of the New York County Democratic Party Executive Committee, I knew I had the votes to support my candidate, regardless of the fulminations of the Congressman from Harlem. As it turned out the Executive Committee gave Mrs. Motley 63 of the 66 votes cast. Interestingly, Congressman Powell abstained. The vote in the Executive Committee meant that in the September primaries Mrs. Motley would run unopposed. As for the November elections, its conclusion was foregone!

My own situation for renomination to the City Council in the September primaries concerned me more: the Powell group had produced an opponent, George Miller, at that time the City's Deputy Licensing Commissioner. Since Mayor Wagner had decided to leave politics and was not running, the Democratic mayoral nomination was up for grabs between Paul Screvane and Abraham Beame, resulting in two contending tickets. Adam and Hulan Jack and their friends had decided to join the Beame ticket against me because I supported Paul Screvane. For some reason Abraham Beame was more popular in Harlem than Paul Screvane, and the reasoning was that in putting George Miller on the Beame ticket, Miller would have an edge over me in the primaries. As it turned out, Miller lost by a 6-to-5 margin because he was not, in my opinion, a very attractive candidate.

But Abraham Beame did win the Democratic Mayoral primary, only to lose to John V. Lindsay in the November elections. Of course, on the basis of registration, Abraham Beams should have won, but 1965 was a very strange year. The party's public squabbles did not invite voter confidence. The party was no longer identified with the disadvantaged, and Beame appeared to be a dim apparition compared to John Lindsay in person and especially on television.

How did this happen? Barbara Carter in her book on this election asked this same question and answered it in this way:

How could a Republican win in a city where Republicans were so pronounced a minority? How could a WASP win in a city where White Anglo-Saxon Protestants were no more than seven percent of the population? In the wee hours of that morning, a team of political researchers at one of the major networks worriedly reexamined their figures and scratched their heads. It didn't add up. Lindsay simply couldn't have won. For their figures showed that Beame had, after all, won all the traditional Democratic constituencies. He had won sixty-seven percent of the Jewish vote, sixty-seven percent of the Puerto Rican vote, sixty percent of the Negro. He even had a slight edge in the Irish vote, which had split three ways, almost evenly, between Buckley, Lindsay and Beame. Lindsay, to be sure, had won the Italian vote, the largest group next to the Jews in the city. But Lindsay's edge there was no more than one percent (and the Italians make up only sixteen percent of the electorate; the Jews, more than a third).

But Lindsay had won, the final vote gave him 102,000 plurality over Beame. And there was an explanation. For Lindsay had dipped into the normal Democratic majorities everywhere in a general way right across the board.[14]

All this was indeed true. Lindsay was a believable candidate, a symbol of new times and new hopes. Our ticket seemed comparatively tired and shopworn, and about that I could do very little. The process had given us our ticket, and so we had concentrated on getting out the vote. That we did, as efficiently as in times past, but it was not good enough. We were now in the era of "personal politics!"

Soon after the election an aide to President Johnson telephoned, seeking my approval for Motley's appointment to a Federal judgeship. Although I gave my immediate and enthusiastic endorsement, I cannot say that I was entirely thrilled by this development. If I had it my way, I would have preferred to have seen her remain in the Borough Presidency and make a run for the Mayor's office in 1969. On the other hand, I had to consider Mrs. Motley's personal desires, and it became clear to me after conversations with her, that she preferred to be on the Federal Bench, in an area for which she had been trained and where she would not have to deal with the hurly-burly and insecurity of politics all her life. In addition, the pay of Federal judges was almost equal to that of the Borough President and the $5,000 difference actually was made up, it could be argued, by the security of the judgeship. I gave my blessings, but as I talked about the appointment with my wife that night, I said: "There goes my candidate for Mayor."

The departure of Mrs. Motley left me two major problems in 1966—one, a replacement for the Borough President, and two, and more important, the race for Governor of New York. The business of the Borough Presidency was easy. In the 1965 elections, the Democrats retained the majority of the seats in the City Council for New York County and, as the press reported, I had been very much involved in the election of two new Democratic Councilmen, David B. Friedland and Carlos M. Rios, the latter our first Puerto Rican on the City Council. I knew I could count on their votes as well as that of Saul S. Sharison in any election for Borough President. In this decision, the Republicans did not figure, because in an election to fill the unexpired term of Borough President, that Borough's representatives in the City Council decide. As was the case of Constance Motley in 1965, the Manhattan delegation was overwhelmingly Democratic; therefore, the choice was ours.

Several names were put forward, among them Percy Ellis Sutton, the Assemblyman from Harlem; Herbert Evans, of my own club, at that time chairman of the Housing Redevelopment Board; State Senator Manfred Ohrenstein; Civil Court Judge Jawna Sandifer of Harlem; and Assemblyman Albert C. Blumenthal of the West Side. My first choice was Percy Sutton. Although he was keeping bad company with the likes of Congressman Powell and his boys, I thought he had the best personality and the best skills for the job. I did not consider any of my own club members, such as James L. Watson, then a Civil Court Judge, because I knew President Johnson was considering him for the Federal Customs Court, a position I knew Watson deserved. As for Herbert Evans, I knew that if Lindsay did not reappoint him as Chairman of the Housing and Redevelopment Board, I would have no trouble finding some place appropriate for him. The key thing to consider here was that Percy Sutton, in the public eye as an Assemblyman, had style and presence, was a better campaigner, and more important, wanted the post more than Herbert.[15] As County Leader, I had to take these things into account because the desire of a candidate in many instances translates into positive vibrations among the electorate. This factor cannot be discounted in winning campaigns. Sutton became my candidate, because he was widely known in the City and the State as the co-parent of a new divorce law that made it easier for people to rid themselves of the misery of unhappy marriage in New York State. Given the rising tide of divorce in the 1960s, this was an extremely popular bit of legislation! Furthermore, in the State Legislature he was also Mr. Civil Rights. Yet he pursued his ends with such grace that at no time was he seen as confrontational or hostile. This man had style, and in him I thought I saw our first Black mayor.

The other five Manhattan Democratic Councilmen may not have been thinking along those lines, but I knew that once it was understood that I wanted Sutton, there would be little opposition. Certain Councilmen like Saul S. Sharison made noises about other candidates, but all this was a smokescreen. And when this same Sharison announced to the press that it was "illegal, unethical and improper" for any city office to be set aside for Negroes or other ethnic group, we all knew he was merely anticipating the hypocritical criticism of the *New York Times*.[16] In the end, Councilman Robert A. Low nominated Sutton, and Saul Sharison, who had said he supported Louis DeSalvo, seconded the motion. The Republicans did their duty and made the election unanimous. Everyone was happy, even Mayor Lindsay.

Chapter 8

A Time of Troubles: Robert Kennedy and Me

IN 1966 A DEMOCRAT had to be found to challenge Nelson Rockefeller for the governorship of New York State. By January everyone in the Democratic Party realized that Rockefeller had turned out to be a most formidable character, and that anyone we chose to run against him, despite the overwhelming majority of Democratic voters in the State, would indeed be a very long shot. Nonetheless, the Party had a responsibility to put up a candidate and to put the best showing on the face of things.

I felt as early as May that interest in the gubernatorial race was not very high. In the New York area, I thought that a little excitement could be generated early, from which some momentum could be sustained into summer. With this in mind, I made the announcement in early May that for the convention, to be held in Buffalo, in early September, I personally would be backing former Mayor Wagner as a favorite son for governor. I also told reporters that, in my position as County Leader, I would try to persuade the entire New York County delegation to back Wagner, at least through the first ballot. This statement generated some excitement in the press, because it was generally known that City Council President Frank O'Connor, and Franklin D. Roosevelt, Jr., both from New York City, were interested in running.

I knew only too well that since the Mayor had left office, his disenchantment with the battles of public office prevented him from considering running unless the odds were strongly in his favor. For the governorship, this was clearly not the case. But one never knows in politics, and a lot could happen between May and November. As it turned out, however, Wagner was not interested, and when the convention met, Howard Samuels, an early contender had faded, and the New York City delegation promoted their own boy, Frank O'Connor. We arrived at this decision easily, perhaps because most people thought that a win against "Rocky" would be the equivalent of the proverbial snowball in hell.

But the choice for Lieutenant Governor, where a real possibility for winning existed, was a more difficult one, made even more so by the intervention of Senator Robert F. Kennedy. What had happened was Robert Kennedy had secretly flown into Buffalo and met with Stanley S. Steingut, the State Chairman, and others at a meeting at which I was not a guest. Kennedy, I learned, had quickly made known his preference for Orin Lehman—nephew of former Governor Lehman.

This action made me furious, for Orin Lehman was from my county, and never before in my experience had a candidate for such a high post, or any post for that matter, been selected from a county without the County Chairman's knowledge. Not only was I not notified of this development, but neither was the rest of the Manhattan delegation. So I went down to the convention floor in a state of high umbrage, and there, of course, were the newspaper and television boys. As I came in, one of the television reporters grabbed my arm and asked if I would make a statement. I did not have to ask the topic. Without much thought for the consequences, I said, "New York State has made progress in eliminating the boss rule, and I am not now going to allow it to return." As it was, the press knew more about the affair than I did, and about the role that Robert Kennedy had played in this nefarious meeting, so the fellows tried to extract exciting statements from me while a crowd gathered round.

At this time certain members of the Kennedy group, apprised of what was taking place, hurriedly pulled me off-camera. When they had gotten me away from the hall in a hastily gathered meeting, this bunch asked me, "What do you want?" I replied, "Take his name off." They all looked at me incredulously, which prompted me to ask the question during their silence, "Would you have done this to one of your own?" And then it struck me that perhaps they had done it because they did not see me as one of them racially. So I asked the question point blank, "Is it because I am the Black County Leader that you have presumed you could do this and get away with it?" There was no answer, and I then decided this was the psychological moment to give them my alternative, Howard Samuels, a candidate endorsed by both me and, of all people, the Reform boys. Since they knew now that the Reform group was with me, and that we would definitely make a fight and embarrass them, they accepted my compromise, running off in all directions with relief on their faces.

Although I relished this small victory over Robert Kennedy, there was no victory for me or the Party to relish in November. The entire ticket went down to defeat, with our only consolation being that the Assembly and the Senate remained in our hands.

The appointment and election of judges: Robert Kennedy and the surrogate fight of 1966

In New York City during my tenure as Tammany Leader, the Magistrates Court, the Special Courts, and the Domestic Relations Courts, comprised that part of the judicial system where all the judges were mayoral appointments. They amounted to almost one hundred judges. Municipal Court, City Court, County Court in General Sessions, Surrogates, and New York Supreme Court judges were elected. All together, these judges amounted to approximately one hundred and seventy five persons. In the City of New York, too, were even other judges: the Court of Claims, its judges appointed by the Governor, and of course, judges in the Federal Courts, the New York State Supreme Court, the New York Court of Appeals. These last two were elected officials, with the parties playing a role in their nominations.

Prior to my becoming Leader, the nomination of "City" judges was really an exercise in amicable relations between the political parties. New York at that time, and at least for the three decades prior to my becoming Leader, was essentially a Democratic City, and therefore the majority of the judges came from the Democratic Party organization. In the majority of instances, the Republican Party supported these judges, and consequently, only in a few primaries did judges run opposed.

Due to the overwhelming plurality of Democratic voters, the Republican Party, seeing it as unlikely and too costly for a Republican nominee to win, usually supported the Democratic nominee. Professors Kaufman and Sayre put it very nicely in their book on the governance of New York City. Nominees for judicial office, they said,

commonly enjoyed the endorsements of both major parties; this is one of the reasons for their security of tenure. Originally, the custom of joint nomination apparently applied only to judges who had completed a full term on the bench. Judges appointed to fill vacancies in an elective court until the next election, and candidates running for judicial office without any prior service in the positions at stake, ordinarily encountered an opposing candidate from the only major party. Over the years, however, the parties began to make bargains with each other involving temporarily appointed incumbents and even nonincumbents, so that many more candidates for judicial office make their runs uncontested than the "sitting-judge" tradition would lead one to anticipate. For example, twice since the end of World War II, more than 80 percent of the judicial seats to be filled by election were won by candidates having both Republican and Democratic nominations.[1]

For the nomination of judges to elective posts prior to my tenure as New York County Leader, there was a Judicial Convention involving all the five counties of New York City. Again, most of the delegates to this convention merely rubberstamped the nominees put forth by the County Leaders, who received a number of possibilities from their Assembly District Leaders. The Convention then met, not so much to promote or deny nominations, but to ratify the County Leaders' decision and to conduct business of judicial patronage and other cognate issues with which politicians are always absorbed.

During the early sixties, a wholesale reform in the method of judicial appointment, nomination, and election became a very hot political topic for the Reform wing of our party, as well as for the Liberal Party. I watched this development with great interest, first as District Leader and then as a City Councilman and County Leader, because I had seen these reform initiatives before, always in the guise of "good government." In most instances they had turned out to be nothing other than the desire of a group of people interested in seizing power for themselves.

As the rift on this issue became more public, it attracted a varied set of individuals. Some were dissatisfied with the running of the Democratic Party and many were displeased with their rate of upward mobility within the Party. They formed ranks with the Reform Democrats to make the question of judicial nominations and appointments seem a moral crusade, while in fact it was being used as a power play through which they surreptitiously sought to gain power for themselves while decrying it in the hands of others.

It should be noted that when a judgeship straddles two counties, the County Leaders involved confer to decide the nominee and the county from which the nominee should come. This was the situation of the Supreme Court judgeships when Edward Costikyan served as compromise County Leader from 1960 to 1963. Adam Clayton Powell, at this time a District Leader and still the powerful Congressman from Harlem, had taken upon himself the authority to confer with the Bronx County Leader, Charles Buckley, to make a successful deal for a candidate for the Supreme Court. Every now and again, a powerful District Leader, particularly if he's a Congressman, or a leader in the State Senate or Assembly, will try this kind of thing, but it's a situation which no self-respecting County Leader will tolerate. By the time I became Tammany Leader in 1964, I noted that this had taken place, and when I learned that Congressman Powell was trying to effect a similar deal in 1966, I met with Charlie Buckley and told him that I would not appreciate it. I was gratified that Buckley respected my leadership, as I respected his, and we agreed that any such further attempts would not be countenanced. I found out later, however, that the Reform group tried "the Adam Powell play," and while they were at it, Senator Robert Kennedy, always trying to establish himself in all areas of New York politics, stepped into the fray.

Kennedy, of course, tried to give the impression that he was above mere politics, but he used the Reformers to put pressure on me to give greater consideration to the candidates he proposed. I responded to this by informing the Kennedyites that I would agree to consider any candidate recommended by them, provided that there be an agreement between them and the Bar Association on one candidate. The Kennedyites then put out feelers to the Bronx Organization on a candidate whom they knew I would not accept, in the hope that Charlie Buckley would go along with them. But Buckley, as a result of our previous talk, would not be pressured. In fact, the Reform group could not even decide on one candidate to propose to Buckley. They had internal problems of their own! And when Robert Kennedy tried to arbitrate within the group, he found to his utter frustration, that like the Star Wars character, he lacked the "force." As a result, nothing came of the attempts of the Reform Democrats to make a deal with the Bronx Organization, and eventually I met with Charlie Buckley, retrieved three State Supreme Court Judges' slots for New York County, and placed matters once again on an even keel. But the junior Senator from New York had not given up on, if not "reforming" the judiciary of New York, at least dominating its political aspects. The opportunity availed itself when a vacancy in the Surrogate Court in New York County occurred that had to be filled in the next general election.

Jones and Kennedy in the surrogate court battle

A Surrogate Judge is one of the most powerful in the entire judicial system. For one thing, the term is for fourteen years, and since the judge is usually backed by both parties, if he or she has performed the job with passable integrity and intelligence, it is likely that nomination and election to another fourteen years is assured. Besides the fact that the salary is one of the highest in the State—more than that of a Federal Judge—and since this position protects widows and orphans, being the arbiter of wills, estates, adoptions, guardianships, and the like, the range and value of its patronage is also very large. The nomination and election of a Surrogate therefore, is a very important matter for both the major and minor parties and for lawyers. The election is also of great interest to a wide range of appointed staff, including clerks, court stenographers, and secretaries, as to County Leaders, District Leaders, and even Election District Campaigns.

In 1966 the Liberal Party and the Reform Democrats saw the nomination of Arthur Klein for the Surrogate vacancy by both the Democratic and Republican County Leadership as evidence that a "deal" (which meant something most unsavory) had been made. What had in fact happened was this: I had convened the Executive Committee of the New York Democratic County Committee and had tried hard to get the Executive Committee to agree on a candidate. This turned out to be impossible, and, as the Committee members' exasperation grew, Vincent Albano, the New York County Republican Leader, suggested that Judge Arthur G. Klein would be acceptable to him. He thought that Klein would also be a fine candidate for the Democrats. At this point as County Leader, it was my duty to assess the worth of his suggestion, and so I immediately checked Arthur Klein's credentials. Besides having been a Congressman and now a sitting Supreme Court Judge, I also found that if he were to come up for another term on the Supreme Court Bench, he most certainly would have the endorsement of both political parties. I checked also with a number of Supreme Court Judges and they considered Klein competent and fit for the Surrogate's job. I therefore placed his name before the Executive Committee, and we agreed on Judge Klein.

There was nothing new in this procedure except that, in this particular instance, Republicans had thought of Arthur G. Klein first. With the announcement that Republicans and Democrats of New York county had agreed on the candidacy of Mr. Klein, vitriolic opposition surfaced immediately from the Reform Democrats and from the Liberal Party. I then realized that I had made a severe political mistake by not conferring extensively with the Reform Democrats, and neither had I conferred with the "great leader" of the Liberty Party, Alex Rose. The trouble was that I was not in any mood to confer at that time with Alex Rose on any issue, but I also suspect that I had based my reluctance to do so on the information that Klein's people had consulted with Rose and found him already opposed to Klein's candidacy. Perhaps if I had made a courtesy call, the force of the attack would have been less; however, I thought we had the votes to elect Arthur Klein, and I was very, very wrong.

In this matter I should have anticipated the reaction of the junior Senator from New York. The first I had heard of Robert Kennedy's involvement in the controversy was in the *New York Times* under the headline "Silverman to Get Liberal Support." Until that day, we had understood that the Liberal

Party had endorsed Civil Court Judge George S. Starke to run against Klein in the June 28 primary. But the paper claimed that Starke had withdrawn as the Liberal Party's candidate in favor of Supreme Court Justice Samuel J. Silverman, because as Starke put it, "Justice Silverman's candidacy affords the opportunity for a broad coalition of good government forces to oppose this deal. . . . " The *Times*, noting that it was not just a Liberal Party activity, said, "The principle celebrity of the hastily formed coalition behind Justice Silverman is Senator Robert F. Kennedy."[2] In this instance the *New York Times* correctly noted that this "celebrity" candidacy was not very persuasive, yet it weighed in on May 8 with an editorial in which it characterized Justice Klein as having been a mediocre Congressman as well as an "undistinguished judge." Perhaps not realizing that the Republicans had suggested Klein to us and perhaps not understanding how the politics of this situation worked, *The Times* continued: "Under these circumstances, it is imperative that the Republican and Liberal parties unite in choosing a truly impressive lawyer."[3] This I should have recognized as the first move on the part of the *New York Times* to endorse Silverman, for it must have known already that he was the Liberal Party's foremost candidate. The suggestion that the Republicans join together with the Liberals was foolish, because, as I said before, Klein was suggested to us by the Republican Party. Indeed, after the primary, he did remain the Republican Party's candidate!

On Tuesday, May 24th, the press reported that the Liberal Party and the Reform Democrats had indeed selected Justice Silverman. The *New York Times* reported Mr. Kennedy as saying,

I intend to support Justice Silverman for the surrogate's nomination. He will make an outstanding surrogate. As a lawyer, a citizen of New York, and a public official, I am concerned about the integrity of the judiciary, and I have serious reservations about the manner in which Justice Klein was selected.[4]

Towards the end of May, in an attempt to drum up support for his candidate, Mr. Kennedy claimed that the manner in which Justice Klein had been selected was "tainted by the suspicion of corruption of a deal."[5]

Kennedy's statement angered me very much because although I had been in politics for many years and knew that smear attempts were part of the political process, this did not mean that I condoned, endorsed, or practiced such tactics myself. Attempts had been made to smear me before and I had been before several investigating committees, and at no time in my career had I ever been found guilty of any illegal, criminal, or even unethical behavior. The charge by Robert Kennedy that I was involved in corruption, when I was the elected County Leader and representative of my party in Manhattan, was just too much to take without a response. I called a press conference for Thursday, June 2, and stated:

The current outburst over the selection of Supreme Court Justice Arthur G. Klein as designee for the office of Judge of the Surrogate's Court has produced such a series of unfortunate distortions that it becomes necessary to search the record, to clear the air, and bring out the truth.

Characters have been wrongfully maligned, the Supreme Court has been demeaned, integrity of commitments is shown without value— and for what? To satisfy a combination of boundless and burning ambitions, the ruthless court quest for power, a vendetta to seize control.[6]

I told the press that the charges of a corrupt deal was an unmitigated lie, and I let it be known that Vincent Albano, the Republican Leader, has asked nothing of me. I reminded the press (and the reporters knew this) that the two-party support of Klein was standard procedure, and that there were other judicial races in which dual sponsorships were at that moment taking place. I pointed out that the only reason anyone had interjected himself into this race was because the Surrogate judgeship was a position with patronage worth millions of dollars, a very juicy plum, sought both by the Reformers and Liberals. There was no question in my mind that Robert Kennedy thought he would win this contest, unlike previous ones, because of his great personal popularity. If he were successful, then of course he would be the leading Democrat in New York City and State, considering that the Mayor was a Republican and so was our Governor.

Soon after this, Alex Rose, leader of the Liberal Party and friend of Senator Kennedy, stated that Albano and I had indeed made a deal, and that if the candidate were unchallenged, then the election was as good as over. Of course he was correct. There was nothing new about this, as I have pointed out before, this procedure had been used for years and produced very good judges. The question to be raised, which Messrs. Rose and Kennedy did not raise, was the worthiness of the candidate, Arthur G. Klein. The emphasis placed by both of them was on a deal having been made, with allusions to suspicions of corruption.

The Committee to elect Jason Silverman also issued a statement. It said:

For the first time in history, the Democratic and Republican organizations have given their joint endorsement for a candidate for a vacancy on the Surrogate's court. The circumstance of that cynical coalition is a real threat to the independence and integrity of the judiciary.[7]

This statement, as I pointed out to the press, was also untrue. I reminded them, for example, that William T. Collins had had joint Democratic and

Republican endorsement when he was elected Surrogate Judge in November 1946. In fact, other examples could be cited without fear of refutation. At this point it is important to note certain important details. It was generally understood around New York at this time that Alex Rose's position on the supposed deal between Albano and me emanated not entirely from his desire for good government, but because a deal had been made with the Democrats by the Republicans instead of with the Liberals. In fact, when John V. Lindsay ran for mayor in 1965, the Liberal Party had moved nimbly from its usual relationship with the Democratic Party to "fuse" with the Republicans in order to elect Lindsay. Indeed, Alex Rose was annoyed at the Republican Leader, Vincent Albano, for breaking the coalition they had enjoyed since the Lindsay election. That was why in its desperation, the Liberal Party had nominated Civil Court Judge Starke, at that time a registered Republican! It was at this point that Robert Kennedy interjected himself more on the side of the Reform Democrats than of the Liberal Party, by pushing a compromise candidate, Jason Silverman. The Liberals saw Silverman, a nominee of the Reform Democrats, as an opportunity to get back at the Regular Democrats by joining behind a candidate more popular than Judge Starke, persuading Starke to withdraw in favor of Silverman. In fact, on June 5, 1966, the *New York Times* under the byline of William V. Shannon, noted:

For his part, Mr. Rose not only arranged for Judge Starke to decline the Liberal nomination, but he also drew the partisan line sharply by attacking Deputy Mayor Robert Price, the Chief Advisor to Mr. Lindsay, on political strategy. In a formal statement last week, Mr. Rose accused Mr. Price of being a backstage participant to the Klein nomination.[8]

Shannon also noted the following:

The purely patronage aspects of the contest, however, have now been overshadowed by the larger political significance. Privately, Senator Kennedy insists that he stands to lose much and gain very little by becoming entangled in this controversy. Nevertheless, observers see several possible gains for him. His intervention further consolidates his support among local liberals who have been increasingly attracted to him by his stand on Vietnam and other issues. *If he is successful, he will seriously weaken and perhaps be able to overthrow Mr. Jones as Manhattan party leader, thereby depriving former mayor Robert F. Wagner of his strongest political ally.* Senator Kennedy does not look favorably upon Mr. Wagner's "dark horse" gubernatorial candidacy which Mr. Jones has been promoting. (Emphasis added)

Most important, by his opposition to the Klein candidacy, Mr. Kennedy has patched up his relations with Mr. Rose which had seriously deteriorated in the less than two years since he received Liberal party endorsement for the U.S. Senate.[9]

This was an astute analysis, because the Surrogate situation was actually being used as an excuse for Mr. Kennedy to consolidate his power in New York City and State. By getting rid of J. Raymond Jones, he would have achieved much to prevent any possible resurgence of Robert Wagner as a major political power in the state of New York.

Inevitably, race entered into this contest. My friend, Dr. Kenneth Clark, called an interracial group together and issued a statement that, "This struggle could be interpreted, even by moderates, as an attempt to constrict the power and prerogative of any political office attained by a Negro or as a desire to control or remove a Negro who seeks to exercise the usual authority of an office."[10] Chuck Stone, at that time, an aide to Congressman Adam Powell also supported this view. Although Stone did not invoke the racial aspect, he noted that there was an "aura of suspicion towards those who support Silverman."[11] Dr. Clark and others' denunciation was potent stuff, which the Kennedy and Rose people found difficult to confront, but in a very short time they found a Black respondent in the former leader of the Congress of Racial Equality (CORE), James Farmer. Farmer rejected the notion that race was involved in any way. He stated that the larger question was whether Blacks were "going to let the bosses make their election choice for them, thereby depriving them of their right to vote."[12] Although I had always had a high regard for Mr. Farmer, this statement depressed me. He had exposed himself to great physical danger and had worked tirelessly in the interest of Black people through CORE; yet he remained untutored in the normal political process. To suggest that the New York County Executive Committees of the Republican and Democratic Parties were boss-ruled was ridiculous! Farmer had forgotten that Blacks had elected their representatives on the County Executive Committees. His statement signified the danger of having someone of Farmer's stature talking about a process of which he had little knowledge.

Not only was Farmer dredged up by the Kennedy people to counteract the statements of Dr. Clark and others, but also James Meredith, who a few days before had been shot in his Mississippi "Freedom From Fear" walk, was brought to the scene to make the statement that for leaders of political parties to nominate judges for election was somehow anti-democratic and denied people the right to vote. Of course, I saw through the whole plan when Meredith publicly admitted that he had been brought onto the scene by Steven R. Smith, the brother-in-law of Senator Kennedy. Clearly Meredith had his own agenda, seeing in this issue the possibility of injecting himself into politics for some future possible political appointment. In fact, a few years later he made an abortive attempt to run against, of all people, Congressman Adam Clayton Powell in Harlem. From this ill-advised decision, he was forced to withdraw very soon, and the position he coveted went to one of my own associates, Charles Rangel.

The onslaught of Farmer, Meredith, and others, the expenditures of large sums of money, and the slick way in which the Silverman campaign was waged was too much for that uncharismatic and unseasoned candidate, Arthur Klein. A few days before the election he stated that he regretted getting into the whole business, that he never thought it would be anything like it had turned out to be, and that he would have preferred to remain on the Supreme Court. Clearly, Klein had not prepared himself for the ruthlessness of the campaign, and as I listened to his comment it became obvious to me that his selection, although perfectly ethical and proper from a legal point of view, was a political mistake. The "New Politics" was beyond him.

As primary day drew nearer, some of the Reform Democrats even floated the rumor that there had been an agreement between Vincent Albano and me, on a four-judge deal that involved Jacob Fuchsberg, Civil Court Judge Alfred Ascione, and Civil Court Judge William S. Shea for nominations to the Supreme Court. This, too, was nonsense. At that time the County organization was considering approximately twenty names for the Supreme Court. Among them were the names of Mr. Fuchsberg and Judge Ascione, all of whom would be submitted, as had been the practice since 1962, to the Bar Association. I, of course, challenged the Reform group to substantiate their accusation, but of course, no substantiation was forthcoming. A few days before the primary, the whole situation had degenerated into an unseemly and vicious quarrel. On June 24, the *Times* printed a letter from Clark written in response to its criticism that Dr. Clark and his group had accused Robert Kennedy of racism. Clark's response read in part as follows:

I am surprised at the reaction of *The Times* (June 22) to a statement I issued jointly with other community leaders warning Senator Robert F. Kennedy of the adverse impact in the Negro community of his entry of a candidate for surrogate in opposition to the candidate unanimously endorsed previously by the County Executive Committee of the Democratic party in Manhattan.

We did not in our statement charge Senator Kennedy with racism. We simply pointed out that Senator Kennedy has chosen to disregard please for his aid and assistance by Reform Democrats waging political war against Charles Buckley in the Bronx. We pointed out that Senator Kennedy has chosen to disregard please for his aid and assistance from Reform Democrats waging political wars against Brooklyn's Democratic Leader Stanley Steingut. We also pointed out that Senator Kennedy responded to pleas for help only in connection with the fight against J. Raymond Jones, the only Negro county leader in the nation. . . .

Finally Clark noted:

Our statement did not stir up the Harlem community. We stated objectively the feelings of the Negro community, not in Harlem alone, but throughout the nation as well. The reaction in the Negro community in support of Justice Klein demonstrates that we have properly analyzed the racial implications of Senator Kennedy's intervention in the Surrogate's Court race.

(Signed) Kenneth B. Clark New York, June 22, 1966[13]

That same day, the *Times* chose to ignore Clark's letter, but issued an editorial in a seemingly neutral tone on the racial issue. But once again, as it has done so frequently in the past, the *Times* missed the issue. Part of its editorial said:

Less astonishing but almost as irrelevant is a political comment as to how the outcome of this primary will help or hurt the political power of Mr. Jones and Senator Robert F. Kennedy, who are backing opposing candidates. This kind of political speculation is inevitable in a hard fought campaign where leading personalities are involved, but voters should keep it in perspective. The simple fact is that no matter how this primary turns out, Senator Kennedy is going to be a powerful figure in the counsels of the Democratic Party, and Mr. Jones is going to be the Manhattan leader.[14]

The point was not whether or not I would remain as New York County Leader—I would, because my administration had been, in my opinion and in the opinion of most of my colleagues, one free from unethical behavior, free from legal complications. There was little possibility of my being turned out of office by an insurgent group. The *Times* simply missed the point that no leader of a County organization, faced by constant sniping and vicious charges such as trumped up by Kennedy and his group, could enjoy the job of being the leader of his party. By primary day, June 28, the plain truth of the matter was that I was getting fed up with the new "prince of the party," Robert Kennedy, and his court.

As primary day neared, I watched the charade of the Silverman campaign. No one was really interested in Silverman; they were interested in Kennedy. The crowds chanted "Kennedy," and pushed and shoved to shake Kennedy's hand. Very few people paid the slightest attention to poor Justice Silverman. Finally this lack of attention got to him, as I knew it would, and three days before the primary, he was heard to complain in what seemed to be a maudlin state of bewildered unhappiness, "I wish somebody would ask once, who is that man walking with Judge Silverman?"[15] As I read this in the evening's paper I had to chuckle, for indeed despite the seriousness of the campaign and the effects it would have on my own position, at the moment I read that sad plea, I felt very sorry for Justice Silverman. I thought that even if he won the primary and won the final election, he would never make it as a reformer on the Surrogate Bench. In fact, he never did.

On primary day, our candidate lost to Silverman by a substantial margin. The total votes were 47,625 for Klein, 70,771 for Silverman. Klein carried the central Harlem neighborhood by more than one thousand votes; in East Harlem, there was a virtual tie; but in South Harlem, the situation was the reverse and Silverman carried it by approximately one thousand votes.

Both contestants were very gracious to each other in their post-primary statements the next day, but once again, as I analyzed the statements, I saw in Silverman's character something that made me feel better that I had not supported him originally as the Party's standard bearer. He thanked a number of people, including Steven Smith, Kennedy's brother-in-law, but he also thanked "all the others who gave so generously of their time, not to mention that vulgar commodity, money."[16] The phrase, that "vulgar commodity, money" struck me as somewhat disingenuous, because Silverman was denying the medium of exchange so necessary for winning elections, while at the same time he could not have won without it. I thought him to be something of a hypocrite, and once again I had the feeling that he would never be able to live up to his stated ideals.

The aftermath of the surrogate primary

In the aftermath of the primary, the *New York Times* claimed neutrality, as always, and insisted that its only aim was the improvement of the judiciary as well as good government in the City of New York. It said of Mr. Silverman:

His victory is bound to weaken the influence of J. Raymond Jones, Chairman of the Regular Democratic organization in New York County, thereby strengthening the Reform wing of the party.[17]

This remark also amused me, because earlier the *Times* claimed that the race had very little to do with me, that I would remain as County Leader and Kennedy would remain as Senator, etc., etc. But now, with Silverman's victory assured, the *Times* readily admitted that Silverman–Kennedy victory would indeed weaken my position as County Leader. The *Times* editors, as usual, were as politically naive as was their candidate Samuel J. Silverman. Why? Because four years after defeating Klein in the November elections, Judge Silverman resigned from the Surrogate bench with the astonishing announcement that he had found it impossible to change the system![18] This great reformer now made it possible for Governor Rockefeller to fill the vacancy with a Republican, which is what the Governor promptly did. There was no question that the Surrogate battle was a setback for me. I had no time to dwell on this, however, for August 1 was soon approaching, when the Judicial Convention for nominees to the New York Supreme Court would be decided on. The Liberal Party had already established their line of attack when they accused me during the Surrogate race as having made a deal with Republican County Leader Albano, when along with our dual support for Klein, we had agreed to support Republican Justice Shea, as well as Jacob Fuchsberg and Judge Ancione, for seats on the Supreme Court. I knew no deal had been made, and all suggestions for nominees placed before the county leadership had been passed on to the Bar Association. I knew also that my Republican counterpart had done the same thing, and it was clear that unless I had some invisible magic powers, the Judicial Convention would select whomever it wanted. But down in Washington, as a consequence of what he saw as his victory in the Surrogate fight, Senator Kennedy could not resist stirring the judicial political pot: he soon issued a manifesto that the proposed names for judicial candidates should be given to the Bar Association and the public long before being sent to the Judicial Convention. This way, he said, the public could rate the candidates before the conventions of both parties. He suggested also that the Judicial Convention should be open to the public so that it could participate! How this was to be accomplished, no one had a clue. A silly idea indeed, but to many, it sounded persuasive. The suggestion was so stupid that even his publicity agent, the *New York Times* chided him on its editorial page. It said:

What Senator Kennedy is urging is in essence what the City Bar Association and others interested in improving the administration of justice, have been proposing for years—that the political leaders submit the names of prospective candidates to the city and county bar associations sufficiently far in advance to permit careful study of their qualifications.

But, realizing how asinine and impracticable the Senator's suggestions were, the editors concluded:

But the Senator went a bit too far, in our opinion, when he proposed that any lawyer who had ever been rejected by a city or county bar association should not be considered for judicial nomination in that district. That rule could blackball forever a lawyer of great ability who in his earlier years might have been declared not qualified solely for lack of experience.[19]

What Mr. Kennedy may not have known is that a better but similar scheme had been explored earlier, when Edward Costikyan was the County

Leader. In his book, Costikyan recounts that when he tried to enlist the New York City Bar Association in the selection process in such a way that there would be equal recommendation from the Harlem Bar Association, the New York County Lawyers Association, and any other official group interested in helping the Democratic Party select highly qualified candidates, the City Bar Association had made no response whatsoever. And his was a proposal far less cumbersome and more practicable than Senator Kennedy's.

Mr. Costikyan recounts that when he did not get a response from the Bar Association, he sought to find out why, and was told by a member of the Bar Association that his letter had been seen as a "Tammany trick." So once again, on behalf of Tammany's Executive Committee, he wrote to the Bar Association:

The Executive Committee took no position whatsoever concerning so much of the proposal of your special committee as dealt with the subject of appointive judges. Indeed, it strikes me that what your committee proposed was merely institutionalizing the present system which the mayor has been pursuing voluntarily and, while I understand there are some questions as to the composition of the committee which you propose, this did not concern us and has not concerned us.

The thrust of my proposal related to assistance to the political leaders in the performance of their functions in relationship to all elective judges, including the State Supreme Court.

I hope the above will clarify what may have been a misunderstanding of my early communication.

To this communication, Costikyan recounts, he received a "polite acknowledgement but no response to my suggestion."[20]

Having explored the possibility of screening by the Bar Association as well as having input from various groups into the selection process before nomination, Costikyan in 1966 came to this conclusion:

I suggest that it is time for those concerned with the quality of the judiciary to forget their theories about who ought to have the power, abandon their efforts to create artificial and mechanical restrictions upon the exercise of political power in the selections of candidates (which merely camouflages the political selection of judges), encourage and support the selection of the right kind of political leaders in both parties, and agree to submit the names of highly qualified candidates to those political leaders, and finally accept the political leaders on the basis of their own best myth—that they are responsible citizens rendering public service through Party activity—and help them do their job.

I should add that screening committees to eliminate unqualified candidates are most helpful. The New York County Democratic Committee has had a Committee on the Judiciary charged with this duty since 1962. It has done a first rate job. The Mayor's Committee on the Judiciary has done the same job.[21]

Perhaps because the *Times'* editors did not support Senator Kennedy's selection plan, on July 20 he called me to arrange a meeting on the issue. I did not see any real cause for this meeting, but to insure peace, I agreed to it. We met and discussed the situation; we agreed that all proposed Democratic candidates would be announced in good time before the nominating convention, and the list of people submitted to the Bar Associations. There was no reason for disagreement here, because what the Senator had suggested in this meeting was exactly what we had been doing all along.

In fact, on July 29, even the *New York Times*, his press machine, editorialized:

Some progressive steps to reduce politics in the nomination of judicial candidates are being taken in the wake of the upset by Robert F. Kennedy and the Reform Democrats of the Bipartisan deal for Manhattan surrogate. Although the new measures do not go far enough, they are welcome signs of the changing attitude in both major parties.

The first indication of the new trend was an announcement by J. Raymond Jones, leader of the New York County Democratic organization, that he and Senator Kennedy had agreed on a procedure for publicly screening candidates for vacancies on the State Supreme Court before the Democratic Judicial Convention, next Monday.

Mr. Jones also made public a list of 20 candidates approved by his organization's judiciary committee as possible nominees for the three vacancies. *In fairness, it must be acknowledged that Mr. Jones had issued a similar list last year—without fanfare.* (Emphasis added.)

I read that editorial with a feeling of justification, because I thought the discerning voter would now perceive that Robert Kennedy, the Reform Democrats, and the Liberal Party had based their "fight" with me and Regular Democrats, not upon the truth or upon an examination of my record, but rather to cynically use "public relations," garner for themselves the aura of truth and virtue. They were, indeed, anything but true or virtuous.

But Kennedy was used to having his way, and when on the 31st of July, on the eve of the Judicial Convention, I read that he had ceased participating in the negotiation for judgeships for the Supreme Court, I was not surprised. In this instance he had to deal not only with me, but also with Republicans from the Bronx and Manhattan, as well as Democrats from both counties. This was a place where serious negotiations took place, where sober compromises had to be made, where many parties had to be satisfied, and where it was impossible for Robert Kennedy to be above it all. What he desired was to state what he wanted, and have it approved by acclamation as if he were a monarch. But this was not forthcoming, and on the eve of the convention he left the negotiations claiming to be fed up with the deals and negotiations taking place! What were these deals and negotiations that were so insufferable to Mr. Kennedy?

The Judicial Convention: Deals, negotiations, and outcomes

Apparently Senator Kennedy had never been to a Judicial Convention. This convention selected nominees for the State Supreme Court of New York, and since the Supreme Court's jurisdiction covered Manhattan and the Bronx, both boroughs sent delegates. The Republicans selected nominees from both boroughs, and likewise, the Democrats.

On the day of the convention, Congressman Adam Clayton Powell opened with a speech, expressing his desire that the convention place a Negro on the ballot. He insisted that he did not have any particular Negro in mind, and said, "No other ethnic group in New York City or New York State suffers from such disproportionate unfairness in representation on the bench as Negroes." Of course, Adam being Adam, he could not resist adding the following. "It would also help the tension on the streets of New York City when the young voter realizes that he has been recognized."[23] On the Manhattan list were indeed three Blacks. They were Civil Court Judge Jawn A. Sandifer, Criminal Court Judge Kenneth M. Phipps, and Andrew R. Tyler, a lawyer. Interestingly, none of these people were from my own Democratic club; Sandifer was from Powell's political club, but Adam did not mention this! As soon as the convention opened, arguments began that the five judgeships should be distributed in such a way to permit an Irish, an Italian, a Jewish, and perhaps a Negro candidate. The fifth slot was held by an incumbent, Justice Abraham N. Geller.

Powell's speech was actually the first move in the chess game during which he hoped he would be able to name one of the judges, having Judge Sandifer in mind. At the 1964 Judicial Convention, he had worked out an alliance with Charles Buckley, the Bronx County Leader, and had been able to place Darwin W. Telesford on the State Supreme Court bench. This time, however, I was not going to allow Adam to make any more deals, when the job belonged to me as a County Leader representing the larger Manhattan delegation. I have noted before that Charlie Buckley and I had agreed that there would be no more private deals with Congressman Powell. When on the first day of the convention Powell's speech was not supported by Buckley, Powell suspected me and became very angry.

Robert Kennedy had tried in the preconvention hours to create a ticket that would have a Reform candidate, two Regular candidates, and what he called a "high-quality Negro." He had in mind Robert L. Carter, the General Counsel for the NAACP. Mr. Kennedy thought this satisfied all factions, but nobody supported Carter. Powell himself was not satisfied with Carter. Once those at the Convention had refused to consider Carter, Powell tried to make it appear as if no Negro had ever been proposed. But if Powell had supported Carter, he would have won the nomination because the Manhattan Regular Democrats would have not contested his candidacy too vigorously. The fact that finally no Negro had been nominated was more Powell's fault than anyone's, but he blamed J. Raymond Jones. "I do not believe in violence," he began,

therefore from now on, whenever a Black man in Harlem sees Ray Jones in the streets, he ought to spit on him. His betrayal of the loyal black voters in the New York Democratic Party surpassed the combined treason of Judas, Benedict Arnold, and Quisling.

All this was the usual stuff to which I had become accustomed, and so I was relatively unperturbed by this. But I must admit that my eyes opened wide when I read the next paragraph:

What Ray Jones did may have well destroyed the Democratic Party's chances for complete victory by rejecting Senator Robert Kennedy's candidate and all the Black and Puerto Rican Candidates of Harlem in view of the Republican Party's nomination of a Negro.[24]

This statement was entirely false.

I had to respond to this, so I issued a statement of my own:

I can well understand Congressman Powell's need to get a Supreme Court Justice-ship for one of the lawyers in his club. But I am concerned more with the thousands of young Negroes who are out of work in Harlem. Congressman Powell ought to be devoting himself to straightening out the problems of HARYOU-ACT so that these young men and women can get to work. My job as County Leader makes it necessary to act as a referee between the conflicting interests of the various leaders. I am not a boss, and cannot dictate who the candidates should be. Perhaps if Mr. Powell had not attempted to make a deal behind my back with Mr. Buckley, the leaders might not have taken the attitude they took.

Having said all I wanted to Mr. Powell, I used the opportunity to clear the air on the whole question of the judicial nominating process, which had become such an emotional, strife-ridden subject in recent months. I addressed the problem as follows:

In my 43 years in this business, I have not been through a more harried 2 weeks in my life. . . . If I were convinced that the method of elections by direct primaries would not make it impossible for a poor man to become a Supreme Court Justice, I would be in favor of that process. And if some safeguards can be found that would prevent the nominations from becoming the exclusive properties of rich men I should back that process to the hilt. In the negotiations just finished, there were demands from Negro groups for a Negro Justice, demands from Puerto Rican groups for a Supreme Court Justice of Puerto Rican extraction, demands from Italian groups that an Italian be put in on the ticket, demands from Irish groups that an Irishman be put on the ticket, demands from Jewish groups that the two Jewish judges be replaced by two Jewish candidates.

In this I agree with the Senator, that as far as these groups were concerned, they had less interest in the caliber of candidates than they did in their ethnic backgrounds. I think that the district leaders in Manhattan did a very excellent job together with the leaders of the Bronx county. I feel proud of the ticket and I am sure that it will succeed.[25]

My statement was not political. I was happy with our slate, which included Judges Ascione and Samuel S. Spiegel, both from the Civil Court, Administrative Judge John M. Murtagh, from Manhattan, and Francis J. Bloustein, Vice-Chairman of the City Planning Commission, from the Bronx. In the November elections the entire slate was elected.

Although the November outcome was satisfactory, the attacks made on me by Kennedy, Powell, and others, created a clear split in the Democratic Party, which try as I might I could not mend. Furthermore, the increasing fragmentation along ethnic, racial, and religious lines indicated that our party was becoming less a party of organization and procedure and more a party of personalities. Instead of concern for orderly progress, concern for constituents, concern for loyalty, compromise and pragmatism, the party was shifting to individual enterprisers whose coalitions changed from week to week, day to day. It created a situation in which one could not depend on anyone for any useful period, a situation that I thought caused anxiety and insecurity in our organization.

As the year drew to an end, I increasingly thought that this new environment was not for me. I wondered if I had become too old-fashioned, and too traditional. I decided to take the Thanksgiving holiday to think it over and make a decision whether I would continue beyond the year, but trouble was placed on my plate much sooner than the turkey.

Silk stockings and Puerto Ricans:
The travails of redistricting

On November 22, 1966, I picked up the *New York Post*, glanced through it, and stopped at a column written by the distinguished columnist Murray Kempton. The title read "Ray Jones' Property." I could not resist. Kempton said, in part,

J. Raymond Jones, leader of the Democratic Party of New York County, came to the Commodore at noon yesterday to contend with newest assault from the Reformers upon his tyranny. He was a great rock ready to bear up under the kick of the butterfly against his surface.[26]

Things had been very tough for me all during the year, and as simple a thing as the auspicious beginning of an article by such a careful and respected columnist thoroughly lifted my spirits. I had known of Murray Kempton for some time and had spoken to him on one or two occasions, so I was not foolish enough to believe that the column, having started this way, would necessarily end on a felicitous note. Besides, I already had an inkling of what he was talking about. Nevertheless, I read on to see how he would characterize the previous day's event. He said:

The Reformers, or some of them, were aroused because, given the terminal horrors of the last electoral campaign, Ray Jones had taken 25 election districts from the control of Richard Lane and Alice Sachs, of the Lexington Democratic Club and assigned them to George Osborne, a youthful Reformer in disfavor with the family for excessive tolerance of Ray Jones' effort to make Justice Arthur Klein a Surrogate. . . .

Yesterday the County Committee met to consider the Lexington Club's complaint that Ray Jones had violated all law and justice.

What then was all this about? Just before the primaries of the previous September, petitioners came into my office complaining that Richard Lane and Alice Sachs, 66th Assembly District Leader and Co-Leader, needed help if the party were to improve its chances in the November elections. This "Silk Stocking" district at that time stretched from 96th Street down to the mid-50s, and from Third Avenue to Central Park West. This was the area that produced John V. Lindsay. I looked into the complaints and decided that, indeed, both Lane and Sachs could use some help.

Similar complaints had come in during the previous August and September from District Leaders all over the country, because prospects for the upcoming elections were not as encouraging as they had been in past years. The reasons centered on the fragmentation of our party, the divisiveness brought about by the Reformers, the development of elite cliques from the activities of Senator Robert Kennedy, the continued sniping of the Liberal Party, and the emergence of what I call "personal politics." Because of all these developments, other members of Executive Committee of the County Committee and I knew we needed new and loyal blood. In those areas which had become too large for present District Leaders, additional leaders, preferably dependable and loyal ones, had to be found.

We decided this just when the State Legislature had mandated redistricting. This reapportionment had actually reduced the number of Manhattan Assembly Districts from 16 to 15. Thus Assembly District lines had to be redrawn all over Manhattan; during the summer and early fall, I had worked with various District Leaders to bring about fair and equitable reapportionment.

In the "Silk Stocking" Assembly District, we had redrawn the lines somewhat by dividing the district into two parts, A and B, assigning 25 of the 96 Election Districts to George Osborne, a former Assembly District Leader who had lost his position because of redrawn lines. This was done in mid-September. We heard no complaint from Richard Lane and Alice Sachs until a month later when they accused me of "unilateral, arbitrary, and illegal acts." It should be noted that, in all my dealings with other Assembly District Leaders, decisions had been made, lines had been redrawn, and new assignments had been accepted in the spirit of camaraderie and unity, except for this and another challenge. I knew the County Committee would eventually have to approve all alterations, but I already had the backing of the majority of the County Executive Committee; therefore, I was not worried about the outcome. Disturbingly, though, these two leaders represented the Reform group, and I regarded their complaint as an unnecessary, unfortunate, and very depressing, divisive assault on the leadership of the county organization.

This was not because of any unjust or illegal activities on my part, but because I now detested certain groups, the constant bickering, vacuous demands, and insatiable appetite for unnecessary and gratuitous conflict. In early November of 1966, I had considered resigning because of all that, but the thought of resigning under unfair pressure was anathema to me, and I decided not to give the Reformers, particularly the 66th Assembly District Leaders, any satisfaction. Furthermore, I was determined not to leave the impression by resigning at that time that I had somehow done something wrong. So I put away thoughts of resigning and girded myself for the battle.

I knew that Alice Sachs and Richard Lane were mouthpieces for the Reformers on the West Side; therefore I decided to make sure that readers of the press and watchers of television would realize in the end that their charges were untrue. As it turned out, the County Executive Committee gave little satisfaction to Lane and Sachs, and Murray Kempton described the end of the meeting this way:

In the end, six lawyers were conscripted to prepare an opinion as to the legality of Ray Jones' proceedings. There was no impulse to sit up late awaiting the verdict. Miss Sachs ended matters with the final complaint that she had been given to

George Osborne without her consent. The laughter was a compliment to her charm. Ray Jones' responsive smile was all resignation. He still had the property: being colored is a condition with few advantages, but it does instruct you in how little the property is worth.[27]

As soon as this problem was resolved, a similar problem arose, this time from the Puerto Rican element headed by Joseph Erazo. Before the September redistricting, Erazo had shared the leadership of the 70th Assembly District with Hulan Jack, the former Borough President, and Anthony Mendez. Both Jack and Mendez had complained earlier that Erazo had not taken care of the ten Election Districts that he represented out of the approximate fifty encompassed by the 70th A.D. Besides, it was pointed out, he did not even live in the neighborhood. Because of this, Jack and Mendez suggested that the Erazo territory be divided and shared between them. I agreed and redrew the lines. But since the neighborhood was in the heart of so-called Spanish Harlem, Erazo apparently thought he could play on the Puerto Rican theme to prevent elimination of his leadership. Sensing support and the popularity of the ethnic representation theme, Erazo picketed the County Headquarters at the Commodore Hotel on the eve of the meeting of the entire County Committee. What puzzled me was, why would Erazo make this protest at this late date? And, indeed, why was he protesting when the Puerto Rican theme did not seem to me to make sense?

In the first place, he had a weak case because he could not defend himself from the charge of not having serviced his district. His not living in the district further undermined his credibility. And wasn't Anthony Mendez just as Puerto Rican as he? I concluded that there must have been some reason, despite the weakness of his case, why Erazo should have chosen this particular day to bring his group to the Commodore Hotel. I decided to make a few telephone calls. These calls revealed that this was part of a plan to embarrass me and the County Committee before the meeting the next day. I found out that Erazo's sudden burst of energy and his confrontation tactics came at the suggestion of certain Reform elements who thought that, if Erazo made a joint cause with Lane and Sachs, somehow both would be reinforced.

As it turned out, less than half of the full County Committee members were present at the Manhattan Center, and the Puerto Ricans became so violent as I entered the Center, that a number of my colleagues thought it safest to form a cordon to protect me from their jeers and fist waving. In the meeting I had expected more fireworks from Lane and Sachs, but it turned out that Puerto Ricans seized the floor, and with much frenzied shouting made wild charges of discrimination against them. Fortunately, I was not in charge of the meeting. This burdensome task had been given to Assemblyman Frank G. Rosetti. Rosetti, who succeeded me as County Leader when I resigned the following year, showed a great deal of aplomb and self-restraint throughout the raucous jeering, boos, and catcalls. Once all sides had been heard, he brought the question to a vote. The motion that the Assembly District remain as it is and that Erazo retain his leadership lost by a vote of 966 to 516. When the vote was announced, Erazo leapt onto the platform demanding a role call, and was ruled out of order by Louis Grossman, the Democratic committee Law Chairman. Despite fist waving, wailing, and gnashing of teeth, the ruling stood.

Perhaps the loss of the Erazo motion had given a signal to Lane and Sachs, because the fireworks I expected from them did not materialize. It turned out that Ed Wiesl, the Democratic National Committeeman, and former Mayor Robert Wagner together suggested a compromise that the district be retained as one, with the understanding that no longer could Sachs and Lane run it in their usual autocratic and independent manner. This I accepted because people such as Weisl, Wagner, Rosetti, and others were anxious, whenever possible, to make accommodations with the Reform group in the interest of maintaining a semblance of unity. I was always comfortable with compromise as long as it did not undermind my own principles. In the end, I felt pleased with the resolution of the redistricting problem, although I wondered if what we had accomplished would remain stable for very long. In the winter of 1967 I felt the ground under Tammany slowly shifting, and no one, it seemed, had the vaguest idea how long the edifice would remain standing.

Chapter 9

The Party is Over

IN NOVEMBER 1969 I would be seventy years old. The year 1966 had been a most strenuous one for me, and 1967 presaged no surcease. The conflicts I had with the Reform wing of my party continued; the sniping from the Kennedy forces showed no signs of abating; the practice of personal politics, seemed on the rise; the press, particularly the *New York Times*, kept up its regular drumbeat on behalf of Reform, managing all the while to portray Regular Democrats as tainted souls. The close and sometimes friendly relationship the Regular Democrats had enjoyed with the Liberal Party now seemed no longer possible. In addition, Mayor Robert Wagner was long gone and although the new Republican Mayor, John V. Lindsay, was a thoroughly decent person, it was not the same thing as if he were a Democrat.

At sixty-eight years of age I was not only Tammany Chief, but a District Leader and a City Council member. As a City Councilman, I was chairman of two major committees, the Committee on the State Legislature and the City Affairs Committee, and a number of ad hoc committees. In addition, there was my own Carver Club to consider, in which I had a number of very promising young men and women, who from time to time needed my advice, or so I persuaded myself. Under normal circumstances I would have relished this multiplicity of roles.

But in early 1967 my role as County Leader was no longer to referee and conduct that elegant interplay of political forces I had enjoyed in previous years. No longer was there the joy of combat with well-known rules and the combatants' understanding of limits aesthetic, ethical, and political. The passing of this ethos was discouraging and I viewed my personal future with uncertainty. Ironically, at this time, Anthony Hiss chose to write what

221

appeared to be a flattering article about me in the magazine section of my nemesis, the *New York Times*. Hiss noted quite correctly in the lead to his article that, "Tammany Hall isn't what it used to be, and its boss—the chairman of the New York County Democratic Committee—is no longer a power . . . he is only a powerful influence."[1]

This would have seemed to the lay person as not an auspicious beginning, but I recognized immediately the statement's uncomfortable truths. I thought that at last the *Times* had come to its senses. I read on with astonishment as the article continued:

J. Raymond Jones, the chairman of the New York County Democratic Committee—or, as some people prefer to call him, the boss of Tammany Hall—is a man of principle. Two of Mr. Jones' most frequently expressed principles are, "Never say 'Never' in politics," and "Nobody ever does anything for nothing." The first is a rule-of-thumb and the second an insight into human nature that is the product of extensive readings in the works of Edward Gibbon and even more extensive participation in the politics of the city for the past 45 years.

At present, Mr. Jones holds down three jobs. In addition to being county chairman (the only Negro county chairman anywhere in the country), he is also a district leader and a member of the City Council, and he puts in a very long working day filling these positions.

After an efficient synopsis of my political life, Hiss wrote:

Jones is proud of being the first Negro to occupy the office, but he never forgets that—like a number of other places that Negroes have waited a long time to integrate—the office itself is not what it once was. But if Tammany Hall is less important than it used to be, it is also less important than it could be— "the organization," in the words of one district leader, "is split three ways to Sunday." . . .

The first person to drop in for a bit of talk was Judge James Watson. Judge Watson sits on the United States Customs Court, and he is one of the people whose careers Ray Jones helped to promote. Others include Robert Weaver, Secretary of Housing and Urban Development; Dr. J. Dayton Brooks, Deputy Mayor of Chicago; United States Judge Constance Baker Motley; Percy Sutton, Borough President of Manhattan; Justice Edward R. Dudley, Administrative Judge of the Criminal Court; Civil Court Judge Herbert Evans; Judge Harold Stevens of the Appellate Division, Supreme Court; and Robert O. Lowery, Mayor Lindsay's Fire Commissioner, Jones' comment is: "We've had some damn fine boys come out of here."

The article was lengthy and filled with anecdotes and references to my alleged cunning. Could the *Times'* publication of this article be a left-handed acknowledgment that I was not the villain they had so often portrayed? Since there was no definitive answer to such questions, I decided in the affirmative.

I liked best the section on my support of men such as Judge Watson and Fire Commissioner Lowery. These men would have done well without me, of that I am certain. What they accomplished through me was not so much elevation to judgeships and the like in personal terms, but elevation to serve Black people and the people of Harlem. This is a difficult concept for many people to understand, and harder still to practice. In other words, all the individuals I helped understood that the price for my endorsement was a willingness to perform in an exemplary manner, thereby setting the best possible example for other aspiring Blacks. It was understood also that they would consciously and continually search for and encourage other Black people to aspire to their levels.

Why were these our rules? Because all too often I had observed other politicians gathering the rewards only for themselves and their close friends. This was something I have always believed that Black people should not and ought not do. I believed this most passionately, because even in the 1960's, the Negro, as a consequence of years of bigotry, discrimination, and murder (yes, murder!), had been so shortchanged that he needed all the help he could get. I felt strongly that it was up to the Black politician, office holder, and bureaucrat, as few as these were, to actively attempt to balance this skewed equation. All my friends and everyone in the Carver Democratic Club understood this, and to this day only one or two have disappointed me.

Hiss's comment on the fragmentation of the Democratic party and its concomitant effect on the power of the County Leader was absolutely correct. Tammany Hall by this time was not much more than a myth. We were, indeed, "split three ways to Sunday." Since assuming the Tammany leadership, this split had occupied more of my time than any other issue. I had thought that since even the *Times* had had to admit that the Reformers and Senator Robert Kennedy were grossly wrong in their indictment of the Regular Democrats and on the selection of judges, there would now occur, at least, some small rapprochement among our various factions. But soon after that event it became obvious that the situation would remain the same. This was no longer a quarrel among friends. Our quarrels had assumed ideological dimensions and I was beginning to think these would soon become fights to the finish. I did not relish such a prospect.

Mr. Hiss, in his article, had spoken to someone "in the know" who had said:

'There is an awful lot coming up in '68 and '67. . . . There's the state constitutional convention, and Ray has gone to a lot of trouble getting a lot of experts to think up some ideas—which is more than any other County Leader has contemplated doing. There's a judicial bill in the Legislature—a lot of new judgeships there. Then there's the new leadership districting lines to be mapped, and that's a mighty big chess game—and Ray's a mighty good chess player. I don't figure him resigning from the game at this point.'[2]

This person was certainly "in the know." In truth, I had wanted to remain in office because I had indeed gathered an array of experts to suggest ideas to be taken to the Constitutional Convention. I knew I had more reports on a larger number of issues than any other County Leader. However, the more I thought about what I would have to endure, the more I began to believe it not worth the cost.

As I've said before, I was 68 years old in 1967, and had, long before decided to retire at 70. But by 1967 I felt that I carried too much of a burden and had too much opposition to justify carrying on. I decided that I ought to resign as County Leader now that the districting problems were solved, and since I had demonstrated to my own satisfaction, if not to Senator Kennedy's and others, that they could not easily push me around. There were other things on my mind too. If I were to resign as County Leader, it would also be wise to resign as District Leader. Thus, I would be left with one main responsibility, that of a City Councilman. That term would end in 1969, when I would be exactly 70 years old. I was not in good health and although politics had been my game for a long time, I thought that 70 would be the age for me to retire to flowers, books, and music.

Having been so engrossed with my work, I had not thought too much about spending time in the Virgin Islands. But as problems mounted, I began to long more and more to return to the peace and quiet of my home there where my wife was already living and working as Collector of Customs for the 51st Customs District. I envisioned recovering my health, and caring for my small affairs. As I contemplated the joys of retirement, the battles looming in the Democratic Party gradually began to seem not as compelling as they once had. Yet, by the end of February, I had not made up my mind. These were merely contemplations.

My ruminations soon took a different direction because of my old sometime friend, sometime enemy, Congressman Adam Clayton Powell. By 1967, Powell was one of the most powerful men in Congress. As Chairman of the House Labor and Education Committee, he had been instrumental in passing a number of bills, considered by everyone—his friends and enemies alike—to have been in the best interest of all our citizens. This was not surprising to me because Adam Powell, an extremely intelligent, brilliant man, powerfully persuasive, charming, debonair and suave, had the ability to convert even his worst enemies when he wished. Until now his political career had been distinguished. There was, however, a perverse side to Powell. When all the elements of this perverse configuration consumed him, he was quite capable of doing things that even a high school politician would avoid.

Adam, although he himself looked white, had nothing but extreme contempt for most white people, and a determination as Congressman, and a powerful one, to show white people that he could do anything they did with equal impunity. If congressmen were going on junkets to Europe at the taxpayers' expense, he would go on junkets as well; if other politicians had people on their staff beyond the limits of the rules, so would he. Not only would he outdo white politicians in their good aspects, but to show his equality, he sought to outdo them also in their bad. His troubles began in 1960 when for calling a woman in New York City, a Mrs. Esther James, "a bag woman," he was taken to court, found guilty of defamation of character and fined the sum of $45,000.[3] Adam, of course, always bristled at being told what to do by anyone, including a judge. He refused to pay, and the case dragged on from 1963 into 1967, all the while creating very negative and damaging publicity. This case, in part, also caused him the loss of the chairmanship of the House Education and Labor Committee in March 1967. The saga of Powell's trials and tribulations at this time did nothing to ease my mind and, in an oblique way, reinforced my desire to retire.

In the conduct of my own club, the Carver, and in my own political life I operated expressly on people's merits. I think all of those who knew me would agree that I abided by that principle. So, in early March of 1967, I looked around my own club and identified several people who could carry on as well as I had, and even better because they were younger. One of these, 39-year-old David N. Dinkins, was a former Assemblyman and now a delegate to the 1967 State Constitutional Convention. I thought Dinkins could carry on quite capably as District Leader in Harlem should I resign. I also thought that Frank G. Rosetti would make a very good County Leader. My view that in my own area of Harlem there were people capable of taking my place, and that at Tammany Hall Rosetti would do a good job, allayed my fears that perhaps my timing would be wrong. Therefore, in the first week of March, at a County Executive Committee meeting I announced my retirement as County Leader and as District Leader.

I explained simply that I felt it was time for new blood; that I'd spent a long time in politics; and that I was not supported by the new power in the state, Senator Kennedy. I informed the Executive Committee that, in my opinion, the ideological dispute now paralyzing our party would get worse before it got better and that means had to be found to foster unity. I suggested that perhaps very little could be done and that it would be best to let the present violence run its course. I was not suggesting "benign neglect" but something analogous. At various times in history it is best to do very little until passions cool. In this regard I decided that my absence would aid Tammany Hall, and so I bade my comrades a fond farewell.

The response of the press

As soon as the press learned that I had decided to retire they sought me out. The answers I gave them were essentially the same I'd given to the Executive Committee: I was 68 years old, I said, and it was time for younger people to carry on. Furthermore, instead of support, I had received nothing but continuous attacks from Senator Kennedy, and I deplored the absence of a consensus within the county leadership, mostly because of the divisive behavior of the Reform Democrats and Senator Kennedy. As usual, the *New York Times* botched the story: one of their reporters, James F. Clarity [sic], speculating on my reasons for retiring, wrote:

The growth of the Reform movement in the last 10 years has also eroded the power of the county leader by splitting the party and weakening his once unquestioned authority in party affairs.

To a similar extent, the power of district leaders, who comprise the county executive committee, has also waned. As Federal, state and municipal jobs began to fall in increasing numbers under Civil Service regulations, there were fewer positions available for distribution by the leaders. . . .

The county leader and the district leaders control little else but a smattering of patronage in New York City perhaps fewer than 500 middle- and low-level jobs, and the designation of candidates for the City Council and the State Legislature. Elected officials, like Senator Kennedy, now control almost everything else that was once in the domain of local party leads (sic).[4]

To a great extent Mr. Clarity was correct in everything he said about the party's state of affairs, but the declining patronage was not as important as many people thought. For me the problem was not so much the loss of patronage, but the loss of confidence in the county organization and the development of the "cult of personality." Clarity was also wrong about the weakening of the "once unquestioned authority" of the County Leader. In earlier times that characterization of authority would have been true, but it had not been the case at least since the election of Robert Wagner in 1953. Even Carmine DeSapio, beginning in 1949, had not enjoyed unquestioned authority. Indeed, it was his assumption of this authority that caused him a great deal of trouble and eventually led to his downfall. While Mr. Clarity's piece was relatively factual and thoughtful, his editors' comments were not. With their usual gift for ignorance, they editorialized:

J. Raymond Jones voluntarily stepped down from the leadership of Tammany Hall yesterday, apparently convinced that he could not function effectively against the opposition of Senator Robert F. Kennedy. His place was secure enough—for the moment, at least; his followers had just voted down a Kennedy proposal to put Tammany on record for Surrogate Court reform.

But, with little power or patronage left in his once powerful post as chairman of the New York County Democratic organization, Mr. Jones wanted out of the ceaseless battle with the party's reform wing. So he has quit to devote himself to working for the re-election of his old friend Adam Clayton Powell.

Mr. Jones is wrong, however, in blaming Senator Kennedy for having split the party by successfully backing Supreme Court Justice Samuel J. Silverman for Surrogate last fall. The party split was the inevitable result of the unsavory deal Mr. Jones has made with like-minded Republicans for the place. The public outcry that arose was a result of Mr. Jones' disservice to the party, not Senator Kennedy's.[5]

Since I had now retired, I could read such an editorial with disdain, without any compulsion to respond. For the record, however, the editors were wrong on all counts. Again, as late as March 1967, the *Times* insisted that the Republican Party and I had made a deal, an impossibility given the processes for nomination, and the *Times* editors knew this. Secondly, to suggest that Senator Kennedy had not fostered fragmentation of the party was ridiculous. Anyone who now takes an unbiased look at the record, beyond the powerful pull and charisma of the Kennedy group, will see that Kennedy supplied not a single idea for progressive reform better than those previously suggested by others, including myself. Nor did he ever suggest a platform to make the party more attractive to ordinary people. The *Times* was wrong also when it stated unequivocally that I was quitting to devote myself to "working for the re-election of [my] old friend Adam Clayton Powell." This was arrant nonsense! Neither Adam nor I had contemplated anything of the sort. The fact that I had accused bigots in Congress of treating Congressman Powell unfairly did not mean that I would be working for his reelection, and I would certainly not resign to work for Adam Clayton Powell.

It was left to a newspaper that was not part of "the establishment," *The Worker*, to lend "clarity" to the situation. It said:

Whatever other factors were involved, and there were many, the resignation last week of J. Raymond Jones as Manhattan Democratic leader, reflected the powerful pressures menacing the gains Negroes have recently made in their fight for representation in the two major parties.

Jones announced his resignation in the midst of a stepped-up campaign to "get Powell" by the Republican high command which unsuccessfully sought to enlist James Meredith in its conspiracy to split the Negro community.

Thus in a period of a few weeks, Harlem, the largest Negro community in the nation, was stripped of its representation by a racist Congress, the only Negro chairman of a House committee was removed from his post, and Jones, the only

Negro head of a major Democratic organization in the nation felt compelled to resign.[6]

All this I felt to be true, although I would not have called the entire U.S. Congress racist, just some of them. *The Worker* went on to describe the importance of Powell's and my positions as symbols of Negro leadership, and then described the Reformers' campaign to undermine my influence as Tammany leader:

Nor did they understand then, as many Reformers still do not understand now as regards to Powell, that their failure to display the expected sensitivity in such situations toward the aspirations of the Negro people helps drive a wedge between them and liberal and progressive forces.

Jones' situation was further made impossible by the opposition of Kennedy, who apparently viewed him as an unnecessary liability in the latter's effort to "unify" regulars and Reformers around his leadership.

Thus a dangerous gap is opening up between the Negro people and many white liberals and progressives, particularly on the issue of Negro representation.

It is a division which racists and reactionists can and will effectively exploit to the detriment of both.

It is in this sense Reformers and liberals and progressives generally need to reevaluate the meaning of the unseating of Powell and the resignation of Jones[7].

I read this article with admiration, since *The Worker* was, as a Communist sheet, supposed to be biased at all times because of its Marxist interpretation of events. Nevertheless, as I reread it, it became clear to me that the writer, Mike Davidow, was far more perceptive than the supposed liberals of the *New York Times*. Indeed, Davidow saw Robert Kennedy and the Reformers as people with a bothersome tendency to talk down to people. They could not abide any deviation from their world view, and by the mid-sixties theirs and that of the Afro-American community simply were not one and the same. But while Blacks were willing to make compromises with Kennedy and the Reformers in the name of progress, they attained very little, for these people always regarded compromise as a dirty word.

Tying loose ends

I felt relieved after resigning as County and District leader. Contemplating my resignation, weighing the pros and cons, and questioning whether I would suffer from psychological withdrawal, I concluded that, withdrawal or not, it had to be done. And, as most people leaving office do, I hoped that someone with views similar to mine would replace me.

For District Leader, this was not a problem because the Carver Club, which I had lead so long, was the dominant club in the 71st Assembly District and boasted many promising young people. As mentioned before, David Dinkins filled the bill. Dinkins, a 1950 graduate of Howard University, obtained his law degree from Brooklyn Law School in 1965, some fifteen years after graduating from college. I admired him because of his dedication and his steady political development. He was easily elected to succeed me as the Leader of the 71st Assembly District C, a few days after my resignation.

The ease of making Dinkins District Leader was not to be replicated on the choice of the new County Leader. Frank Rossetti, who, as the chairman of the County Committee, was a sort of a Deputy County Leader, became Acting County Leader after my resignation. Rossetti shared my views and therefore I found it easy to support him. Furthermore, as a Regular Democrat, he would most likely attempt to carry out the initiatives I had set in motion.

The Reformers, however, did not share this point of view. The March 17 *Times* quoted Frank Baraff, a Co-Leader in the 69th Assembly District, as saying that Rossetti was "completely unacceptable to Reform leaders," and that, "In the selection of a county leader we are going to vote as a block. . . . This is significant because Reform leaders have never been able to unite before behind a common position." The same issue of the *Times* quoted Senator Kennedy: "I personally like Mr. Rossetti, and I've always enjoyed working with him. In the last analysis, we need somebody who can unite the party. I don't know whether Mr. Rossetti can. He's being given the chance right now."

I enjoyed a silent laugh when I read these reports because Hugh Ferry, the Co-Leader in the 69th Assembly District had also said: "We don't want Senator Kennedy picking a candidate for us, but once a candidate's picked we'd welcome his support." The whole affair was laughable because the Reformers announcing themselves as *unanimously* opposed to Rosseti was unimportant. Being opposed to Rossetti was one thing; finding someone they could *unanimusly* support to defeat Frank was another. Reformers had always fought each other to the last bell and I did not think this time would be any different. "Frank," I said at one point to Rossetti, "don't worry about Kennedy and that gang. They will be fighting amongst themselves on the day of the election." As it turned out, that prediction could not have been more accurate.

I was amused, too, by Hugh Ferry's statement regarding Senator Kennedy's not picking a candidate for them. Why was I so amused? Because I felt vindicated! The Reformers were beginning to show unmistakable signs of nervousness about this camel they had let into their tent.

They did not want the voters of New York to think that Kennedy bossed them around, which he essentially did. Ferry's statement was not only revealing, it was naive.

In the interim between my resignation and the election of my replacement as Tammany Chief, Rosetti did all he could to ensure his candidacy and bring the disparate factions of the party together. But his best efforts at conciliation and unity were of no avail, and when the County Executive Committee met on July 10th, the Reformers opposed him.

As I had predicted, however, the Reformers were not unified on election day. At the eleventh hour, Mrs. Ronnie Eldridge challenged the announced candidate, Shanley Egeth. Through the maneuvering of Charles Kinsolving, the Reformers finally chose Egeth. Rossetti, however, won handily for, despite concerted opposition by the Reformers, he had more than nine solid Regular Democratic votes of the sixteen on the Executive Committee. I was satisfied with this outcome and turned my attention to my job on the City Council, where there were a few loose ends to tie up.

My last two years as city councilman

It is a law of politics that the more you are known, the more people come to you with their problems. When I retired from the County and District Leaderships, I had further decided that I would fully retire at the end of my term as City Councilman in 1969. Until then, I would not seek out controversial issues, nor would I go out on any limb. Since my burdens were now fewer, I could afford to work only with those projects with odds good enough to achieve something, those projects my colleagues on the City Council would support. I was not to be afforded this luxury!

Soon after my resignation, the long smoldering controversy between Columbia University and Harlem exploded into a public confrontation. Columbia had been involved with the City for some time on a number of projects: at one time it had contracted to train or retrain a number of Black and other minority medical doctors; although there had been some problems, the program had been satisfactory. This new affair had its origins in 1960 when after extreme pressure had been brought to bear upon the City Council through its representatives in the State Legislature, Columbia had been granted a one-hundred year lease on approximately two acres of Morningside Park, which connected the University to Harlem. Morningside Park was, of course, public domain and, although the lease granted by the City and the State was completely legal, it was somewhat irregular, because park property was technically the property of all the citizens of the City, the authority to grant a lease would probably have been better done through a referendum. Since a referendum was not mandated, the City Council granted the University a lease, on the condition that Columbia would build a basketball court and exercise room for neighborhood kids as part of the athletic building they proposed for the property.

In 1960 a deal like this seemed fair and equitable. Seven years later, though, the ambience of politics, and of towngown relations had drastically changed. Race had entered politics with a vengeance, not without good reason, and many people in the Harlem community felt the agreement with the University was rife with inequity. Originally, the agreement had been that twelve percent of the building's floor space would be reserved for the Harlem community. But now the community felt that more than that should be allotted to it, perhaps as much as fifty percent, given the fact that the University was, to use a phrase of that time, "ripping off" part of its park. Since technically I represented the area in the City Council, I was asked to chair a community group, which included Borough President Percy Sutton and State Assemblyman Basil A. Patterson, to negotiate the matter.

Sometime in May, my group met with the Mayor at Gracie Mansion. Grayson Kirk, Columbia's president, and David B. Truman, its Vice-President and Provost, represented the University. I proposed that fifty per cent of the gymnasium should be made available to the Harlem community on a time-sharing basis. Columbia rejected this proposal, and instead offered a pool. This counter-proposal seemed to be in bad faith, and it so annoyed Mayor Lindsay that in exasperation, he turned over the whole problem to the Commissioner of Parks. Later the *Times* reported that: "The two sides had drawn such rigid lines that the mayor felt that there was no hope of an agreement and no point in having a further meeting."[8]

The Mayor's anger resulted from the knowledge that the Harlem community would not be satisfied with a pool that would only raise the amount of floor space available to it to only twenty percent. Although such an offer would have been fine in 1960, it was deemed unacceptable in 1967, both because of the floor space problem, and because the University plans called for two separate entrances to the gym. One entrance would be on the top side facing the western entry from the University and the other would be at the bottom of the park facing Harlem. On the face of it, this sounded reasonable, but somehow, in 1967, a mandated entrance on the Harlem side was seen as the "back door." Referring to this situation, Robert McKay, leader of the West Harlem Community Organization said: "In the South it's the back of the bus, up here it's the back of the gym."[9]

I watched this development with alarm between 1965 and 1968 because, in my opinion, the original deal made with Columbia was fair, as it would have been difficult for the University to give over fifty percent of its space to the community. But by April 1967, a number of students decided to support the Harlem protesters and, in defiance of University rules, occupied five buildings. On May 1, through the intercession of Dr. Kenneth Clark and others, the protesting students agreed to leave buildings although some insisted they be arrested and were accommodated.

As a consequence of the takeover of Columbia University, a committee, of which I became chairman, was formed by the City Council. In hearings, John Wheeler, a Columbia University attorney, blamed Thomas Hoving, the former Parks Commissioner, for giving the students ideas about the inequality of the park lease agreement. Certain members of Columbia's Board of Trustees echoed this view. Nothing new or useful came out of these hearings, for we all knew the score, and our committee, really a contingency one, was abolished when the State Legislature later took up the issue. It was allowed to die in committee, and nine months later, Dr. Andrew W. Cordier, Columbia University's new president, acknowledging the lack of community support, issued the following statement which read in part:

Construction on the gym site in Morningside Park was suspended last spring and has not been resumed. . . .

Since overwhelming community support for the plan would be necessary, both in the construction stage and in the long years of its use, I have come to the conclusion that the University should not proceed with this plan, and I shall recommend this course of action to the Trustees. [10]

By the time the University issued this statement the question had long been moot for me and the City Council because of the Legislature's action. In truth, the project had hardly ever pleased anyone and by 1968 we were very happy to be rid of it.

1968 was also a Presidential election year. In time past I would have been excited about the coming November because as District Leader, and later Tammany Leader, I would have been in the thick of things. But 1968 was a peculiar year. Lyndon Johnson had decided not to run again and though I regarded Hubert Humphrey most highly, the rivalries, jealousies, and competing ideologies, so fragmented the Democratic Party in New York City, that I felt relieved at having no official responsibilities other than those of a City Councilman. I participated very little in that campaign, voted for Hubert Humphrey, and persuaded those that I could to do so. I believed then and do so now that Hubert would have made a most excellent President, for he was a man of great humanity, very bright and capable, as his entire record shows, and someone upon whom people great and small could have depended. Although he never achieved the highest office in the land, I believe he died happy knowing that he was so beloved by so many in America, that country about which he cared so passionately.

Although the Presidential election did not concern me greatly, the bungling and scandals surrounding the Human Resources Administration of the City of New York became a severe strain on my energies, often tested my belief in the ordinary sanity and reasonableness of human beings. In 1966, New York established the Human Resources Administration (H.R.A.) through the Mayor's Office, with federal, state, and city funds, to oversee and coordinate poverty relief efforts. Numerous little programs operated under this agency, including the Neighborhood Youth Corps, which had received a lot of negative publicity in February 1968 when three of its former employees were indicted on charges of stealing more than half a million dollars from the program.[11] Other claims were that more than $2.7 million had been stolen from the Agency since it was set up.

The City Council decided after these disclosures that I, as one of the senior City Councilmen, should look into the matter. We formed a fifteen-member committee and on March 3, I made a preliminary statement that "there definitely was a lack of organization and clearly there was mismanagement in administering the programs."[12] Although my preliminary announcement did not represent the entire committee, I was joined in it by the attorney for the committee, Joseph P. Hoey, a very learned lawyer and a former United States Attorney for the Eastern District of New York.

H.R.A. had come about from the desire of Mayor Lindsay, Governor Rockefeller, Senator Kennedy, and the President of the United States to do all they could to prevent a continuation of the violence, rioting, and vandalism that had been taking place every summer since 1964 in various cities. They believed that if cities ripe for riots received monies to dispense through agencies like the Neighborhood Youth Corps, block grants, and manpower programs, things would cool off. By March, when I made my preliminary statement, it could be seen that these agencies had been set up in such haste and with such political urgency that they had not been clearly thought through. Accountability was the least considered item in the structure and management of these programs; in fact, they were nothing more than political entities in which large sums of money were invested. New York City averaged about $1.5 billion per year.

Our committee conducted hearings with various people with complaints about the running of the agencies, and it soon became obvious that no one, except perhaps certain politicians, was satisfied with the H.R.A.'s work. Convinced that dissatisfaction was predominant, we next investigated the subagencies themselves to see how they conducted business. This took a whole additional year. We investigated from the bottom to the top, finally reaching to the administrator, Mitchell I. Ginsberg. When called to testify before us in February, 1969, despite the overwhelming evidence of mismanagement, bungling, and outright theft, he declared,

Certainly we have accomplished less than we had hoped to do, . . . Serious problems remain. But I remain convinced of the absolute necessity for comprehensive planning, centralized management, decentralized delivery of services, and community participation—the foundation stones of H.R.A.[13]

Of course, no one could argue with this, for he simply stated what should have been done and ought to have been done. But Ginsberg, knowing the circumstances under which the agency had been set up and which to a great extent had been responsible for its poor performance, said, in reference to the highly charged political atmosphere at its inception:

At that time, the highest priority was placed on operational results, not on careful planning and management. In fact, Federal programs did not provide sufficient funds for planning, management and accounting staff.[14]

I listened to Mr. Ginsberg's testimony that day with a great deal of sympathy, having been in politics for so many years and involved in similar programs in which I warned of potential serious deficiencies because of too much haste. Everybody was at fault here, including Mayor Lindsay who did not want any more riots in the city, and Governor Nelson Rockefeller who did not want riots either in New York City or elsewhere in New York State since he had presidential ambitions. Robert Kennedy, having greatly assisted in making these funds available to the city, also had presidential aspirations, and with his strong national identification with New York City, certainly did not want any more riots. Furthermore, the President of the United States had to consider the problem of civil disturbances not only in New York City but in the rest of the nation's cities. Here was a clear case, stated concisely, of haste making waste.

In July we finally completed the investigation and issued our report. In brief, I told the press that it had not been our charge to investigate charges of fraud, theft, and things of that nature. The District Attorney and other federal agencies would be looking into those matters since the funds involved came from the federal government as well as from the city and state. The committee and I did point out that the entire agency was so fragmented that no useful delivery of services could take place. Our review revealed waste, duplication, and a lack of accountability beyond belief.

Our report offered fifty-five recommendations, including the institution of proper accounting procedures with clear lines of authority and accountability. But most important, we recommended that the Commissioner of

Social Services post be abolished, along with those of the Commissioners for the Manpower and Career Development Agency and for the Community Development Agency, which oversaw the Anti-Poverty Program and the Youth Services Agency. I did not expect that our report could go unchallenged: the moment it was issued Ginsberg issued a statement taking "strong exception" to our charge that the entire running of the H.R.A. had been a failure.[15] But I had not anticipated a four- man minority who did not agree with the majority report. This minority, led by Councilman Joseph Modugno, a Republican from Queens, charged that the majority report had not gone into the issues of relaxed standards for relief, of fathers of illegitimate children, and of the need for the urging of birth control on welfare recipients!

Much too detailed for our concern, these issues were not in our charge. Our concern was the running of the department and recommendations for its accountability so that it could provide the best relief possible for its clients. The minority's action reflected a willingness to seize on sensational and, at that time, reactionary popular issues such as birth control. I thought then, and I think now that ours was an excellent, fair and even-handed report, given our mandate and its financing. A few days after issuing the report I felt gratified by this comment in the *New York Post* by columnist Murray Kempton.

The life of City Councilman J. Raymond Jones has been lived and has had its rewards from consistent fidelity to the mechanics of the Democratic organization and from occasional outbreaks of his dignity and his hopes for a better world.

The report of Ray Jones' committee to study the city's welfare and poverty programs will probably be his last act in government; and those who doubt that the life of a machine politician can be worthwhile can read it and have their answer . . .

Jones' primary lesson is that we do not know very much how anything works, simply because we lack the basic figures that might tell us . . .

J. Raymond Jones' abstention from the search for scandal and his refusal to blame the poor have alike been associated by his critics with the condition that he is a Harlem politician. Yet the two commissioners upon whom his hardest judgment falls happen both to be Negroes and no enemies of his. You may say if such be a sin, that he is tender towards women and children of his people; but you cannot say that he will cover up for its bureaucrats.

He has left the City of New York a statement of its duty towards its poor and a model for salvaging the performance of that duty. That monument is all his, fought through with the patience, the cunning and occasionally the main force of a man almost too tired by now to climb the stairs. Almost by himself, he kept the Democrats from making their war upon the poor. He leaves and goes to Saratoga, the proper resort for men of old-fashioned tastes. He has shown us a model for any man's exit time.[16]

I read the Post column with gratitude because, although over the years I had developed a thick skin to the slings and arrows of outraged politicians, enemies, opponents, reporters and columnists, one always feels better when good things are said. Perhaps because I was not as busy as I used to be, I spent much time reflecting on the *Post*'s comments, for I could not help feeling that with time I would be vindicated — the most for which a prudent and passably decent person can hope. Certainly, in New York politics, that is hoping for a lot.

My last days in politics: Opposition to Mario Procaccino and vindication by the New York Times

1969 was a city election year and Mayor Lindsay was running again. As I have said, I had no official responsibilities other than those of City Councilman and my Carver Democratic Club had been taken over by David Dinkins, now Borough President. Since I planned to retire, Jessie Gray was running for my seat on the 5th City Council District, and I was free to support whomever I wanted for Mayor.

In the primaries, John Lindsay lost the Republican nomination to State Senator John Marchi, and was forced to run on the Liberal and Independent tickets. The Democrats endorsed Controller Mario A. Procaccino, causing a three-way race for the mayoralty. Things began to heat up in early September, and I gradually realized that times had changed drastically, at least from my point of view.

Sensing the mood of the country and realizing the manner in which Richard Nixon had won the presidency the year before by appealing to the reactionary mood of the American community, using slogans like "forced busing" and "law and order," Procaccino picked up and emphasized similar themes. To someone in politics for more than forty-eight years and to all my other colleagues who recognized political code words, "law and order" simply meant that no quarter should be given to those protesting racial discrimination in the streets; that all people disadvantaged as a consequence of hundreds of years of discrimination should now be viewed as "ne'er-do-wells" and "vagrants"; and that the provisions of the Civil Rights Acts of 1964, 1965, 1968, and the Supreme Court rulings in between if not reversed, should be severely curtailed to fit what Nixon had called a "strict constructionism."

As Procaccino continued his speeches, and as his campaign aides put out the word privately that as mayor, Procaccino would bring law and order to the streets, I decided that Mr. Procaccino's whole campaign was repugnant to me. I saw the drastic change in the mid-sixties, and I knew I had no control over the way in which politics were now being conducted. Nonetheless, at least I could register my protest and use whatever influence I still had in support of a more considerate and humane approaches to politics in New York City. But before I did anything, I phoned Mario and told him of my concern about the buzz phrases he used, like "law and order," which Congressman Powell had cited correctly as anti-Negro code words. I expressed the hope that he would stop using them. His response was that nothing was meant beyond what he had said. I suppose he thought because I was retiring from politics and was no longer the County Leader, I now had very little influence. His tone and answers were cavalier and flippant. I decided then to take action.

I called a news conference on September 10 and announced my support of John Lindsay for Mayor in the coming elections because, as the *New York Times* correctly quoted me, I thought Lindsay, "the only candidate who is in the tradition and maintains the attitudes and philosophy of the Democratic party that I have known."[17] I made it clear to the reporters that in my opinion Mr. Procaccino himself was not a bigot, but rather was under the influence of the people around him. Of course I did not expect my comments to go unanswered, and so Procaccino in response called his own news conference. He characterized my comments as vicious and denied everything I had said.[18]

My announcement and Procaccino's response created a mild sensation, and reporters scurried to interview my colleagues to see why I had done so. The *Times* speculated that this was my "Last Hurrah," that I wanted to create some sensation before I retired from politics. Then one of its reporters, Richard Reeves, using my own axiom, "Nobody does anything for nothing", suggested that perhaps I had some ulterior motives. Reeves said,

"The actions and words of Mr. Jones surprised many people in city politics because the Councilman's long career has always been marked by two things—gentlemanly, almost courtly manners and language, and intense loyalty to the party he began working for at the old Cayuga Democratic Club in 1921.[19]

I liked the part about "gentlemanly and almost courtly", but Reeves' speculations were far off target. I had no ulterior motives and nothing to gain personally from supporting Lindsay, because I would be leaving politics at the end of the year. I expected no jobs from the City or from Lindsay, and therefore I was free from all compulsions to do this for myself. What had become clear to me was that not only in New York City but also in the rest of the country, both North and South, there was a conservative backlash developing, encouraged to a great extent by the President of the United States, Richard Nixon. It deeply disturbed me to see this tendency make its appearance in New York City, and I meant what I said of Mayor Lindsay, that we had in him the best person to counteract this trend. Support for my views came from the most unlikely source, the *New York Times*.

Although their reporter had earlier called me "courtly and gentlemanly," I did not expect this to be the view of the *Times* editors. But a few days after my press conference, the editors wrote:

New York is a Democratic city. In terms of voter-registration, the Democratic party enjoys a better than three-to-one margin over the Republican party, which in turn enjoys a better than five-to-one margin over the Liberal and Conservative parties combined. In terms of philosophical outlook, the notable figures of the Democratic party in this city—in the Smith-Roosevelt-Lehman tradition—generally reflected its spirit of enlightened tolerance.

Because this is so, it is important that Democratic leaders not now permit their party to become the captive of conservative, backward-looking elements or to acquiesce in the election of a mayoral candidate who gives no promise of following along in the path of the most honored New York Democratic leadership of the past.

It is possible that it was with these considerations in mind that City Councilman J. Raymond Jones, long a wheelhorse in Democratic party affairs and a former county chairman, turned his back on his party's nominee, City Controller Mario Procaccino, and endorsed Mayor Lindsay, a registered Republican running a fusion campaign. In the Councilman's view, Mr. Lindsay stands as "the only candidate who is in the tradition and maintains attitudes and philosophy of the Democratic party I have known". . . .

Mr. Procaccino won his party's nomination because moderate and liberal Democrats failed to get together and because their votes were divided among four other candidates, none of whom has subsequently endorsed the Controller for election. The thrust of his campaign has been to appeal to the fears of citizens rather than to their hopes. As Mr. Jones, Mr. Hogan and others have proved, it has divided the Democratic party. Its success could wreck the city.

Mayor Lindsay's fusion effort, endorsed by some Democrats, deserves to be endorsed by more. The Mayor for his part has announced support of a number of Democrats for election to a variety of local offices. His reelection campaign is hardly a partisan cause. The choice for moderate and liberal Democrats, concerned about the direction of their party and of their city, cannot be considered a choice between endorsing a fusion effort and remaining silent. To remain silent is simply to aid Mr. Procaccino.[20]

This editorial pleased me for many reasons. Despite previous fights with the *Times*, on this issue the editors fully supported my view. This I knew would certainly have a significant effect upon a number of voters. I also took the editorial to mean that the editors had now seen that I was never as wrong or as machine-oriented as they had always characterized me.

Perhaps the *Times* had come to realize that in politics one had to deal with the cards one was dealt. Their previous excoriation of me for associating with Adam Clayton Powell had never made any sense, since he was a powerful Congressman from my neighborhood, a fellow District Leader, and a member of the County Committee with whom I had to work. The *Times* in its ignorance had never seemed to consider that I had no choice in the selection of the people on the City Council, on the Democratic Committee, or in other political organizations. This support, if not accolade, coming from my long-time nemesis, the *Times*, gratified me. And when in early October the *Times* called me, "J. Raymond Jones, a former Tammany Hall leader and a man of immense personal and political prestige,"[21] I thought "my cup runneth over."

As it turned out John V. Lindsay won handily in November. Although his victory gave me satisfaction, it was mixed, for I mourned the passing of the caring leadership the party once possessed. Yet there was little more I could do. I was seventy years old and felt it was time to "lay my burdens down." Fortunately in the waning days of the year, friends—various and sundry—called and visited to pay their respects. My support for Lindsay was privately applauded by all. My old friend Mayor Robert Wagner paid me tribute as he had always done. But the Carver Gang was most nostalgic. They preferred to recall the battles fought, lost and won, the difficulties over which we had triumphed, and the long cold nights and hard wintry days we had weathered. We had persevered together and we, like our brothers and sisters in the larger civil rights struggle, had "overcome." In the midst of all this I thought that my efforts over the years must have yielded something of real value, and I felt I could retire and withdraw to the Virgin Islands with an untroubled conscience knowing that I had done the very best I could.

Chapter 10

Reflections on a Life in Politics

THE DISTINGUISHED political colum-
nist and reporter, David Broder, in his book, *The Party's Over: The Failure
of Politics in America*, noted the following:

In the autumn of the pre-presidential year—the time at which these words are
being written—the residents of the nation's capital have reason to recall the found-
ing father's warnings against the "danger of factions." Partisanship runs riot and
Washington begins to turn testy. However much he may insist that he is governing
as President of all people, the first-term incumbent begins to measure policy
decisions by their effect on his re-election chances. He gauges the opposite field
and finds occasion to point up the contrast between his statesmanship and his
potential challengers' unseemly scrambling for office. These gentlemen protect
themselves as best they can against the President's intimation of unwarranted
ambition, meanwhile elbowing each other for advantageous position in the spring
primaries and the public opinion polls.[1]

After cataloguing certain similarities between problems in 1960-65 and
in 1971, and citing such problems as having in fact been continuous since
1955, Broder expressed the view that:

American politics is at an impasse, . . . we have been spinning our wheels for a
long time; and . . . we are trying to dig ourselves ever deeper into trouble, unless
we find a way to develop some political traction and move again. I believe we can
get that traction, we can make government responsible and responsive again, only
when we begin to use our political parties as they are meant to be used. And that
is the thesis of this book.[2]

A few pages later Broder restated his thesis in this way,

The reason we have suffered governmental stalemate is that we have not used the one instrument available to us for disciplining government to meet our needs. That instrument is the political party.[3]

In the early pages of this book, I spoke of my great surprise when I was introduced to the American political system in New York City, once I realized that I was in fact an American citizen and that I could exercise all the rights and privileges of that estate, and that all I had to do was register to vote. This is what I was told and this was what the law said. But it did not take me very long to perceive the gulf between the promise and its realization. Thus began my education in how to "use the one instrument available to us for disciplining government to meet our needs." That instrument, as Broder says, was and is the political party!

In the New York City of 1920, although many of the barriers constructed to forbid blacks from voting in the South were missing, two very potent ones remained to restrict the growth of the Black vote: the literacy test and apportionment of districts. The law required that all new voters applying for registration at the Board of Elections during a prescribed registration period prove their literacy by taking a test. That is, the election inspectors would send them to the designated testing school whereupon the assigned instructor would administer a prepared test. Only upon presenting to the Registration Board a slip indicating that the test had been passed could one gain permission to vote. This was simple enough, except that literacy test inspectors in the 1920s were usually school teachers from other than Black neighborhoods who seemed more concerned with failing than passing the applicants, and the officers assigned to protect the testing area were all white, entirely without sympathy for the general proceedings.

During this time I moved to the northernmost part of Harlem. The new Dunbar Garden Apartments built by the Rockefeller family had just opened for occupancy and I served as District Captain for the Democratic Party in this area. It was my good fortune to have a constituency of such people as Dr. W. E. B. DuBois, Paul Robeson, and A. Philip Randolph. The entire area comprised 15 Election Districts out of a total of 45 in the Assembly District. The district then was two-thirds white and one-third black, but with a voting strength of 1 in 5 rather than 1 in 3. Thus it became necessary for the fifteen captains in this section to make every effort to close the gap in voting strength.

In the District Clubs of both parties, a feeling of family ran high in New York City. Party members respected one another, cared about the welfare of one another, and, in times of misunderstanding, resolved differences in the interest of good working relations. The rules of the Tammany organization required that each Assembly District have at least one recognized clubhouse (in some cases there were two or three); that each club be open twice a week to enable communications among clubs within the county and city. Thus clubs became both political and social entities, and out of these conditions the feeling of family grew strong.

By 1952, with the election of Dwight D. Eisenhower and the defeat of Adlai Stevenson, I already identified a certain transmogrification of party politics, party discipline, and party loyalty, and the gradual erosion of the party as a family. Since then, in my view, the steady erosion of party politics has also had a negative effect on the ability of our government to perform its duty of delivering goods and services to the electorate. David Broder was absolutely correct in his assessment, and from my vantage point of 88 years, with more than sixty of those years as a participant in Democratic politics, I believe that party deterioration is still taking place, and that our federal, state, and local governments suffer from the absence of partisan politics. Broder's concern is with the role of the federal government, and the presidency, and the effects of the absence of party discipline and party politics on the efficiency of the federal government. He is essentially correct, and, both intellectually and experientially, I can speak similarly with some authority on the relationship between parties, partisan politics, and the efficiency of government, and the opportunities for Black leadership on the local level, with New York City as an example.

In the period between World War I and II, on registration day the district clubs usually provided the District Captain with campaign money. The amount of money varied according to the district, but no district received less than fifty dollars. In Harlem, however, the maximum was thirty-five dollars.

Fortunately, we had captains in the 22nd Assembly District with a personal interest in helping new applicants pass the literacy tests. It was necessary to "neutralize" the officers assigned to the test group (neutralization consisted of an honorarium out of our own pockets); and instead of sending registration applicants directly to the testing room, we took them in groups of five to an apartment in the district where some of our own schoolteachers drilled them, using copies of test sheets. In this manner we succeeded to some degree in increasing our registration rolls and in increasing participation of a few Blacks in the predominantly white clubs in Harlem. We participated in the rewards, if even on a reduced scale. Then as now, the redrawing of new district lines after each decennial census created problems. Since Harlem was an area in transition—whites moving out, blacks moving in—white District Leaders kept charts of demographic change enabling them to redraw district lines in such a manner that they could retain control. This gerrymandering was not in the interest of the increasing Black population of New York City.

Such problems characterized New York City and the rest of the country. In the South and the Midwest, the hooded hounds of hell were rampaging the countryside, lynching, burning, and bombing (even the House of God). Sharecroppers and plantation workers huddled in the fields, muted voices rising to the silent stars, as they sang their hymns of supplication, hope, and faith in deep communication with their God. In the cities, conditions were hardly better. A people who had shown excellence in government in the ten brief Reconstruction years after the Civil War, was by World War I now reduced to no more than the ten percent of its population allowed to vote; in some areas of the South, the percentage was less. Not until 1924, when Dr. L. A. Nixon, an El Paso, Texas, Democrat, brought suit to regain the right to vote for Negroes, triggering a long series of successful cases finally restoring Blacks' right to the franchise in *Terry v. Adams* (1952), was there any certainty that Black people would regain their rightful place in American society. Even so, it took a Voting Rights Act thirteen years later to bolster the ruling of the United States Supreme Court. Not for any other people in America have such struggles and sufferings been necessary.

Yet there always has been in America a segment of the white population adhering faithfully to the humane principles upon which our nation has professed to be founded. Members of this group in cooperation with Blacks founded the National Association for the Advancement of Colored People in 1910 and a similar group, the Urban League, the next year. These two organizations worked hard throughout the years in the fight to reclaim for Negroes what was rightfully theirs. Working outside the ordinary political institutions they achieved great success, but it is a sad and unhappy commentary on our society that even now their job is not done.

Despite discrimination, terrorism, and disdain by the majority of our population, Black people have themselves, against terrible odds, managed to fashion lives of dignity. In the midst of their struggle, they have produced individuals such as Booker T. Washington of Tuskegee, Mary Mc-Cleod Bethune of Bethune-Cookman College, Dr. W. E. B. DuBois of Atlanta University, all in the field of higher education. In the arts there have been the very great poet Langston Hughes, composer and writer J. Weldon Johnson, novelists Nella Larsen, Zora Neale Hurston, Richard Wright, Ralph Ellison, and the many others in the latter half of the twentieth century. Think of the contributions Black people could have made for a better America if they had been given an equal chance. The prospect overwhelms the mind.

The party and the Black politician

In 1949, when offered the leadership of Tammany Hall, I had been in Democratic politics some twenty-nine years. Had I accepted the job then, possibly some historian would have assessed my progress between 1920 and 1949 as meteoric, considering that I was a Black immigrant from the Virgin Islands, without property and without money—the prime qualification to vote for the Municipal Council in the Virgin Islands. How was it then that in twenty years I was being offered the leadership of Tammany Hall? My view is that there is a lesson in this for aspiring Black politicians, a view which corresponds to Broder's. If Black politicians are to do well in this country and find the mechanisms and means for making the social changes eminently desired not only by the Black community but also by all Americans, then their best route is through the political parties.

I have not ruled out Black participation in the Republican Party, although I might hasten to add that those Black men and women in the Republican Party today are usually not of my persuasion. In fact, they do not project or reflect views in the best interest of either the Black community or all Americans. Even in 1987, I have seen nothing proposed or practiced by the Republican Party that suggests support or even sympathy for the Black population—or even for the disadvantaged white population. The Reagan Republican Party has placed America and the rest of the world in a position of military competitiveness, the cost of which is so great that in order to accomplish and improve that position, it must destroy some and reduce substantially all social programs developed under the New Deal and the Great Society. Because of its competition with the USSR in the techno-logical field, funding for educational and social programs has been all but eliminated. In his obsession with the "Evil Empire," as Mr. Reagan calls Russia, has made it possible for other nations such as Japan and Korea to seriously undermine our economic position in the world. The irony, of course, is that superiority in technology requires intellectual superiority elsewhere as well, and that can only occur with the expansion and upgrad-ing of all our educational systems. The most adverse fallout will be on those who cannot attain an education without financial assistance—many of our Black Americans will therefore become obsolete.

When I think of Blacks and other minorities, I automatically think of my own Democratic Party. Blacks, Hispanics, Native Americans, and women have always fared better in the Democratic Party, since the administration of Franklin Delano Roosevelt. With the election of 1932 there was a marked movement of Blacks away from the Republican to the Democratic Party; and it is indeed an historic fact that by the Congressional elections of 1934, and certainly by the Presidential election of 1936, Blacks were for the first time voting Democratic by an overwhelming majority. The record of the Democratic Party in addressing in an increasingly serious manner since 1934 the problems of the Black population has been a progressive and most encouraging one. Given the rigidity and seeming insensitivity of the Republican Party, the obvious home for the Black politician in the United States, at least for the moment, is the Democratic Party. I recognized this in the 1920s, and to this day have had no reason to change my view.

I am aware of the fact that the Republican Party was the party of justice and fairness until 1876, and the party of the Negro from its inception until the early twentieth century. At the same time, however, when "the Party of Lincoln" was making an about-face and becoming anti-Negro, the Democratic Party, seeing the possibilities for its own enhancement, welcomed Negroes with open arms. While in the late nineteenth and early twentieth centuries this was essentially a Northern development, it is an incontrovertible historical fact that beginning with the New Deal years, even Southern Democrats began to see the need for recruiting Black voters. It is indeed most interesting to note that in 1987, the South compared to all other sections of the United States now has the highest percentage of Black elected officials relative to its Black population; there, as in the North, very few of these officials are in the Republican Party. It is obvious, therefore, that the primary source by far for Black political development and participation in the wealth and welfare of America is, at the moment, the Democratic Party.

My election as leader of Tammany Hall in 1964 supports this view, for my election was no accident. In 1961, when I had contributed mightily to Robert Wagner's reelection as mayor of New York City, he expressed the wish that I become New York County Leader. By then I represented the watchful and powerful constituency of Harlem, and despite my on-and-off relationship with Adam Clayton Powell, there simply was no question that together we were a powerful voice in New York City politics.

I did not ascend to the post as County Leader in 1961 because the Reform Democrats would not have me. At that time former Governor Herbert Lehman, Eleanor Roosevelt, and others of that ilk pressured Mayor Wagner to have someone of their own as County Leader, furthering their effort to take over the Democratic Party from the top. The Mayor, in striving for party unity, decided a compromise would be best. That person was Edward Costikyan, who served from 1962 to 1964. The objection to me was *not* based on race as some have argued, but rather on the conflicting ideologies of the Regulars and the Reformers. I felt then that it would be only a matter of time before the County Leader position would be mine if I desired it, for the tenure of County Leaders (DeSapio excepted) was getting increasingly short over the years, and as Costikyan, merely a compromise candidate, would not last very long.

But the point is that I had been in the party for many years and had paid my dues. Apart from the Reformers, almost all members of the Regular Democratic Party knew this. I had done almost everything asked of me and, frankly, within the Tammany organization there was nowhere I could go but up. By 1964 I was already a City Councilman and chaired the powerful Committee on the State Legislature as well as the ad hoc committee investigating the Human Resources Administration. As District Leader, 13th A.D. East, I held the influential chairmanship of the district's County Committee, sat on Tammany's Executive Committee, and served as Chairman of its Rules Committee, holding one and one-quarter of its votes. I could of course run for the lateral position of Chairman of the County Committee, but in that I was not interested. When I was finally nominated and elected in December 1964, I was happy, satisfied, and pleased, but I was not astonished. The press made much of my color, and inflated the point that I was the first Black person so chosen in the country; but privately I felt that my "elevation" was a normal progression, as it should be for Blacks or anyone.

My ascendance to the New York County Democratic Leadership resulted from years of active party participation, a mastery of the mechanics of the system, the building of a network of dependable colleagues, and to some extent the tenor of the times. It is my view that although the political environment has deteriorated appreciably since 1980, and that the present social and political atmosphere bears little comparison to the fifties and early sixties, a Black person in most localities in America today can, with skill, ingenuity and hard work, obtain the approval and support of his peers and achieve positions of leadership. There is no better way than by starting low and climbing the ladder. Yet, in too many instances, attempts have been made to begin at the top. At times this is necessary and useful, but beginning at the top usually results from a draft, and not from forced entry. The case of the Reverend Jesse Jackson is instructive.

Jesse Jackson and the case of race and charisma

Jesse Jackson's campaign for the presidency is a classic case of an attempt of an imposition on the party from the top, and of the danger of an overemphasis on race. Because of his charisma, the sense of unredressed grievance of his presumed constituency, and a presumption of moral righteousness, Jackson thought he could "seize the time" in pursuit of the Democratic nomination for the presidency of the United States. But while

Jackson's ambience is necessary and useful in projecting a career as leader of a political-social movement, such ambience is seldom successful in the promotion of a purely political career. The Jackson approach is even less likely to be successful when the individual is Black. Why is this so?

If one were to juxtapose the careers of Daniel Patrick Moynihan and that of Jesse Jackson, several interesting factors can be observed. Moynihan, prior to becoming a politician, was a professor at Harvard University and a sociologist of fine repute. While there, he co-authored a well-received book, *Beyond the Melting Pot*, which, despite its designation as a work of scholarly sociology, could be used as a source book for politicians concerned with the solution of social problems. On the basis of this work and a report published in 1965 sponsored by the U.S. Department of Labor, entitled, *The Negro Family: The Case for National Action*, Moynihan found himself a prominent advisor in the Nixon Administration. In *The Negro Family*, Moynihan had certain prescriptions for Negro family improvement. Certain of his observations, analyses, and prescriptions were found to be flawed, but most viewed his report as a genuine attempt to solve a problem that was becoming a matter of increasing concern for social welfare agencies and politicians. By 1968, the public perceived Moynihan as a concerned academic with original thoughts and original prescriptions for the curing of one of the nation's major ills. This made him an attractive, draftable individual to either political party.

While advising at the White House, he was often thought of as a Republican, but since he had no overwhelming commitment to any party, the Democrats successfully drafted him in 1976 to run for United States Senator from New York. He had been shrewd enough to establish a residence in New York after leaving Harvard University, and at the time of his announced desire to enter politics and from the top in New York, I found myself involuntarily involved.

Because of the misunderstandings and controversy surrounding Moynihan's "benign neglect" memo to President Nixon, the United Elected Negro Leadership of New York, a semi-formal political group, contemplated opposing his candidacy. During their deliberations, they contacted me. My counsel was simple. No one could be entirely certain that Mr. Moynihan's advice, if properly translated, was inappropriate. Furthermore, if it would have been inimical, the furor already expressed had attenuated its potential injury. On the other hand, Patrick Moynihan was otherwise popular. His lectures as U.S. Representative in the United Nations had made him so. His chances were fairly good without the Black vote. Apart from his call for "benign neglect," there was no stigma attached to his name relative to Blacks or otherwise.

I said that considering all the possible alternatives, Moynihan was a very attractive candidate. His particular and peculiar qualities were perfect for overcoming the conservatism of the Republicans. After the turbulence of Robert Kennedy and the conservatism of James Buckley, as Senators from New York, we needed in New York a smart and attractive candidate, actually, "a man for all seasons." Since the Democratic Party in New York County and the rest of the state was in a state of disarray, it needed political glue, some cohesive force to ensure success in the senatorial race. I concluded that Moynihan was a superior candidate and I so informed my colleagues. Of course, in 1976, I was not in a position to mandate, or significantly influence decisions, and I am not sure that I persuaded anyone; nonetheless, I do know that Moynihan received a majority of the Black vote, and that pleased me. He remains a fine Senator. Here then, was a case in which the Party needed Moynihan as much as Moynihan needed the Party. There was no question of any imposition, and no question of pressure, but rather a felicitous confluence of personal ambition and party needs. Indeed, some quarters considered getting Moynihan to run on the Democratic ticket as something of a coup, since it was sometimes rumored that the Republicans were also interested in him.

This happy development did not characterize the 1984 campaign of the Reverend Jesse Jackson. To state it this way, admittedly, is to oversimplify the complex maneuvers of the Jackson campaign. Yet Jackson's political life in many ways parallels Moynihan's. Despite the difference of one being Black, the other white, one being an academician and the other a social worker, the point must be taken that they were both public figures before their attempt at electoral politics.

Jackson had been present in Greensboro, North Carolina, in May and June of 1963 in the successful battle there to desegregate public facilities. Jackson, President of the Student Council at North Carolina A & T College (to which he had transferred from a school in Chicago), had been a football hero, and a big man about campus. As related by Professor William Chafe in his book, *Civilities and Civil Rights*, Jackson was "the hero who led the troops into battle and inspired the rank and file. Dynamic, flamboyant, a figure who thrived in the limelight, Jackson provided the charismatic attributes necessary to rally the movement and re-invigorate if energy lagged."[4]

For his endeavors, Jackson was eventually jailed, creating a massive outpouring of support for him in the streets, which contributed, to a great extent, to the capitulation of Mayor David Schenck, and the end of segregation in Greensboro. As everyone now knows, Jesse eventually became a minister of the gospel, returned to Chicago, and subsequently became an outstanding civil rights activist notably, through the organization called PUSH.

It appears to me that Jackson's successful involvement in Mayor Harold Washington's campaign stimulated his desire to run for President of the United States. Perhaps because in his student days he had been drafted into the Civil Rights Movement, Jackson believed that a similar draft would be successful if he positioned himself strategically. But while he was drafted as a student in Greensboro, there simply was no draft for Jackson in electoral politics as there had been for Moynihan. And Jesse did not show the required humility when on the night of Harold Washington's election as mayor of Chicago, he made the mistake of appearing in front of the cheering campaign workers to declare, "We won, we want it all!" This ill-advised exclamation immediately created a serious backlash among Chicago's white population. But for many Blacks, the gesture was welcome. They viewed it as a gesture of long-denied success, part of a matrix of defiance and independence, impetuously surfacing after long years of frustration and unredressed grievance. That gesture reinforced the image of Jackson as a national figure, a charismatic one, and somebody to be reckoned with.

In many quarters, at this time, Jackson came to be seen also not only as a figure in his own right, but also as a successor to the martyred Dr. Martin Luther King, Jr. His long experience in protest from North Carolina to Chicago, his presence at the scene of Dr. King's murder, and his similar rhetoric, were persuasive. Armed with a righteous sense of grievance, and psychologically protected by the appropriated bloody mantle of the revered Reverend Dr. King, Jackson began his epic odyssey for the presidency of the United States.

Certain ingredients present in the Moynihan attempt to become Senator from New York, however, were absent from Jackson's campaign for the presidency. What were they? The first and obvious missing ingredient in this case, was the right color: Jackson is Black. Yet, from his speeches and responses to reporters questions, he seems to have thought that being Black was a plus! But merely being Black in the United States today is not in itself as valuable a political currency as Rev. Jackson may have believed. There is no question that being Black and charismatic, he had a tremendous appeal for the majority of the Black population. His primary victories in certain districts in the South as well as the North with overwhelmingly Black populations, with liberal and progressive whites, support, were encouraging.

Yet despite designating his campaign the Rainbow Coalition, there was always the view by the larger segment of the white community that Jackson was still a Black person concerned mostly with Black problems. Therefore, the second missing ingredient was an ability to persuade skeptical white voters of Jackson's equal concern for them. This observation is not to say that white voters reject Black candidates out of hand. Such a contention has been consistently disproved. Rather, it is important to remember that Jesse Jackson, as a Black man identified with protest and confrontation, was seen as the quintessential Black protester, Black confronter, an image not comforting to the ordinary white voter, nor for that matter to the increasing numbers of middle-class Black voters.

Mr. Jackson was seen as even less comforting by the leaders at all levels throughout the Democratic Party. Although a public figure, although charismatic, and although he could undeniably garner Black and liberal white votes, he was not to be drafted. In fact, his candidacy was interpreted as a coercive attempt to make the Democrats draft him—in other words, a forced draft. This indeed was what Jackson was attempting, apparently in the belief that no other route would get a Black person on the Presidential ballot.

Of course, Jackson's attempt failed because Walter Mondale and the Democratic Party were appealing to the nation's center, and in their view Jesse Jackson was pushing the Party too far left. With this approach, obtaining the Democratic nomination for the presidency was hopeless, for the Democratic party wished desperately to remain in the middle.

Missing also from Jackson's background was political dues-paying and administrative experience. Let us suppose that someone of the stature of Mayor Tom Bradley of Los Angeles, or even Mayor Coleman Young of Detroit, had attempted to place his name on the presidential ballot. What would have been the response and how would it have been different from that of Jackson?

In the first place, Bradley and Young have labored for a long time in the vineyards, have made contributions to the Party, and have proven capable of administering large cities with a plethora of problems and a matrix of competing demands. Over the years, such men have demonstrated that Black concerns are not their sole agenda, but rather the welfare of all of their constituents. They have made it impossible for anyone credibly to charge them with a predisposition towards Blacks or other minorities at the expense of whites. In other words, they have developed an even-handed approach to the administration of their governments, perhaps even more so than their white predecessors, who always have shown varying degrees of disregard for the problems of Blacks, Hispanics, Asian Americans, other minorities, and women. I think that this case can be made for all Black mayors in the 1980s, including even Harold Washington, who has often been accused of being unconcerned with problems of his white constituents. If any of these men had contested for the Presidential nomination, or even the Vice-Presidency, white people throughout the country would know as a matter of historical record that here is someone with administrative experience to whom they could look for assistance, and for redress of their grievances without fear of unfair treatment.

A similar prospect does not obtain at this time for someone like Jesse Jackson, who does not have this background, and who consequently, presents an uncertain image. If Jackson, or someone like Jackson, is to aspire to the highest position in the land, he will necessarily have to start somewhat lower and demonstrate as Coleman Young, Tom Bradley, and others have done, that he is capable of even-handed administration, and is not just a Black person with an essentially Black agenda.

That is why, in all my years as leader of the Carver Democratic Club in New York, I always attempted to find the best educated, and if not formally educated, the most intelligent, circumspect, savvy, and personable men and women to be sponsored by my club. In most cases, I started my protegés in positions of low responsibility such as Election District Captains, and then, when they had shown an understanding of how the political system worked and a willingness to contribute to the party, they would be sponsored for offices such as State Assemblyman, City Councilman, State Senator, judges of all ranks, and so on. The objective behind all this was to develop in the individual a sense of responsibility to the party and its constituency, and with it to provide public exposure. In this manner the aspiring politician or officeholder enlarged his constituency and enhanced his reputation not only among the Black voters, but also among the white electorate. When such a person runs from a constituency that is, for example, sixty percent white and forty percent Black, then his race becomes a less weighty factor. Unfortunately, the Reverend Jackson has never been through this process. It may, therefore, be wiser for him to run for Congress and move on from there. Given his skill at oratory, his energy and intelligence, I believe he can yet play a large and useful role in national life.

In New York County during my years as Leader of the Carver Democratic Club, as City Councilman, District Leader, and "Tammany Chief," my program and that of my collaborators involved "paying dues," recruiting the best possible people, and promoting them strongly when they were ready. If anyone were to check the record, it would be seen that we were enormously successful. We have had several Black Borough Presidents, male and female; we have had City Registrars and City Clerks; a number of State Assemblymen; and of course, two Congressmen. I believe this is an enviable record, better than any other in the United States to this very day.

In these days we are faced with a conservative reaction, the sort of backlash about which President Lyndon Johnson always warned me. This development calls for careful planning and subtle maneuvers by Black and other minority leaders. It will not do to overemphasize race. Rather, sophisticated and persuasive strategies, though difficult, must be found to make all constituents see that only through collaborative action will common problems be resolved. It is not an easy task, yet there is no other viable alternative. My approach in New York City over the years to strategize, securing influential jobs and offices at all levels, is an approach that I believe could be emulated with great profit for all.

Preface

1. Interview with Mayor Robert F. Wagner, Jr., New York City, March 27, 1984.

2. Interview with Judge James L. Watson, New York City, August 11, 1983.

3. Julius C. C. Edelstein to author, January 7, 1984, in response to a questionnaire.

Introduction

1. Al Smith was elected in 1918 only to lose in 1920 because of the "Republican Reaction" throughout the nation in the Harding-Coolidge presidential sweep. Smith was reelected in 1922 with strong Tammany support and remained governor until 1928.

2. Edwin R. Lewinson, *Black Politics in New York*, (New York: Twayne Publishers, 1974), p. 64.

3. Lewinson. See also Anthony Hiss, "Boss Jones of Tammany Hall," *New York Times Magazine*, February 19, 1967.

4. Robert S. Allen, ed., *The Fair City* (New York: Vanguard Press, 1947), p.49.

5. Warren Moscow, *The Last of the Big-Time Bosses: The Life and Times of Carmine DeSapio and the Rise and Fall of Tammany Hall*, (New York: Stein & Day 1971), pp. 2425.

6. Moscow, pp. 143144.

7. For a succinct narrative and analysis of the relationship between organized crime and Tammany politics, see, for example, Moscow, esp. chaps 3 and 4

255

8. Moscow, pp. 4445.

9. Malcolm Cowley, *Exile's Return: A Literary Odyssey of the 1920's* (New York: Penguin Books, 1979), pp. 2728.

10. Shirley Chisholm. *Unbought and Unbossed*. Boston: Houghton Mifflin, 1970, p. 151.

11. Edward Costikyan, *How to Win Votes: The Politics of 1980* (New York: Harcourt Brace Jovanovich, 1980), p. 73.

12. Costikyan, p. 77.

13. Steven F. Lawson, *In Pursuit of Power: Southern Blacks and Electoral Politics, 19651982*, (New York: Columbia University Press, 1985), p. 276.

14. *National Roster of Black Elected Officials*, 15th Edition (1986), pp. 15.

15. *National Roster*, p. 5. (BEO means Black Elected Officials)

16. *New York Times*, August 6, 1986.

17. *New York Times*, August 6, 1986.

Chapter 2

1. Ray Stannard Baker, *Following the Color Line*, New York (1908 New York, Harper and Row, 1964), ch. 7.

2. John Henrik Clarke, *Marcus Garvey and the Vision of Africa*, (New York: Vintage Books, 1973), p. 426.

3. Professor Ivan Light notes in his excellent book, *Ethnic Enterprise in America: Business and Welfare among Chinese, Japanese and Blacks* (Berkeley and Los Angeles: University of California Press, 1972) that the *esusu* remained intact among Caribbean Blacks in the form of *asu* and "hands," and contributed greatly to the West Indian immigrant success in the U.S.. See: p. 3244.

4. *New York Times* reporting on this incident labels Oscar Waters as "recently a messenger in the employ of Gerhard M. Dahl." *New York Times*, October 14, 1925.

5. *New York Times*, August 23, 1925.

6. Oscar H. Waters was true to his credo of making the most of his time, for after the primary, he promptly switched his support to the Republican ticket led by

Frank D. Waterman. Presumably he received a payoff for that too. See *New York Times*, October 14, 1925.

7. Herbert Mitgang, *The Man Who Rode the Tiger: The Life and Times of Judge Samuel Seabury (New York: J. B. Lippincott , 1963), p. 162.*

8. Mitgang, p. 169.

9. Mitgang, p. 163.

10. Mitgang, pp. 242243.

Chapter 4

1. McQuade was called "Forty" because of the more than forty relatives he placed on the city payroll.

2. Wallace S. Sayre and Herbert Kaufman, *Governing New York City: Politics in the Metropolis*, New York: Russell Sage Foundation, 1960, p. 269.

3. Sayre and Koufman, p. 270.

4. Sayre and Kaufman,pp. 269270.

5. Sayre and Kaufman, p. 270271.

6. *New York Times*, June 28, 1948.

7. *New York Times, June 28, 1948.*

8. *New York Times*, December 18, 1948.

Chapter 5

1. *New York Times*, August 12, 1948.

2. *New York Times Magazine*, February 19, 1967.

3. *New York Times*, December 13, 1950.

4. *New York Age*, March 7, 1953.

5. Hulan E. Jack, *Fifty Years a Democrat* (New York: The New Benjamin Franklin House, 1982), p. 7374.

6. Jack, page 76.

7. Jack, page 8587.

8. *New York Times*, August 6, 1986.

9. John Hope Franklin, *From Slavery to Freedom*, 4th ed. (New York: Alfred A. Knopf, 1974), p.475.

10. Franklin, p 475.

Chapter 6

1. Adam Clayton Powell Jr., *Keep the Faith, Baby!* (New York: Trident Press, 1967), pp. 7879.

2. *New York Times*, September 1, 1961.

3. *New York Times*, September 1, 1961.

4. *New York Times*, September 1, 1961.

5. *New York Times*, September 1, 1961.

6. *New York Times*, September 4, 1961.

7. *New York Times*, September 4, 1961.

8. *New York Times*, September 5, 1961.

9. *New York Times*, September 5, 1961.

10. *New York Times*, September 8, 1961.

11. *New York Times*, September 8, 1961.

12. Barbara Carter, *The Road to City Hall* (Englewood Cliffs, New Jersey: Prentice-Hall, 1967), pp. 3738.

13. *Amsterdam News*, December 9, 1961.

14. *New York Times*, September 7, 1963.

15. Quoted in Carter, p. 65.

16. Edward N. Costikyan, *Behind Closed Doors: Politics in the Public Interest* (New York: Harcourt, Brace and World, 1966), p. 115.

17. Costikyan, p. 113.

18. Costikyan, p. 123.

19. *New York Times*, March 19, 1964.

20. *New York Post*, November 6, 1964.

21. *New York Times*, December 5, 1964.

22. *New York Times*, December 5, 1964.

23. *Newsweek*, December 14, 1964, p. 27.

24. *New York Herald Tribune*, December 6, 1964.

25. *New York Post*, December 6, 1964.

26. *New York Times*, December 5, 1964.

27. *New York Times*, December 5, 1964.

Chapter 7

1. Costikyan. p. 100.

2. *New York Times*, January 6, 1965.

3. *New York Post*, January 29, 1965.

4. Telegram: Richard A. Lukins to J. Raymond Jones, January 29, 1965. Executive V. P., Interstate Security, Inc. Jones' files.

5. *Time*, February 6, 1965.

6. *New York Times*, May 9, 1965.

7. *New York Times*, November 9, 1965.

8. *New York Times*, November 9, 1965.

9. *New York Times*, November 12, 1965.

10. *New York Times*, November 19, 1965.

11. *New York Times*, February 23, 1965.

12. *New York Times*, February 10, 1965.

13. *New York Times*, June 14, 1965.

14. Carter, pp. 9899.

15. Sutton was also very well thought of by his colleagues in the State Legislature. On the occasion of being sworn in as Borough President, a colleague in Albany was heard to say: "Anybody who lives in his area has to claw his way up." "Not Percy—he *glided*," replied a bystander. *The New York Times*, September 20, 1966.

16. *New York Times*, September 10, 1966.

Chapter 8

1. Sayre and Kaufmann, p. 546.

2. *New York Times*, May 3, 1966.

3. *New York Times*, May 8, 1966.

4. *New York Times*, May 24, 1966.

5. *New York Times*, June 2, 1966.

6. Copy in files of J. Raymond Jones: See Also *New York Times*, June 3, 1966. p. 26.

7. *New York Times*, June 3, 1966.

8. *New York Times*, June 5, 1966.

9. *New York Times*, June 5, 1966.

10. *New York Times*, June 14, 1966.

11. *New York Times*, June 10, 1966.

12. *New York Times*, June 14, 1966.

13. *New York Times*, June 24, 1966.

14. *New York Times*, June 24, 1966.

15. *New York Times*, June 26, 1966.

16. *New York Times*, June 29, 1966.

17. *New York Times*, June 29, 1966.

18. *New York Times*, November 27, 1970.

19. *New York Times*, July 22, 1966.

20. Costikyan, p. 208209.

21. Costikyan, p. 209.

22. *New York Times*, July 29, 1966.

23. *New York Times*, August 1, 1966.

24. *New York Times*, August 4, 1966.

25. Copy in Jones' personal files.

26. *New York Post*, November 22, 1966.

27. *New York Post*, November 22, 1966.

Chapter 9

1. Anthony Hiss, "Boss Jones of Tammany Hall," *New York Times Magazine*, February 19, 1967, p. 3253.

2. Hiss.

3. In those days the term "bag woman" meant an informer and collector of payoffs for the police. For a brief but useful description of the case see: Chuck Stone, *Black Political Power in America*, (New York: Dell Publishing Co., 1968), pp. 199201.

4. *New York Times*, March 14, 1967.

5. *New York Times*, March 11, 1967.

6. The *Worker*, March 21, 1967.

7. The *Worker*, March 21, 1967.

8. *New York Times*, July 30, 1967.

9. *New York Times*, July 30, 1967.

10. Press Release, February 27, 1968. Copy in files of Office of Public Information, Columbia University.

11. *New York Times*, March 4, 1968.

12. *New York Times*, March 4, 1968.

13. *New York Times*, February 15, 1969.

14. *New York Times*, February 15, 1969.

15. *New York Times*, July 25, 1969.

16. *New York Post*, July 29, 1969.

17. *New York Times*, September 11, 1969.

18. *New York Times*, September 11, 1969.

19. *New York Times*, September 11, 1969.

20. *New York Times*, September 17, 1969.

21. *New York Times*, October 5, 1969.

Chapter 10

1. David Broder, *The Party's Over* (New York: Harper & Row, 1972), pp. xiii.

2. Broder, p. xvi.

3. Broder, p.xx.

4. William H. Chafe, *Civilities and Civil Rights: Greensboro, North Carolina, and the Black Struggle for Freedom* (New York: Oxford University Press, 1980), p. 175.

Selected Bibliography

Alsop, Stewart. *Nixon and Rockefeller: A Double Portrait.* New York: Doubleday, 1960.

Baker, Ray Stannard. *Following the Color Line: American Negro Citizenship in the Progressive Era.* New York: Harper and Row, 1964.

Bellush, Jewel, and David, Stephen M., eds. *Race and Politics in New York City: Five Studies in Policy-Making.* New York: Praeger, 1971.

Bernstein, Barton J., and Matusow, Allen J., eds. *The Truman Administration: A Documentary History.* New York: Harper and Row, 1966.

Brauer, Carl M. *John F. Kennedy and the Second Reconstruction.* New York: Columbia University Press, 1977.

Bridges, Amy. *A City in the Republic: Antebellum New York and the Origin of Machine Politics.* Cambridge: Cambridge University Press, 1984.

Broder, David S. *The Party's Over: The Failure of Politics in America.* New York: Harper and Row, 1972.

Burk, Robert Frederick. *The Eisenhower Administration and Black Civil Rights.* Knoxville: The University of Tennessee Press, 1984.

Cannon, Poppy. *A Gentle Knight: My Husband Walter White.* Chicago: Johnson Publishing Company, 1952.

Carson, William H. *The Unfinished Journey: America Since World War II.* New York: Oxford University Press, 1986.

Carter, Barbara. *The Road to City Hall: How John V. Lindsay Became Mayor.* Englewood Cliffs, NJ: Prentice-Hall, Inc., 1967.

Carter, Dan T. *Scottsboro: A Tragedy of the American South.* London: Oxford University Press, 1969.

Carter, John Franklin. *La Guardia: A Biography*. New York: Modern Age Books, 1937.

Chafe, William H., and Sitkoff, Harvard, eds. *A History of Our Time: Readings on Postwar America*. New York: Oxford University Press, 1987.

Chisholm, Shirley. *Unbought and Unbossed*. Boston: Houghton Mifflin Co., 1970.

Connery, Robert Howe. *Rockefeller of New York*. Ithaca, NY: Cornell University Press, 1979.

Costikyan, Edward N. *Behind Closed Doors: Politics in the Public Interest*. New York: Harcourt Brace and World, 1966.

——*How to Win Votes: The Politics of 1980*. New York: Harcourt Brace Jovanovich, 1980.

Cross, Theodore. *The Black Power Imperative: Racial Inequality and the Politics of Nonviolence*. New York: Faulkner, 1984.

Dewey, Thomas Edmund. *Public Papers of Thomas E. Dewey, Fifty-first Governor of the State of New York*. Albany: Williams Press, 1946.

Farmer, James. *Lay Bare the Heart: An Autobiography of the Civil Rights Movement*. New York: Arbor House, 1985.

Franklin, John Hope. *From Slavery to Freedom: A History of Negro Americans*. New York: Alfred A. Knopf, 1974.

Frye, Hardy T. *Black Parties and Political Power: A Case Study*. Boston: G. K. Hall and Co., 1980.

Garrett, Charles. *The La Guardia Years: Machine and Reform Politics in New York City*. New Brunswick, NJ: Rutgers University Press, 1961.

Haley, Alex. *The Autobiography of Malcolm X*. New York: Ballantine Books, 1965.

Hapgood, David. *The Purge That Failed: Tammany v. Powell*. New York: Holt Press, 1959.

Hentoff, Nat. *A Political Life: The Education of John V. Lindsay*. New York: Knopf, 1969.

Huggins, Nathan Irvin. *Harlem Renaissance*. London: Oxford University Press, 1971.

Jack, Hulan E. *Fifty Years a Democrat: The Autobiography of Hulan E. Jack.* New York: The New Benjamin Franklin House, 1982.

Jacobs, Andy. *The Powell Affair: Freedom Minus One.* New York: The Bobbs-Merrill Co., Inc., 1973.

Jacques-Garvey, Amy. *Philosophy and Opinions of Marcus Garvey.* New York: Atheneum, 1970.

Karnig, Albert K., and Welch, Susan. *Black Representation and Urban Policy.* Chicago: The University of Chicago Press, 1980.

Klein, Woody. *Lindsay's Promise: The Dream That Failed.* New York: Macmillan, 1970.

Lawson, Steven F. *In Pursuit of Power: Southern Blacks and Electoral Politics, 19651982.* New York: Columbia University Press, 1985.

Lewinson, Edwin R. *Black Politics in New York City.* New York: Twayne Publishers, 1974.

Lindsay, John V. *The City.* New York: Norton, 1970.

Mann, Arthur. *La Guardia Comes to Power.* Philadelphia: Lipincott Press, 1933 (2nd ed., 1965).

McAdam, Doug. *Political Process and the Development of Black Insurgency, 19301970.* Chicago: The University of Chicago Press, 1987.

Meier, August, and Rudwick, Elliott, eds. *Black Protest in the Sixties.* Chicago: Quadrangle Books, 1970.

——*CORE: A Study in the Civil Right Movement, 19421968.* New York: Oxford University Press, 1973.

Mitgang, Herbert. *The Man Who Rode the Tiger: The Life and Times of Judge Samuel Seabury.* Philadelphia: J. B. Lippincott Co., 1963.

Moscow, Warren. *The Last of the Big-Time Bosses: The Life and Times of Carmine DeSapio and the Decline and Fall of Tammany Hall.* New York: Stein and Day, 1971.

Mushkat, Jerome. *Tammany: The Evolution of a Political Machine, 1789 1865.* Syracuse, NY: Syracuse University Press, 1971.

——*The Reconstruction of New York Democracy, 18611874.* London: Fairleigh Dickinson University Press, 1981.

Newfield, Jack. *Robert Kennedy: A Memoir*. New York: Dutton, 1969.

——*The Abuse of Power: The Permanent Government and the Fall of New York*. New York: Viking Press, 1977.

New York (State). *State Study Commission for New York City: Task Force on Jurisdiction and Structure. Reported by Edward N. Costikyan*. New York: Praeger, 1972.

Oates, Stephen B. *Let the Trumpet Sound: The Life of Martin Luther King, Jr.* New York: Harper and Row, 1987.

Painter, Nell Irvin. *The Narrative of Hosea Hudson: His Life as a Negro Communist in the South*. Cambridge: Harvard University Press, 1979.

Pinkney, Alphonso. *The Myth of Black Progress*. Cambridge: Cambridge University Press, 1984.

Powell, Adam Clayton, Jr. *Marching Blacks*. New York: The Dial Press, 1973.

Record, Wilson. *The Negro and the Communist Party*. New York: Atheneum, 1971.

Riordon, William L. *Plunkitt of Tammany Hall*. New York: Alfred A. Knopf, 1948.

Rockefeller, Nelson A. *Public Papers of Nelson A. Rockefeller, Fifty-third Governor of the State of New York*. New York, 1959.

Salinger, Diane. *An Honorable Profession: A Tribute to Robert F. Kennedy*. New York: Doubleday, 1968.

Sayre, Wallace S., and Kaufman, Herbert. *Governing New York City: Politics in the Metropolis*. New York: Russell Sage Foundation, 1960.

Schlesinger, Arthur M., Jr. *Robert Kennedy and His Times*. Boston: Houghton Mifflin, 1978.

Shannon, William Vincent. *The Heir Apparent: Robert Kennedy and the Struggle for Power*. New York: MacMillan, 1967.

Shaw, Frederick. *The History of the New York City Legislature*. New York: Columbia University Press, 1954.

Sitkoff, Harvard. *The Struggle for Black Equality, 1954-1980*. Toronto: Collins Publishers, 1981.

Sorenson, Theodore C. *The Kennedy Legacy*. New York: Macmillan, 1969.

Stone, Chuck. *Black Political Power in America*. New York: Dell Publishing Co., Inc., 1968.

Whalen, Charles, and Whalen, Barbara. *The Longest Debate: A Legislative History of the 1964 Civil Rights Act*. New York: Seven Locks Press, Inc., 1985.

White, John. *Black Leadership in America, 18951968*. New York: Longman Group Ltd., 1985.

White, Theodore H. *The Making of the President 1960*. New York: Atheneum House, 1961.

White, Walter. *A Man Called White: The Autobiography of Walter White*. New York: The Viking Press, 1948.

Wilson, James Q. *Negro Politics: The Search For Leadership*. New York: The Free Press, 1960.

Wirth, Louis. *The Ghetto*. Chicago: The University of Chicago Press, 1956.

Index

Wright, Richard
  novelist, 244
Young, Coleman
  Mayor, Detroit, 251–252
Young, John III
  candidate, Councilman-at-large, 164
Youth Services Agency, 235

Zaretski, Joseph

candidate, Senate Majority Leader,
  184–185
new Senate Majority Leader, 186
Senate Minority Leader, 183–184
Zaretsky, Joseph
  Senate Majority Leader, 12
Zichello, Philip
  Deputy Commissioner of Hospitals,
  116